INVISIBLE ALLIES

INVISIBLE
ALLIES

ALEKSANDR
SOLZHENITSYN

Translated by Alexis Klimoff and Michael Nicholson

COUNTERPOINT
WASHINGTON, D.C.

English translation by Alexis Klimoff and Michael Nicholson
copyright © 1995 by Aleksandr Solzhenitsyn

First published in Russian under the title *Nevidimki*

Library of Congress Cataloging-in-Publication Data
Solzhenitsyn, Aleksandr Isaevich, 1918–
[Nevidimki. English]
Invisible allies / by Aleksandr Solzhenitsyn;
translated from the Russian by Alexis Klimoff & Michael Nicholson.
"A Cornelia and Michael Bessie book."
1. Solzhenitsyn, Aleksandr Isaevich, 1918– —Friends and associates.
2. Authors, Russian—20th century—Biography.
3. Political prisoners—Soviet Union—Biography.
I. Klimoff, Alexis. II. Nicholson, Michael (Michael A.) III. Title.
PG3488.04Z4713   1995
891.73'44—dc20
[B]   95-33079
ISBN 1-887178-08-2 (alk. paper)

FIRST PRINTING
Printed in the United States of America on acid-free paper that
meets the American National Standards Institute Z39-48 Standard

Designed by David Bullen
Typeset by Typeworks

☥ A CORNELIA AND MICHAEL BESSIE BOOK

COUNTERPOINT
P.O. Box 65793
Washington, D.C. 20035-5793

Distributed by Publishers Group West

I sit down to write these pages and in my mind's eye all my loyal companions in arms, my collaborators, my helpers, almost all of them still alive and still in danger, gather around me like affectionate shadows. I see their eyes and listen intently to their voices—more intently than I ever could in the heat of battle.

Unknown to the world, they risked everything without receiving in recompense the public admiration that can mitigate even death. And for many of them the publication of these pages will come too late.

FROM CHAPTER ONE

Contents

INVISIBLE
ALLIES

To the Reader:
Asterisks in the text refer to the translators' notes,
which begin on page 319.

I

Nikolai Ivanovich Zubov

Every historical period produces its share of otherwise inconspicuous individuals who have the gift of preserving the past, though not by setting down their memoirs for posterity. Instead, they evoke it in conversation with their contemporaries; their recollections can be borne across decades even to the very youngest listeners and when the narrator's own life is drawing to a close. As long as the head holding these memories remains steady, as long as we stay receptive to its kindly silver-haired glow, we can continue to draw on it for the past it has preserved. But the use we make of these insights is then entirely up to us.

Nikolai Ivanovich Zubov had this special talent from an early age. At the time of the revolution, he was an observant twenty-two-year-old with a retentive memory, and he managed to preserve astonishingly clear recollections of the Russian world that had been irretrievably shattered in the space of a few short months. Because Nikolai Ivanovich did not see the world in political terms, those recollections did not add up to a comprehensive picture of the whole, but consisted of a myriad of brilliant fragments, any one of which N. I. could readily extract from deep within his memory, well into old age. These might concern the organization of the railroads, local geographical features, the world of bureaucrats, daily life in small-town Russia, or various other minor but fascinating aspects of our history. He would always relate the kind of thing you could not have deduced by yourself or have picked up from a book. Yet strangely enough he could say virtually nothing about the Russian Civil War, even though he had been its contemporary. At the time, he had lived far from the hub of events, he had not personally taken part in the conflict, and it was as if his mind had refused to absorb the chaos and horror of this bloody turmoil.

The life of any individual is so full of its own problems and events that it can proceed in a direction completely unrelated to the flow of historical circumstances. N. I.'s father had died while he was still a boy, and the early age at which he had been left fatherless had made an indelible impression on his personality. This was the source of his eternally youthful outlook on life, his boyish pride in being good with his hands (he always carried a penknife), and his secretive, gentle, and timid attitude toward women. He loved and respected his mother to the end, never daring to flout her wishes, even though she was full of set ideas that she was determined to impose on her son. One such notion was that he, as a delicate and overprotected young intellectual, should marry a woman "of the people" and that in order to do so he should "go to the people."* Thus, as soon as N. I. had graduated from medical school, she packed him off to the Novgorod region to work in a butter-producing cooperative. And indeed the young man learned enough about butter-making and the Novgorod area to last a lifetime—but his choice of a wife proved to be an utter disaster. By the time I met him, no one in N. I.'s home was willing to speak of this hysterical woman "from the people," and I know nothing about her, except that she made his life such a misery that he was forced to leave her and take his three children with him: a silent, expressionless son who grew up a stranger to him and could not become N. I.'s successor in any way, and two daughters who inherited their mother's mental instability.

It was this divorcé with three variously handicapped children whom the thirty-year-old Elena Aleksandrovna nevertheless chose to marry, even though she was still grief-stricken at the death of her first husband, a man who had been twenty-five years her senior and with whom she felt she had experienced the pinnacle of earthly happiness. But now she fell under the sway of her new mother-in-law, for N. I. could never challenge his mother's will. So in the Soviet Union of the 1930s—decidedly not a time when women were content to be chained to hearth and home—E. A. successfully came to terms with this new role, adapting to life under these "neofeudal" circumstances. Then the wrath of the almighty NKVD struck, and both N. I. and his wife were cast into prison camps. (I related their story in *The Gulag Archipelago*, Part Three, Chapter Six, and in *Cancer Ward*, where they appear as the Kadmins.)

After his stint at butter production, N. I. had been able to return to medicine, and had chosen gynecology as his specialty. There was nothing accidental about this, since it brought together the delicate sensitivity of N. I.'s hands, his gentle yet persistent nature, and perhaps some aspect of his youthful indecision about all those creatures of an alien gender with whom he shared the planet. I believe that he must have made an extraordinarily successful gynecologist, a joy and comfort to his patients. And indeed they retained a deep and lasting sense of gratitude toward him, while he continued to practice his profession well into old age. Unable to draw his pension until he reached seventy (the years in camp were not counted toward that goal), N. I. remained eager to respond to calls involving difficult deliveries or serious illnesses. And he was seventy-five when he finally realized a pet project of his: introducing a brief course for girls in the graduating class of the local secondary school. The course concerned those "shameful" subjects that they needed to know about but that their parents could not bring themselves to discuss openly; rather, the students would pick up what they could from each other, typically in vague and inadequate form, with disastrous results in later life. N. I. wanted to write a book on the subject, a manual for teachers.

Being a doctor made it possible for N. I. to survive for ten years in a labor camp, and it allowed him to arrange for his wife to be a nurse at the same camp. But his versatility and skill at working with his hands continually inclined him toward all manner of handicrafts, with bookbinding a long-standing favorite. Before his arrest he had owned all the equipment essential for this task—paper trimmer, vise, and so on—and in the camp he managed to have these things produced for him during a quiet spell in the workshop. Later, when living in exile, he once again contrived to procure a set. He literally craved to bind books, particularly volumes he considered worthy. This was another manifestation of his delayed boyhood, as was his great love for Latin: in camp he became friendly with a noted Latinist, Dovatur, and used his position as doctor to organize Latin lectures for the nurses! This boyish enthusiasm also drew him to a game especially close to his heart: conspiracy. While N. I. cared little about politics and had no actual need to engage in conspiracy (though a spell in the camps has a way of setting people to thinking, and N. I. did have long discussions on Russian history with the quasi-Bolshevik M. P. Yakubovich*), he never tired of refining various conspiratorial techniques in his spare time. For example, he devised a way of using the regular mails to set up a clandestine link with a distant correspondent unversed in subterfuge. His first message would include some harmless-looking poem and an ardent request for the recipient to commit it to memory. Once he had confirmation that the message had been received, his second letter would reveal that the poem had been an acrostic. Reading the first letter of each line, his correspondent would get the words: "unglue envelope." When he did so, he would uncover a message written on the glued-down strip of this latest letter informing him about the next communication, which might come in the binding of a book, in the false bottom of a box, or—the height of art—inside a simple postcard that, when soaked in warm water, could be peeled apart. N. I. had hit upon a brilliant technique here. He would split apart an ordinary postcard while it was dry, write his message on the inner surface, then glue the two halves back together (he had experimented with many types of glue). Finally he would write a message on the outside of the card, making sure that the new text covered the lines written inside. Postcards are hardly every checked and are the easiest things to get past the censor. (But it must be said that Soviet "free" citizens shrank from such conspiratorial connections and generally preferred not to respond.)

The whole technique was developed by N. I. while he was in camp, but he found no obvious application for it at first. Then he got to know Alfred Stökli, a literary scholar from Moscow who was a prisoner in the same camp. Stökli told him that if he could find a way to keep it hidden, he would write a novel set in the time of Spartacus but drawing an analogy with the present (a favorite device of the daring spirits of Soviet literature) and basing the psychology of the Roman slaves on his observations of zek* behavior. N. I. immediately offered him a brilliant method of safekeeping: rather than hiding individual sheets of the manuscript inside a binding (which would have required an awful lot of books), N. I. suggested making the binding itself out of multiple layers of manuscript pages, glued together in such a way that they could be peeled apart without damage to the writing. The method was tested and found to work perfectly, and Stökli began to write. Whenever he had enough pages for one binding, N. I. would glue them together, keeping the newly bound volume in full view of the wardens as they did their routine searches. Later Stökli was transferred to another camp, possibly after he had already abandoned his novel. N. I. not only preserved everything he had written but also managed to take it out of the camp to his place of exile. He then wrote to Moscow, where Stökli now lived as a free man, inviting him to collect his novel. Stökli responded with polite excuses. I felt great sympathy for this secret author, my fellow conspirator, and we decided that he was missing the hints in N. I.'s letters, thinking that his precious text had been lost forever. In 1956, when I too headed for Moscow, N. I. asked me to look up Stökli and inform him of the situation directly. Alas, once rehabilitated, reinstated in his academic career, and installed in his former apartment in central Moscow, Stökli had lost all interest in his camp scribblings: all this stuff about slavery—who needs it? The whole episode reminded me of the devoted but spurned Maksim Maksimych in Lermontov's *A Hero of Our Time*.

N. I. arrived in Kok-Terek, his place of exile, several months before I did. He had been separated from his wife when she was sent off to the Krasnoyarsk region (not by any design of the secret police but simply due to sloppy work at the Ministry of the Interior), and it was a year before she could rejoin him. N. I.'s aged mother, who was the cause of the couple's arrest, dragged herself out there to join him, as did one of his daughters, already seriously deranged—but all that lay ahead. For the time being he was alone, quite silver-haired yet as agile as a young man, wiry, small in stature, with a ready smile and clear-eyed gaze that was impossible to forget. We first met in the local hospital where I was admitted with an unidentified illness, a malady that struck me right after my release from prison camp. (This was a cancer that had been spreading undiagnosed for an entire year, and N. I. was in fact the first one to suspect what was wrong.) But N. I. was not my doctor, and we met as two fellow zeks.

At one point soon after I was discharged I recall walking with him through our settlement and stopping at a teahouse for a glass of beer. There we sat, both of us without family: he was still waiting for his wife to join him, mine had left me toward the end of my camp sentence.* At the time he was almost fifty-eight (in a kind of ironic accord with the article of our criminal code that had brought us here, these digits seemed to pop up everywhere!*) while I was going on thirty-five, yet our new friendship had something youthful about it. Perhaps it was our lack of family ties, the youthful buoyancy we both shared, and the feeling of a marvelous new beginning that overwhelms the senses of a released prisoner. To some extent it was also the spring on the Kazakh steppe, with the blossoming of the fragrant camel thistle—the first spring after the death of Stalin, and Beria's last.*

But just as N. I.'s age was greater than mine, so too was his optimism. To think that he was getting ready to *begin* life at fifty-eight, as though the whole preceding period had counted for nothing! The past lay in ruins, but life had not yet begun!

I have always formed judgments about people at the very first encounter, the moment our eyes meet. N. I. charmed me so completely and was so successful in unsealing my tightly locked soul that I quickly resolved to confide in him—the first (and last) such confidant during my years of exile. In the evenings we used to stroll to the edge of the settlement, and there, seated on the edge of an old irrigation canal, I would recite selections from the verse and prose I had stored in my head, and would try to gauge his reaction. He was the ninth person in the course of my prison years to listen to my works, but his reaction was unique. Rather than praising or criticizing, he voiced sheer amazement that I should have been exhausting my brain by carrying this burden inside me for years.* But in fact I could imagine no place other than my memory where I could safely keep my works, and I had grown accustomed to the strain this placed on me, as well as to the constant need to review what I had learned. But now N. I. undertook to lighten my load! And a few days later he presented me with his first contrivance, amazing in its simplicity, so unobtrusive that it could not arouse suspicion amid the barest of furnishings, and easily transportable to boot. It was a small plywood box of the type used for mailing parcels, something that could be cheaply acquired in the cities while being quite unavailable in a place like Kok-Terek. That made it something that would be natural for an exile like me to hold on to in order to store small items; and it would not look out of place next to my sorry-looking furniture and the earthen floor of my hut. The box had a false bottom, but the plywood did not sag and only the most sensitive hands—such as those of a gynecologist—could ascertain by touch alone that the inside and the outside surfaces did not match. It turned out that two small nails had been inserted snugly rather than being hammered home; they were easily removed with the help of pliers. That released a locking crossbar and revealed the secret cavity—those dark hundred cubic centimeters of space that I had dreamed about and that, though technically within the U.S.S.R., were yet beyond the control of the Soviet regime. It was a quick task to pop in my texts, just as quick to retrieve them, and easy to ensure that the contents would not knock about inside. With my handwriting grown microscopic by necessity, there was room enough to hold a transcription of everything I had composed during my five years of captivity. (In the original edition of *The Oak and the Calf* I mentioned "a fortuitous suggestion and some timely help" received from another person* and suggested that this happened after my treatment in Tashkent. This deliberate distortion was made to deflect suspicion from N. I. From the day I received his gift in May of 1953, I gradually began setting down on paper the twelve thousand lines of verse I had memorized—the lyrics, the long narrative poem, and my two plays.)

I was ecstatic. For me it was no less of a liberation than stepping out of the camp gates had been. N. I.'s eyes simply shone, and a smile parted his gray beard and whiskers: his passion for conspiracy had not been in vain; he had found a use for it at last!

To think that in a settlement with barely forty political exiles (of whom fewer than ten were Russians) a do-it-yourself underground writer would stumble upon a born do-it-yourself conspirator! It was nothing short of a miracle.

Later N. I. installed another secret hiding place in my crude working table. The storage capacity available for safekeeping kept growing, my work was now easy to get to, and one can imagine the boost this gave to my clandestine writing activities. I could stow my texts away a few minutes before heading for school, quite unconcerned about leaving everything for hours on end in my isolated hut, protected by nothing but a small padlock and windows fit for a dollhouse. There was nothing there to tempt a burglar, and a sleuth from the command post would never know what to look for. Despite my heavy (double) teaching load, I now managed to look at my drafts daily and to add to them on a regular basis. Sundays I would work the whole day through, provided we were not herded out to work on a collective farm, and I no longer had to spend a week of every month on review and memorization as I had to do before. At last I also had a chance to polish my texts, reappraising them with fresh eyes without being afraid that making changes would impair my ability to recall what I had memorized earlier.

N. I.'s help in the loneliest moments of my devastated life and the sympathy offered by Elena Aleksandrovna, who joined him in the fall, were a constant source of warmth and light; they served as a substitute for the rest of humanity from whom I concealed my true self. When E. A. arrived, I was waiting for permission to leave for a cancer ward, with the prospect of almost certain death there.* It was an austere meeting; we spoke in matter-of-fact tones about my impending death and how they would dispose of my belongings. I decided against leaving my manuscripts in their house so as not to burden them; instead I buried my camp poem and plays in a bottle on my plot of land, in a spot known only to N. I. From the Tashkent cancer clinic (and later from Torfoprodukt and Ryazan), I wrote them frequent, long, and richly detailed letters, unlike any I have ever written to anyone else in my life.

The Zubovs belonged to the better half of the zek race, to those who remember their years in prison camp to their dying days and who consider this period a supremely important lesson in life and wisdom. This made me feel as close to them as though we were related or, rather, because of our ages (N. I. was only slightly younger than my late father), as if they were my parents. For that matter, not many people could have enjoyed as interesting and cheerful a time with their natural parents as I did with the Zubovs, whether we corresponded by means of notes inserted under a dog's collar (their smart little dog dashed back and forth between our two houses), attended the local movie house together, or sat in their clay gazebo at the edge of the open steppe. There, with more frankness than one could have with parents today, I talked about the deplorable fact that marrying would jeopardize my manuscripts, and together we pondered ways of getting around this problem.

In the spring of 1954, when I was blessed with a return to health and wrote my play *Republic of Labor** in a delirious surge of creativity, I had in mind virtually no one but the Zubovs as a potential audience, seasoned zeks and dear friends that they were. But staging a reading of the play was no simple matter. They did not live alone, and trusting N. I.'s daughter was out of the question. Furthermore, their hut was wedged in between others, while I wanted to read in a natural voice, acting out each and every role. My own hut was well placed in this regard, all the approaches being visible for a hundred meters or so. But the text was enormous, longer by half again than the version known today, and the reading would take a good five hours, counting intermissions. For the Zubovs to stay so long at my place during the day was to risk arousing the suspicion of the neighbors and of the command post. Besides, we had jobs to go to and household chores to take care of. There seemed to be no other solution than for them to come by after dark and stay the night.

It was a steamy night in late June, majestically lit by moonlight in a way possible only on the open steppe. But we had to keep the windows closed to muffle the sound, and there we sat in my miserably stuffy quarters breathing in the fumes of my kerosene lamp. We aired the place during pauses in the reading, and I would step outside to make sure no one had crept up to eavesdrop. In fact, the Zubovs' dogs were lying close by; they would have barked at any intruder. That night the life of the labor camps reappeared before us in all its vivid brutality. It was the same feeling that the world at large would experience twenty years later on reading *The Gulag Archipelago*. When the reading was finished, we went outside. As before, the whole steppe was suffused with boundless light, only the moon had by now moved to the far side of the sky. The settlement was fast asleep, and the predawn mist was beginning to creep in, adding to the fantastic setting. The Zubovs were deeply moved— not least, perhaps, because for the first time they seriously believed in me and shared my conviction that what was being readied in this ramshackle hut would one day have explosive consequences. And E. A.—already fifty and leaning on the arm of a husband soon to be sixty—exclaimed, "I can't get over how young we feel! It's like standing at the very summit of life!"

Life had not treated us zeks to many summits.

As soon as Nikolai Ivanovich and I had begun to earn salaries as "free" employees—salaries that were no longer on the measly scale of the camp—we were like overgrown schoolboys fulfilling a long-held dream: we each bought a camera. (We went about it systematically, first reading up on the theory of photography; soon afterward N. I. even sent the factory that had produced his camera some critical comments on its construction.) But enjoyment of our new craft did not distract us from our conspiratorial schemes; rather, it stimulated them further: how, we wondered, could photography be harnessed to serve our goals? We studied up on the technique of photoreproduction; on my trips to Tashkent for follow-up medical treatment I procured the more esoteric chemicals; and in due course I learned to make excellent photographic copies of my texts. A half-built clay shed with walls but no roof protected me from the wind and the prying eyes of neighbors. Whenever the sky became overcast—which never lasted long in Kazakhstan—I would rush to my shed, set up the portable equipment, and for as long as the light remained steady, with no breaks in the cloud cover or sudden sprinkles, I would hurriedly photograph my tiny manuscript pages, none of them bigger than five by seven inches. But the most important and delicate task was then up to Nikolai Ivanovich. He had to remove the binding from an English-language book we happened to have; create spaces inside the front and back covers, each large enough to hold an envelope; pack the two envelopes with sections of film, four exposures to each strip; and then close up and reattach the binding in such a way that the book seemed to have come straight from the store. It was probably the most demanding binding job N. I. had ever undertaken, but the result was a marvel to behold. (Our only misgiving was that the silver nitrate in the film made the bindings seem heavier than usual.) Now all that remained was to find that noble Western tourist who should be strolling somewhere in Moscow and who would accept this incriminating book thrust at him by the agitated hand of a passerby. . . . But no such tourist turned up, and in later years I reworked my texts, making the earlier versions out of date. I kept the book for a long time to commemorate the astonishing workmanship of N. I., but at the time of my 1965 debacle* I burned it. I can still see it in my mind's eye—a collection of plays by George Bernard Shaw in English, published in the Soviet Union.

The Zubovs and I had taken for granted that we would live in Kok-Terek "in perpetuity," to use the phrase entered in our documents, but in the spring of 1956 the whole system of political exile was abolished, and I immediately made plans to leave. The Zubovs stayed on, prisoners not of the Interior Ministry now but of their

domestic burdens. It was no easy matter for them to uproot themselves, given their declining strength and the illness of Nikolai
Ivanovich's mother. To make matters more difficult still, N. I.'s deranged daughter, wandering defenselessly through the settlement,
had become pregnant (apparently by the chairman of the village soviet) and had saddled the Zubovs with a baby Kazakh before she herself vanished forever into a mental institution. (The Kazakh heredity
asserted itself in astonishing ways: the boy was brought up in a
Russian family and was taken out of Kazakhstan while he was still an
infant, yet without prompting and with no examples to emulate, he
always preferred to sit cross-legged in the Muslim fashion.) N. I.'s
other daughter committed suicide a year later by jumping out of a
commuter train in a Moscow suburb.

The safekeeping system N. I. had devised was so light and so easily transportable that he sent me another by ordinary post when I
moved to Torfoprodukt* in central Russia. I now had three of these
parcel boxes, and they were to serve me for many years to come; in
fact, I made occasional use of them right up to my expulsion from
the Soviet Union. But when I moved to Ryazan* to be reunited
with my first wife Natalya Reshetovskaya, the availability of a typewriter made a further expansion necessary. (Reshetovskaya had
then been married to another man for six years and returning to her
was a false move on my part, one that would cost both of us dearly.)
Typing three or four copies at a time rapidly increased the volume
of material to be stored, and I had to find more hiding places.
Fortunately N. I. had taught me what to look for, so that I was able
to come up with some pretty decent ideas myself: installing a false
ceiling in a wardrobe, for instance, or inserting manuscripts into the
casing of a record player that was already so heavy that the additional weight would not be noticed.

Kok-Terek had seemed an extraordinarily attractive place as long
as getting a release from exile was hopelessly barred. We had actually grown to love it! But how swiftly it lost its charm once we were

granted the gift of freedom and people all around us started leaving. For the Zubovs there was no way of returning to the Moscow region. ("You can't buy a ticket to the land of the past"—N. I. liked to repeat this melancholy aphorism born of his prison-camp experience.) "The Crimea, then!" his wife would urge. She had spent happy years in Simferopol as a girl, and the Crimean peninsula evoked treasured memories. While changing one's place of residence in the Soviet Union is painfully difficult even for ordinary citizens, one can imagine the problems faced by a former zek, especially one not officially rehabilitated. (The authorities could not forgive the Zubovs for having briefly given shelter to a deserter.) Zeks are simply unwanted everywhere. Still, after lengthy correspondence and endless inquiries, Dr. Zubov was finally allowed to take a position in Ak-Mechet (now renamed Chernomorskoye)—a remote settlement in the barren Crimean northwest. With great difficulty, the Zubovs made the move in 1958, but what they found bore little resemblance to the popular image of Crimea, much less to the Crimea E. A. remembered: there was empty steppe all around, just as in Kok-Terek, and the sun-scorched barren landscape actually resembled their place of exile. (I once joked that it was simply Kok-Terek "next to a sea dug out by Komsomol enthusiasts"—but I realized at once that I had hurt their feelings.) But they did have a smooth beach, the real Black Sea, and, best of all, a bench not far from their home with a view of the bay; the Zubovs would come here in the evenings arm in arm to watch the sun go down. With their astonishing ability to find joy within themselves and to count even their tiniest blessings, the Zubovs declared this to be a happy place, a spot from which they would not stir for the rest of their lives. Although E. A. was still far from old, her mobility became progressively impaired, until eventually she was unable to reach that bench of theirs and was practically confined to her bed. But they had mastered the art of living the inner life—just the two of them together beneath their tranquil roof, listening to music in the evening and exchanging letters with friends. For them, it was a world in its fullness.

Now that I had acquired a typewriter and could produce multiple copies of all my works, it made sense not to keep them all in one place. I should not have imposed on the Zubovs, but I had no one I could trust more. So in 1959 I traveled from Ryazan to leave them copies of all my plays, as well as the narrative poem I had composed in camp and *The First Circle* (in the ninety-six-chapter version that I then considered complete*). And N. I. once again set to work rigging up false bottoms and double walls in his rough kitchen furniture and hid everything away.

From Ryazan I kept up a very warm correspondence with the Zubovs, though I necessarily had to stay within the generalities appropriate to the postal censorship. When Tvardovsky* accepted my *Ivan Denisovich*, there was no one with whom I was more anxious to speak about it than the Zubovs, but no letter could capture everything I wished to say. By Easter 1962 I had typed up a revised version of *The First Circle*, and with a copy of this text in hand I dashed off to see the Zubovs in the Crimea. There, in surroundings so familiar to me and at a round table that resembled my own back in Kok-Terek, I told my favorite couple of the incredible developments at *Novy Mir*. As I talked, E. A. plucked a freshly butchered rooster for a gala dinner, and now and then she would pause in amazement with her hands full of feathers. And because the whole scene was so reminiscent of the cozy chats the three of us had had in Kok-Terek (the only difference now being the electric lighting), the full significance of the miracle was brought home to me as never before: not even in our wildest dreams had we hoped to see anything like this in print during our lifetime. But then again, could we be so sure that we would this time?

I must digress briefly here in order to include a point that does not fit elsewhere. That spring, as I prepared for whatever might befall me after the publication of *Ivan Denisovich*, I made three sets of microfilm containing absolutely everything I had written up to then. Using a summer vacation trip with my wife as a pretext, I set off to deposit them with friends from my prison days. One set went to my dear friend, the incomparable Nikolai Andreyevich Semyonov, the fellow prisoner with whom I had composed "Buddha's Smile" while sitting on a bunk in Moscow's Burtyrki prison. ("Buddha's Smile" eventually became a chapter in *The First Circle*, and Semyonov figures in the novel as Potapov.) Semyonov, who was working at a hydroelectric station in Perm, accepted the film and safeguarded it loyally until I burned it myself. The second set was supposed to go to the Kizel area, to Pavel Baranyuk, a hero of the Ekibastuz camp uprising* (in my plays *Prisoners* and *Tanks Know the Truth* he appears as Pavel Gai). When I went there I had no idea that I would only be able to reach Pavel by vehicles provided by the Interior Ministry and that Pavel had himself become a sort of prison-camp guard, something he had not admitted in his letters to me. This loss was as painful as a wound and has not been satisfactorily explained to this day, though it may be understandable enough, given the way they must have come down on him after the camp revolt was crushed. With a capsule of microfilm that felt like a bomb in my pocket, I roamed warily for a whole day around Kizel, one of the centers of the Gulag empire, fearful of being stopped by one of the numerous police patrols in a random check or due to a suspicious move on my part. I never did reach Pavel, and it is just as well. The third set of microfilm went to Ekaterinburg, to Yuri Vasilyevich Karbe, a high-minded, unflappable, trusted friend from my Ekibastuz camp days. Like Semyonov, he accepted the films and safeguarded them faithfully, burying them somewhere out in the forest. He died in May 1968, almost on the same day as Arnold Susi.* (Both had heart disease, and this was a period of heightened sunspot activity.) I can no longer recall whether Karbe eventually returned the films for me to destroy. Perhaps they are still buried somewhere in a forest in the Urals.

After the publication of *Ivan Denisovich,* my circle of correspondents and acquaintances expanded dramatically, as did my obligations and my ability to collect materials. There was a corresponding increase in the attention paid to me by the Unsleeping Eye. As a result I had less and less time for writing detailed letters to the Zubovs, and the possibility of expressing myself fully continued to diminish. As far back as I can remember, I have been able to produce as much work as half a dozen other people, but while I remained underground, there had always been the occasional brief lull when I could get some letters written or chat with friends. Such opportunities now vanished entirely. True, in the summer of 1964 Nikolai Ivanovich came up from the Crimea to join my wife and me on the first trip we made in our own car—from Moscow to Estonia. The old intimacy and rapport were reestablished. But then he disappeared again into his settlement, which had meanwhile become part of a "restricted zone" (some kind of naval base) and in effect now constituted an exile in reverse: in order to visit the Zubovs one now had to apply for a permit at the local Interior Ministry post. The Zubovs themselves grew ever less active: E. A. was largely confined to her bed, while N. I.'s progressive deafness cut him off from Western radio broadcasts. They shut themselves up in a static world, immersing themselves in the classics and noticing only the random—and usually second-rate—works of new literature that happened to reach them. Our experiences and the rhythms of our lives were beginning to diverge, while censorship considerations made writing letters almost pointless: hints were misinterpreted or failed to register at all.

On the night in October 1964 when the news of Khrushchev's ouster first broke,* the Zubovs burned everything they had held for me and notified me of this action by a prearranged phrase in a letter. That was our agreement: if in their opinion they were seriously threatened, they were free to destroy everything. Nor were they alone in expecting a massive crackdown to begin in a few days. At the same time and for the same reason I took the film I had left over from Kizel and sent it abroad (with V. L. Andreyev). Consequently I was not too upset at the news of the Zubovs' bonfire, since I had enough copies of my work elsewhere. The only problem was that there now remained only one copy of my play *Victory Celebrations*.

A year later when my papers were seized at the Teush apartment,* this fact took on painful significance: I had no more copies of *Victory Celebrations* in my possession. It is true that the Central Committee had printed a private edition for their own purposes,* so the text might at least have survived in that form, but the loss was nevertheless a bitter one. In 1966 I met with N. I. in Simferopol (it was impossible to visit him at home) and asked whether he had really burned absolutely everything. His reply left no room for doubt. The only item that had accidentally escaped the flames was an early version of *The First Circle*, and the two of us burned it then and there in a Simferopol stove.

In 1969 N. I. was briefly in Moscow and visited me in Rozhdestvo,* but he had nothing more to add to the story and now I was altogether certain that *Victory Celebrations* was lost forever. But in 1970 a letter from him contained an unclear passage about an old friend of his in Moscow whom I really should look up. This was a hint I did not understand. (We were no longer on the same wavelength in the way that we had been in Kok-Terek; in those days we had grasped each other's meaning at a word and had wondered at the obtuseness of our "free" correspondents. The years apart had now brought a measure of this obtuseness into our own relationship.) I did not go to see his friend. Then in the spring of 1971, Natalya Reshetovskaya, from whom I was already separated, obtained a permit from the Interior Ministry to visit the Zubovs for a few days. I had myself sent them a letter requesting that they receive her; my hope was that their high-minded influence might have a mollifying effect. At the time I could not have imagined into whose clutches our divorce would drive my wife nor that she was on the verge of becoming (or had already become) more dangerous to me than any spy, both because she was ready to collaborate with anyone against me and because she knew so many of my secret allies. Earlier she had taken from N. I. almost all of my letters to the Zubovs, particularly those dating from the time she had left me for another man; she needed them to fill the gaps in her memoirs. Now, not suspecting any more than I did the direction in which Reshetovskaya was moving, N. I. entrusted her with passing the following sensitive news to me, and he spelled out an address to go with it.

The news concerned the Zubovs' Kazakh grandson, born of N. I.'s deranged daughter in Kok-Terek and brought up by the Zubovs with great difficulty. A retarded boy of thirteen with a vicious temper, he had come on a brief visit from his school for problem children. (Placing him in this institution had been an unbelievable struggle, involving endless rounds of begging and pleading.) He had quarreled violently with the Zubovs, threatening to kill them—not for the first time—and in a fit of rage had blurted out to the woman next door that the old couple were "in his hands," that they were hiding anti-Soviet materials in their furniture, and that he had discovered it! One can only imagine the consequences for the Zubovs if the boy had had the chance to make a real denunciation. At the very least they would have been expelled from the environs of the naval base, a calamity for people of their age and state of health. But the neighbor promptly warned N. I., who after a frantic search discovered a forgotten hiding place containing *Victory Celebrations*, *The Republic of Labor*, and several short items. All the manuscripts were immediately hidden elsewhere. When the grandson discovered that they were gone, he cursed and raged. But N. I. now knew that he must save *Victory Celebrations* and at the same time he understood the danger of keeping it, since the boy might turn him in at any moment. But he had no way of notifying me and was unable to travel himself. So he fearlessly kept the newfound cache for several months more. The conspiracy we had launched so merrily in Kok-Terek seventeen years earlier had dragged on a little too long and was now beyond his strength.

In the summer of 1970 a young Leningrad couple, Irina and Anatoly Kuklin, arrived in Chernomorskoye with their small daughter to spend their vacation. They were friends of friends of N. I. More precisely, Irina was a graduate student of the Latinist and classical historian Dovatur whom Zubov had befriended in prison-camp. The Zubovs' cordiality and warmth attracted the new arrivals to them from the moment they met. Thus N. I. had no misgivings about entrusting my manuscripts to them, on the understanding that they would turn them over to me when they could, or destroy them if things should get out of hand. Soviet transportation rules being what they are, it was impossible for the Kuklins to disembark from the Crimea-to-Leningrad train when it passed through Moscow. Irina came to Moscow on another occasion and passed a note to me through Mstislav Rostropovich, but the message was so cryptic and so many people were then trying to see me on all sorts of frivolous grounds that I stuck to my work schedule and failed to respond.

In June 1971 my warily hostile former wife, who at that point still had some hope of winning me back (we were not yet at daggers drawn), related the whole story to me, along with the Kuklins' address in Leningrad. I tried not to let her see how much this meant to me. (Later, after my return from Leningrad, I told her, when she asked, that I had made the trip for nothing, that they had burned everything long ago.) But in fact, I was in Leningrad only two days later, where this admirably fearless young couple had for a year kept my seditious text safe in the damp clutter of their basement apartment on Saperny Lane, undaunted by the torrents of abuse relentlessly poured on my work through all the official channels. *Victory Celebrations* was once again in my hands!

I grew to love these young people. Though they belonged to an entirely different generation (Elena Chukovskaya and I referred to them in code as "the Infantes"), they had come into my quarter-century-old literary underground of their own accord. Theirs was an episodic role—to save a play—but who could say that their lives might not have been ruined as a result? They wished to help me further; professional historians both, they had grown sick of participating in official lies and longed for a chance to clear their lungs. But there was little opportunity to do so, and in any case they wouldn't have been able to: they soon had a second daughter, their basement apartment was as hopelessly miserable as ever, Anatoly developed health problems, they were barely coping with their own duties, and money was short. It wasn't for them to help me but for me to help them. The last I heard before being deported was that Anatoly had been harassed at work, though that may not have been because of me.

But then again, perhaps it was. The special nature of my ties to N. I. was clear enough. It was made doubly so by Reshetovskaya, who in her rush to publish her memoirs about me during my lifetime (in the samizdat journal *Veche* in 1972) did not spare the Zubovs, stating openly that they had been my closest friends during my Kok-Terek exile, had read all the works I had composed in camp, and had kept a copy of *The First Circle* for me. Furthermore I had myself maintained a correspondence with the Zubovs through the regular mails and had even sent parcels to them during the last year before my expulsion. (Once N. I. directed a very amiable individual, one Andrei Dmitrievich Goliadkin, to me. He brought me a letter from N. I. and became one of the 227 witnesses whose accounts were used in *The Gulag Archipelago*. Later Goliadkin was the best man at my wedding to my second wife.* In this sense N. I. also participated in the ceremony, indirectly playing that paternal role that he had never been able to fulfill successfully in his own family.) Because of all their domestic problems, the Kuklins were unable to return to Chernomorskoye for two or three years, but they made the trip again in 1974, in the summer following my February expulsion.

That fall they brought back the following news, which eventually reached me in Zurich. On the very night I was arrested, in the wee hours of February 13, the Chekists descended on the Zubov home with a search warrant. Dear God, how long will we have to suffer these fiends? I don't know the details, but it is all too easy to imagine the knock on the door, the anxiety gripping the heart of former prisoners, the helplessness of old age, the dressing gowns hastily draped over frail shoulders. N. I. was almost stone deaf by now and for forty, fifty, sixty years had witnessed over and over again the same Chekists, the same ransacked homes. There were questions about Solzhenitsyn. What do you have of his works? They rummaged through the place, confiscating letters (including the few from Kok-Terek that had not been turned over to Reshetovskaya because they were the most intimate ones) and probably other messages from me that I had sent by private means, perhaps even my note of thanks for *Victory Celebrations*. (But no, they were more likely to have burned all notes of that kind. . . .)

As the proverb has it: a rope may have loops and twists aplenty, but it does have an end.

What could I have done to defend them? How could I have saved them? By appealing to public opinion in the West? But was it not already overburdened by all the grief beyond its own shores?

Perhaps the Chekists had heard of the double walls? They would then have scrutinized every piece of furniture, every floorboard. That day they searched for the "principal hiding place" of my manuscripts in a number of other locations besides the Zubov home, mostly in the remote provinces—for some reason they had concluded that I kept everything hidden there. Their mistake! The main depository of my papers was by now a safe in Zurich. They left empty-handed, having accomplished little beyond making the poor Zubovs miserable.

But perhaps this was the last major disruption that the Zubovs had to endure. N. I.'s obdurate mother had died some years earlier, the two daughters had gone to an early grave, the son was alive but not present. E. A.'s only sister had moved away from the Crimea. Always so warm toward the younger generation, the Zubovs were effectively left without direct descendants. Every spring N. I. probably continues to give his brief course to the girls in the graduating class, hoping that their lives will not be ruined by ignorance. At times he is still summoned to help with deliveries in the maternity ward. The rest of the time he goes about his household chores and takes care of his wife, who can now scarcely ever leave her bed.

They did have a life. True, much of it had passed in prison, labor camp, and exile, but it was a life. And now it was coming to an end. I sit down to write these pages and in my mind's eye all my loyal companions in arms, my collaborators, my helpers, almost all of them still alive and still in danger, gather around me like affectionate shadows. I see their eyes and listen intently to their voices— more intently than I ever could in the heat of battle.

Unknown to the world, they risked everything without receiving in recompense the public admiration that can mitigate even death. And for many of them the publication of these pages will come too late.

The irony of it! Here I am safe and sound, while they continue to live with an ax suspended over their heads.

I do have a presentiment, a certainty, that I shall one day return to Russia. But how many of them shall I still be able to see when I arrive?[1]

---

[1] The scoundrel Tomaš Řezáč* tracked down poor Nikolai Ivanovich and tormented him again for his KGB-inspired book. (1978 note)

In 1984 I heard that both Zubovs had passed away. May they rest in peace! (1986 note)

2

Nikolai Ivanovich Kobozev

I once planned to write a short novel about this man. There was nothing to prevent my doing so except for the never-ending race I had with time. The novel would have shown how the Soviet system managed to destroy the best minds in Russia without even having to put them behind bars.

Nikolai Ivanovich Kobozev was one of the most brilliant men I have ever met. He was a renowned specialist in physical chemistry, but he went beyond this field, and in the best tradition of pre-revolutionary Russian science combined his main line of research with reflections on comparable phenomena and problems in parallel branches of knowledge, as well as in philosophy, Russian history, and Orthodox theology. Fate had given him an opportunity for leisurely thought in a way denied to most others in this century.

All the peculiarities of his biography, including the reason he was neither devoured nor crushed by the Gulag juggernaut, were linked to his chronic ill health. Before he was twenty, in the early years of the Soviet regime, he lived somewhere in the Altai region, often on the move, getting about by riverboat and surrounded by fit and healthy companions. But at the end of the 1920s, just as the regime launched its campaign to suppress the surviving members of the old scientific intelligentsia, he was already succumbing to disease. He held a professorship at Moscow University, but stopped giving lectures there in the mid 1930s. Agoraphobia, the fear of open spaces, made any excursions, even to work with students in his laboratory, increasingly rare and soon halted them altogether. He began seeing his students only at home and gradually grew accustomed to a life confined to a couple of rooms in his downtown apartment, with its old-fashioned brown furniture, its library, and its walls covered with the curiously whimsical paintings of his twelve-year-old son.

His windows opened onto Third Tverskaya-Yamskaya Street, which for decades had been a quiet byway but recently had become a thundering, fume-filled thoroughfare with bumper-to-bumper traffic so that the recluse had neither peace nor fresh air even at night. Night was indeed the most important time for him, as is true for all insomniacs and people with disrupted schedules: deprived of exercise and fresh air, they fall asleep later and later each night and eventually only toward morning, until the period of sleep shifts into the daylight hours and the time of awakening comes in the early afternoon. Caused by illness, this topsy-turvy schedule in turn aggravates their maladies and increases the damage caused.

Kobozev suffered from an endless number of physical ailments; I would not be able to enumerate them all. One arm was chronically dislocated at the elbow and lacked all strength; with the other arm he could barely manage his spoon and fork so that his wife had to cut his food up into tiny pieces as if he were a child—this was also necessary in order to control his stomach ulcer. He suffered from a discharge of cerebral fluid into his nasal cavity; his legs became so feeble that he had to be pushed around in a wheelchair; he had several complicated illnesses affecting his bones, his spinal cord, and his circulatory system, along with some kind of perplexing disorder of the brain toward the end. His illnesses invariably came several at a time, with the treatment of one being contraindicated for the treatment of the others. He was frequently hospitalized for weeks or even months at a time; then suddenly he would be up and walking around with a smile on his face, spending the summer convalescing in Uzkoye, either in the luxurious resort for academicians or in a simple log cabin when money was short. Even during the times when he was relatively well, you could never tell whether you would find him sitting up or lying in bed. Afflictions had rained down upon him as though he were God's chosen, perhaps in even greater abundance than those that had fallen upon the biblical Job. But Kobozev never raged against his lot, smiling as he submitted to God's will. He was very short in stature, and when he lay in bed doubled up by his afflictions, he seemed a helpless little bundle of humanity, more like a child than a man.

Despite the fact that he was rarely involved in any of the scientific community's day-to-day concerns, Kobozev was never in good standing with the university administration. He had little support for his efforts to publish his research, and his laboratory was financed only thanks to the energetic efforts of his graduate students. His work outside his narrow specialty in physical chemistry was actively discouraged, as is the case in the land of the Soviets with everything that happens to be truly original. What conventional category of research could possibly accommodate a topic such as Kobozev's attempt to formulate a universal rule governing the optimal proportion in any undertaking between directed effort and Brownian passivity—a proportion he determined to be 2:1? Only by sheer good fortune could such research find a home on the pages of the *Bulletin for Naturalists*—a little-read scientific review that had for unknown reasons survived from tsarist days. By 1948, quite independently of Norbert Wiener and without the least knowledge of his works, Kobozev had single-handedly elaborated—albeit by a different method and using a different terminology—what became known as cybernetics on the other side of the Atlantic and only percolated through to us eight years later. Kobozev was as unpublished as I was, but while I could hardly take offense, given my subject matter, why should this happen to a scientist? Constantly muzzled or ignored, denied the ability to present his discoveries in print, Kobozev had to add this millstone of ostracism to the crushing burden of his ailments and to his mind-numbing confinement in a room without fresh air, virtually without daylight, above the din of a street choked with traffic from five in the morning till late at night.

And yet in his last years he managed to bring out a brilliant study on the thermodynamics of information processes,[1] published in the Soviet Union by oversight and, by no less of an oversight, never translated abroad. In this book he reformulated cybernetic theory in terms of thermodynamics, and in the course of his exposition, he offered a thermodynamic justification for the existence of God.

Kobozev became greatly interested in me after reading a samizdat version of *Ivan Denisovich*, and he asked my first wife, a former graduate student of his, to arrange a meeting. Our very first conversation established a feeling of trust between us, and our discussions grew steadily in depth and scope at each of the all too infrequent evenings when I came by to visit. I let him see my unpublished manuscripts, and he proved a painstaking and thoughtful reader. It was natural enough to allude to the difficulty of safeguarding this material, and he responded by offering to arrange for its storage, on the condition that the texts could be held at a distant location. This

---

[1] *Issledovanie v oblasti termodinamiki protsessov informatsii i myshleniia* (Moscow University, 1971).

kind of deep cover was precisely what I needed. The extraordinary consonance of our views made it possible to trust Kobozev with absolutely any of my texts, and between 1962 and 1969 he was the steadfast guardian of the principal copies of all my major works. (They were kept in the home of a woman whose sister had been married to Kobozev's brother until his death in prison. I saw this woman only once and cannot even recall her name but shall always be grateful for what she did. It was her son Alyosha who carried the papers back and forth for me.) At the time this was the most complete set of my manuscripts in existence; it included unfinished drafts and sketches that I could not possibly keep at home. Like a massive stone foundation, it underpinned all my activity by giving me the assurance that my works would survive, whatever might happen to me.

In 1969 I transferred the entire set to the care of Alya, who was soon to become my second wife.

To spend an evening with Kobozev was to get a sense of the unceasing movement of his restless mind. Every problem would be evaluated in a fresh and independent manner. He was particularly fond of Dostoyevsky and Vladimir Soloviev, and he would present me with vast and original ideas, in this way compensating for the disrupted cultural tradition as well as for my own ignorance. Kobozev was acutely aware of the Russian spiritual collapse in the twentieth century, but in religious terms he was a simple Orthodox Christian free of intellectual pretensions. He loved to quiz me on the key ideas underlying my projected historical epic.* I tended to duck the question: a novelist does not approach his material with ideas already formed, they take shape in the process of literary construction. But Kobozev would insist: yes, but how did I see the overall picture? What did I make of the February Revolution?* Or of the overthrow of the tsar and of the monarchy as a principle? Did the February Revolution necessarily lead to October? Why were the relatively minor Russian retreats in the course of the First World

War perceived as a catastrophe, while the huge German incursions during the Second could somehow be endured? Kobozev forced me to confront questions and entire areas of thought that I, in my perpetual hurry, never had the time to engage properly. I could have profited enormously from my talks with him if things had been less tense. Needless to say, I eventually had to grapple with all these questions myself, but Kobozev must have sensed that he would not live to read *The Red Wheel*, and he wanted to have a chance to discuss these problems with me.

We always met rather late in the evening, and we would never really manage to finish a conversation before it was time for me to rush off to catch the last train.

I invited him to contribute to the collection *From Under the Rubble*.* He was eager to do so, but he could no longer muster the strength.

Finally his spine gave out completely. With the help of Rostropovich we brought in a doctor of folk medicine from Kazakhstan, but to no avail. We also tried the latest medicines from abroad, but nothing could release him from the grip of his ailments. Throughout 1973 Kobozev was semiconsious and on the brink of death.

As the KGB drove me from Lefortovo prison to the Sheremetyevo airport, our route happened to take us by way of Third Tverskaya-Yamskaya Street. I thought of Kobozev as we passed beneath his windows and glanced at the passageway I used to enter after dark, sometimes coming in by way of an open courtyard, often carrying manuscripts, and always on guard against being tailed.

A month later Kobozev was dead.

3

Veniamin Lvovich and Susanna Lazarevna Teush

By the time I met the Teushes, the great difference in age between the two of them was becoming less apparent. They already had a grandchild, and their son taught mathematics at the same institute as his parents. Veniamin Lvovich spoke with bitter remorse about his past as a fierce "non-Party Communist" in the 1930s, when he would have considered it an act of valor to inform the police of anyone's hostile activity. (This did not mean that he had actually done so, but it did give an idea of the "Communist consciousness" of that time.) Historical circumstances have now changed to such a degree that many individuals are incapable of even remembering or believing—to say nothing of having the courage to name—their earlier frame of mind, but V. L. did just that. His wife Susanna, meanwhile, had been brought up in fervent Judaism by her father, Lazar Krasnoselsky. During the early Soviet years she had persuaded some of her girlfriends from school to skip class in order to attend Passover services (this act resulted only in a mild reprimand). In later years, under the influence of the reigning ideology, these sympathies waned, and there was no discord between husband and wife on that score. Their entire circle of friends was well-to-do in the Soviet sense; Susanna's cousin, also named Veniamin Lvovich, was a prominent public prosecutor, a holder of the Stalin Prize (for achievement in the aircraft industry), and a full professor.

The storm broke over them, as it did over many others, at the end of the 1940s with the start of the anti-Jewish campaign in Moscow. V. L. was forced to leave the capital and for several years held a teaching position in Ryazan; Susanna retained her Moscow residence permit but stayed in Ryazan for extended periods. The times changed and so did both Teushes; in this sense they were ahead of many others for they now viewed their former sympathy for Communism as deplorable, and their hearts were filled with an ever deepening love for and faith in Israel. In spite of the usual difficulties of life and the differences in their temperaments, this intense, shared emotional commitment bound them firmly together and overcame the potentially dangerous rift that developed between them in the early 1960s. At this juncture the newly retired V. L. became engrossed in anthroposophy, a teaching that encouraged withdrawal from "normal" life, while Susanna remained a natural and life-loving dweller of this world to the end.

In Ryazan the Teushes got to know Natalya Reshetovskaya and her husband at the time, and their friendly relations with Reshetovskaya continued after the Teushes moved back to Moscow.

In 1960 I was for the first time overwhelmed by the claustrophobic conditions of my literary underground.* I felt like one buried alive, and the friends from prison and prison camp who occasionally dropped by were incapable of evaluating what I had written. My wife, while fervently admiring *The First Circle*, found *Ivan Denisovich* "boring and monotonous," while Lev Kopelev* judged it to be "typical socialist realism." At the time Kopelev was my only link to literary circles, but just as he had dismissed all the works I had brought back with me from exile in 1956, so now on a visit to Ryazan he rejected everything I had written since then, including *The First Circle*. Although I was certain that these judgments were wrong, after twelve years of solitary work I needed to hear someone else's opinion. I had lived in "free" Soviet conditions ever since my release from prison camp, but I still felt like a captive in a foreign land. The only people I felt close to were fellow zeks, but they were invisible and inaudible, scattered all over the country. The rest of the population, in my eyes, consisted of the oppressive regime, the oppressed masses, and the Soviet intelligentsia—that *cultural milieu* which by its active mendacity participated in the system of oppression. I could not even imagine a milieu or social stratum where I would be read and appreciated. But of course there might be happy exceptions, isolated cases of meetings of the mind. My wife suggested that I try an experiment, allowing my works to be read by her friends, the Teushes—and in late summer of 1960 we made a trip to their cottage in the Moscow area.

They indeed turned out to be a striking couple. Their conversation was fascinating: Veniamin Lvovich held unusual, incisive, and quite uninhibited opinions that went beyond politics to touch on spiritual matters, while his wife possessed extraordinary charm, intellectual subtlety, and a kind of emotional iridescence. True, I also noticed that V. L. was somewhat slapdash: as he rushed to speak, for instance, he would constantly interrupt his own train of thought—this was not necessarily an unattractive trait in conversation—and there seemed to be more than a trace of muddle in his practical affairs. But why should I care? It was only a question of whether I should give him a text to read. I decided to go ahead, handing the Teushes a manuscript entitled *Shch-854*, a politically barbed version of *Ivan Denisovich*, but the most harmless work I possessed at the time.* For me this was an earthshaking step: I had never revealed myself to anyone whom I knew so little and of whom I was not yet deeply certain. My tightly sealed defensive shell had *by my own choice* developed a chink, the kind of opening through which the wind whistles as it carries away invaluable secrets. I had acquired two readers, yet I stood to lose the labor of my years in prison camp, in exile, and as a "free" man, along with my very head.

The reading had an explosive effect on V. L., who in his delight lost all peace of mind. He solemnly proclaimed the work not only a literary success but a historic event. And then he undertook a willful act: without even thinking to ask my permission, he called on his friend, assistant professor Kamenomostsky, and then on another academic, his friend and mentor in anthroposophy, Yakov Abramovich (his surname escapes me, but I recall that he lived on Shukhov Street*) in order to read the text to them and to share his enthusiasm. Early on he also lent the work to his son. All these people joined him in expressing delight, while V. L. solemnly intoned Simeon's *Nunc Dimitis*: "Lord, now lettest Thou Thy servant depart in peace." Teush and Kamenomostsky, unable to contain themselves any longer, then came to see me in Ryazan. I was not told of Yakov Abramovich at the time but simply confronted with the fact that Kamenomostsky had read the text. (Among the plaudits they heaped on me was the declaration that they were touched by the gentle attitude of the main protagonist—and of the writer—toward Tsezar Markovich.* Kamenomostsky made a comment that struck me as very strange at the time: in his eyes my work had through this trait "rehabilitated the Russian people.") And now they both expressed their eagerness to read anything else that I might have. What other works did I have in my possession?

I was thunderstruck by this unsanctioned disclosure. My heart sank, gripped by a feeling of a great misfortune, as though a fiasco had already occurred. What right did he have? And V. L. stood there with an unaffected smile on his face as though nothing had happened: is not everyone delighted, after all? Ah, how painful it was to emerge from the underground! It took me several days to recover, but there was nothing to be done about it now. I had to get used to the idea of this breach, this sudden increase in the number of those who knew. There were no further unauthorized disclosures, and I gradually accustomed myself to the new circumstances.

In fact no leak occurred, and I had now gained readers who were intelligent, sincere, and thorough. They immediately judged my text to be epic making—for themselves, for Soviet literature, and for the country at large. How could an author—who, it must be confessed, had said similar things to himself—not be tickled pink? A small circle sprang up in which my works were read and discussed one after another. Kamenomostsky's wife turned out to be a former actress from the Maly Theater; she invited someone from that institution, and I gave a reading of my play *Candle in the Wind* in their apartment, though with limited success. And my decision to offer *Ivan Denisovich* to *Novy Mir* resulted not only from the momentum generated by the Twenty-second Party Congress,* but also from the dramatic success the story had enjoyed a year earlier in the narrow circle of Teush and his friends. This "microsuccess" gave me the certainty that *Ivan Denisovich* could be accepted by non-zeks. (At the time I did not recognize any other distinctions and had not even considered that many different currents might exist among the educated strata of society.)

Such was the origin of the only circle of readers sympathetic to me that arose in Moscow at that time. And when a year later I stood revealed in *Novy Mir* and ceased being an anonymous worn-down little pebble among an untold number of others—just one among the millions of former zeks—I transported a second set of typescripts and microfilm from Ryazan to the Teushes' place inside a phonograph; the first set was already in the care of Nikolai Ivano-vich Kobozev. (Every text was represented by a microfilm that I had prepared, ready to be sent abroad under the pseudonym of Stepan Khlynov, with all passages that seemed too autobiographical touched up so that I could not be identified. However, my bur-geoning friendship with *Novy Mir* changed all these plans.)

Since V. L. was now a guardian of all these writings, it was only natural to allow him to read them one after the other. My play *Tanks Know the Truth* called forth a storm of enthusiasm similar to the one elicited by *Ivan Denisovich*. But concerning the play *Prisoners* he re-monstrated that a denial of bolshevism must not lead to sympathy for the White cause in the Russian Civil War because, he said, the people were unanimously on the side of the Reds and it was no ac-cident that nineteen-year-old boys were promoted to the command of entire regiments. (He also considered the kolkhoz agricultural system a distinct step forward in the rational use of land, and he set enormous store by the Yugoslav version of socialism. All these ideas were left over from the beliefs he had held in his earlier life.)

Veniamin Lvovich had retired shortly before we met, and though bothered by some recurring health problems, he was bursting with intellectual vitality. (A typical Soviet syndrome: upon retirement, those who have turned into robots die, while those who have man-aged to maintain their humanity blossom.) His major preoccupa-tion was now anthroposophy; he read all the books of Rudolf Steiner, prepared summaries of his writings and those of other an-throposophists, and made a serious effort to induct me. (I was not interested.) Anthroposophy armed him with a lofty perspective on life but also allowed him to make specific practical applications of the doctrine, and V. L., who had never before tackled literary criti-cism or delved into the Russian language per se, now undertook a study of the language of *Ivan Denisovich*. This turned out to be a fresh analysis that demonstrated remarkable sensitivity to the phonetic texture of words and to their multiple layers of meaning. He released this article into the samizdat network, where it was read with interest, and then immediately started work on a second essay entitled "Solzhenitsyn and the Spiritual Mission of the Writer," in which he placed the Stalin epoch in the context of the world's spiritual landscape. All but identifying anthroposophy by name ("the newborn spiritual science," "the prescriptions of spiritual science"), he virtually revealed his authorship by expounding its essential tenets. True, he was politically cautious, avoiding all use of terms like "socialism," "Leninism," "communism," or "the Soviet regime." (Come to think of it, this avoidance, rather than being the consequence of caution, was more likely a remnant of his former ideological orthodoxy, for we also find him speaking here, in all apparent sincerity, of the pernicious nature of private property in agriculture, of "the historical crimes of the Church," and " the tsarist and White Guard hangmen." Positive notes are also sounded in reference to the cult of revolutionary leaders and the phenomenon of the revolution as a whole: "What was said [about the crimes of the Stalin era] by no means leads to the conclusion that the cause of the revolution was false or immoral from the very beginning. . . . The revolution did occur and was consequently a necessary historical act, a deed carried out by lofty spiritual forces.") Defending my text from attacks that were by now officially inspired, V. L. nevertheless found the main protagonist to have "an inadequately developed intellect and sense of personal moral freedom," and he passed over brigade leader Tyurin in hostile silence. By this time Teush had also read a number of my works unknown to anyone else, and he could not refrain from hinting that during the years the author had been underground he had "probably written other works still to be revealed." He then proceeded to cite segments of my long prison-camp poem, which remains unpublished to this day, and he used numerous quotes from letters sent to me by my readers. This latter section constituted a significant proportion of the essay, making it easy for the security people to deduce that the essay had been written by someone very close to Solzhenitsyn. At the same time these essays and this particular focus of V. L.'s work had become his central interest; how could one have the heart to block this activity? Yet how could I have been so deprived of common sense as to continue to keep my papers at his home after this? Such a blunder on my part was unforgivable. It is hardly appropriate for a guardian of secret manuscripts to take on the role of their public reviewer. It would have been one thing if his essay had been written "for the drawer."* But whenever he was on to something that he viewed as spiritually important, V. L. was incapable of restraining his ardent desire to share it with others. He started to lend out his second essay, and although it seems that at first he gave it only to "chosen" readers, the text inevitably escaped his control and floated free, albeit under the pseudonym Blagov.

Now whenever I visited Moscow, I would always, even if I was laden with bags of groceries, make a lengthy detour to Mytnaya Street to see the Teushes. There I had no need to hide or to dissemble, my heart would be at peace, and I could speak openly about the events of my life and seek their advice. I grew extremely fond of them. They were excellent listeners, particularly Susanna Lazarevna with her extraordinary gift of understanding and empathy. She was the kind of woman whose mere presence encouraged one to speak. The Teushes thus became the first to whom I would unburden my soul whenever I came to Moscow and the first to whom I related my troubles with *Novy Mir*. One might say that my relationship with them assumed the same kind of role in my life that the friendship with the Zubovs, and my endless conversations with them, had played during my years in exile. The Teushes became such close friends, in fact, that in 1964, when a deep rift developed between my wife and me, the Teushes acted as proxies for both of us in an effort at conciliation. (The fissure was then papered over for six more painful years.)

For his part, Veniamin Lvovich believed that the closeness of our friendship included the right to deal with my unpublished manuscripts more or less as he saw fit, including lending them to a circle of relatives and associates, among whom was his young friend and disciple in anthroposophy, Ilya Zilberberg. I did not know about this, and there ensued a repetition of the earlier incident with Kamenomostsky: in June 1964, V. L., without warning me or seeking my permission, arranged for Zilberberg and his wife to come to the Shteins' apartment where V. L. and I had agreed to meet. He introduced the Zilberbergs to me as his relatives.

In the years when my manuscripts were kept at the Teushes, I would often give them an account of the latest events in considerable detail. Thus I acted out my conversation with Dyomichev,* making great fun of him; I suspect that a clandestine recording made on that particular occasion was then sent on to Dyomichev at the Central Committee. At the time the Teushes lived in a single room of a communal apartment with a thin partition separating them from their neighbor, a pensioner with an ugly mug who happened to be a former employee of the Interior Ministry. The Teushes assured me that this man was an utter idiot and that his grown-up daughter was no better. Maybe so, but his connection with the security apparatus was nevertheless a fact. Former zek that I was, how could I have let my guard down so completely? True enough, in Moscow at that time we weren't very much aware of the use of hidden microphones, and the concept of "the ceiling"* had not yet become commonplace. People were not really on their guard. But there could easily have been an ordinary break-in and search of the place when the Teushes were away. If the ugly mug from the Interior Ministry did not think of this himself, he would have been put onto it by the "Organs of State Security" once the trail had led to this apartment. When I think about it today I'm astonished at the degree to which I threw my usual caution to the winds in dealing with the Teushes and at the fact that I kept my precious papers there for more than three years.

Considering the uncertain and cramped quarters that the Teushes occupied, I had also imposed a heavy burden on them.

V. L. was quite careless on the telephone (like most of the rest of us, I must say, until we all began to sense the danger), and in other conversations as well. Thus he told some chance acquaintances at the resort of Druskeniki about his friendship with me, and no doubt added some mention of my unpublished works. By this time one of the copies of his second essay had not only escaped from his control but had certainly landed on a desk at the Central Committee or at the KGB.

When I learned about this in early June of 1965 (V. L. reported it to me at once and I took it as a sign of imminent danger), I picked up the phonograph holding my papers from the Teushes and without incident trundled it over to my new friends the Anichkovs (see Chapter Six). It thus seemed that, walking the usual tightrope, I had once again made a successful escape, even though I was surrounded by the eyes and ears of the KGB. And it would indeed all have ended happily if we had checked the shelves of V. L.'s bookcase to make sure that nothing had been left behind by mistake. Or if V. L. had strictly followed the procedures we had agreed upon—namely, that he would remove only one manuscript at a time from the phonograph as he reread the texts for his own purposes and would return each item without fail to the same place as he finished. This is where V. L.'s carelessness in everyday affairs did its damage: he had extracted nearly a dozen manuscripts, had not put them back, and had in fact forgotten about them. I had taken away the phonograph but these texts had remained behind, among them the dangerously subversive *Victory Celebrations*, some verse of similar orientation composed in prison camp, the play *Republic of Labor*, and various irreplaceable rough drafts.

Still, the situation could have been salvaged even at this point. As V. L. was preparing for a summer trip a few days later, he discovered my dangerous texts. He still could have summoned me from Ryazan by telegram, and all could have been saved if only V. L. had had a clear understanding of the facts and of the danger I faced. Instead, he unthinkingly, indeed uncaringly, stuffed all my secret texts into a little packet and, without having the right to do so or informing me of the fact, gave them to Zilberberg to keep for the summer. But V. L.'s links with Zilberberg were so open that he might as well have left everything in his own apartment. (The list of confiscated materials shows that apart from this packet there was also a paragraph willfully copied from *The Gulag Archipelago*—ten years before its publication!)

And that was not the half of it! The issue seemed so insignificant to V. L. that when I dropped by at the end of the summer and when, blinded as I was by my own concerns, I later came back to burden the poor Teushes with a suitcase containing the *First Circle* typescript from *Novy Mir*, V. L. did not even remember to tell me that he had come upon the manuscripts and passed them on to Zilberberg.*

Meanwhile Zilberberg was still away on vacation, and the KGB was waiting for him to return. On the evening of the day he came back, September 11, 1965, they pounced on both Teush and Zilberberg.

The confiscation of *Victory Celebrations* and of my prison-camp verse was the most painful blow I suffered in what is now a quarter century of literary conspiracy. Eighteen years of unceasing effort had been ripped up and trampled underfoot. Worst of all was the timing: the future *Gulag Archipelago* was then entirely in my possession; it was barely begun in terms of the final text, but included more than two hundred statements from former zeks that had not yet been fitted into an overall plan. Would all this material now be lost? Never to be made public by anyone? And would those voices from beyond the grave never be heard?

I immediately began to burn the papers I had been keeping in Ryazan, including certain items that could never be replaced.

I was overwhelmed by feelings of bitter failure. Through his lack of care and his negligence, V. L. had broken the thread that I had patiently been spinning out of the darkness of prison cells, a thread that extended through the Black Marias, transit prisons, labor camps, and exile to my secretive life in Torfoprodukt and Ryazan—he had broken it and did not even understand what he had done, since he assumed that we would resume a lively interchange right after the confiscation.

The KGB, meanwhile, pretended that it was only looking for "Blagov," the author of the essay on *Ivan Denisovich*, and both Teush and Zilberberg were summoned for interrogation. Needless to say, the first grilling in the Lubyanka prison is always a difficult experience; it must have shaken them badly. But it is also true that Teush's essay could not have carried the risk of a prison sentence. And for some reason, the Dragon was not yet prepared to target me directly. This was surely a misjudgment. Moreover, the KGB seemed not to notice *Victory Celebrations* at first, although several months later they did begin to make use of it. The case against the Blagov essay, meanwhile, was soon dropped.

What tormented me most was the awareness of my own blunders. How could I have missed the chance to save everything earlier? It became difficult for me to meet with V. L., and I withdrew from the Teushes for a long time.

Some years had to pass, the wound had to heal, and the cause itself had to regain strength—not only avoiding defeat but turning into victory—before the bitterness receded and it became possible to meet again.

Our meetings resumed in 1970, although they now lacked their former warmth. The Teushes had grown noticeably older and were often in ill health; they inspired compassion. Nevertheless, Susanna Lazarevna generously agreed to try to help soften the blow to my wife in our final marital split. V. L. was experiencing more and more memory lapses. He was trying to complete a treatise on the historical fate of the Jewish people, a piece on which he had been working for many years. It was a high-minded study containing many important insights, and I read it with interest and profit. Since he had no links to the outside world, V. L. asked me to make a microfilm and to send it to Zilberg, who had by then emigrated to the West, with the instructions that it should be published without changes, corrections, or omissions. I made the film and sent it, but there was no response. Thinking that the film had not reached its destination (it had), I prepared a second copy in 1972 and sent it off. But Zilberg has been in no hurry to publish it to this day.

My relationship with the Teushes in the last few years before my expulsion was warm, although the former level of friendship could not be reestablished.

Veniamin Lvovich died in May 1973.[1]

[1] In 1976 Zilberg brought out a book that surprised me very much. Published in London, it bore a title that could have been produced by a Party committee: *A Necessary Conversation with Solzhenitsyn.** In it, Zilberg reproaches me for knowing full well that my papers had been transferred to him; he claims that at our only meeting "V. L. began to tell you something in a quiet voice and I heard him say 'at his place' as he pointed to me, and you gave a nod of assent." This is a latter-day product of Zilberg's imagination: he has absentmindedly (I hope not consciously) moved the meeting of June 23, 1964 (this date is firm, since it was on the eve of our departure for Estonia for a summer of work there) to June 1965. Zilberg errs again by referring to an "archive" as though this were a standard set of papers kept in a perfectly normal way by Teush and now legitimately transferred to him for safekeeping. In truth these were random fragments that Teush had forgotten to return to me and had thus thrust upon Zilberg for that reason alone. Zilberg bases many of his accusations—particularly in formulating the moral indictments to which he is partial—on these two errors. In his view, the central event was the investigation launched in connection with the "Blagov essay" (although he notes that their treatment by the KGB men "did not call to mind Stalin-era interrogators" and that "not one of them provoked strong antipathy"), and he accordingly expresses astonishment that I did not immediately rush to their side for consultation on "what to do next." At the same time Zilberg writes that he "did not attempt to and could not grasp the true goal of the search." (For unknown reasons he suppresses the names of the KGB men when he cites the official record of the search in his book—a regrettable omission.) But I learned from reading Zilberg's book that Teush had received suspicious visits in early 1965 from persons interested in "math lessons" and others seeking "technical translations" and that there had even been an instance of tape-recorded eavesdropping when Zilberg and Teush had had a lengthy discussion in the courtyard. V. L. had never warned me about this, nor had he become more cautious as a result.

Zilberg is also mistaken when he asserts that, at the meeting with the secretariat of the Union of Soviet Writers in 1967, I was the first to name Teush publicly.* I mentioned Teush then because his name had already been bandied about by Party lecturers for some time, and by linking it with mine I was in fact strengthening his position. But Zilberberg's book goes far beyond these errors; it amounts to a diatribe against me.

Adopting a schoolmarmish tone, Zilberberg produces 150 pages of reminiscences and commentary based on a single unsolicited fifteen-minute meeting with me. He cites unnamed friends and individuals at third and fourth remove who all said something to someone else. With unremitting tactlessness and self-assurance Zilberberg sermonizes and patronizes me. He echoes other small-minded opponents in his eagerness to point to my own published confessions and remorse and even states that he wishes to help me achieve spiritual harmony. Seeing me as a zek hopelessly corrupted by the Gulag (a point of view also held by Vladimir Lakshin),* he instructs me on moral behavior in normal (Soviet) society. In his opinion I had adopted "low" methods in my struggle with the Soviet regime, while more "lofty" methods were required; I had entered literary life with an "inner falsehood" (against the Communist Party), and this quality "shows up like rust stains" in the sketches of my life and in many of my public statements: it even penetrates my purely literary works. In my public statements there is an "aberration of vision" that is so characteristic of me. The manner of my struggle with the regime was only the "typical behavior of a Soviet man"; how could I have sunk so low as to present the certificate of rehabilitation (when I had been accused of working for the Gestapo*)? On the other hand, why had I admitted my authorship of *Victory Celebrations*? (Because the play is all too autobiographical, and denial would have been senseless.) He had read *The Oak and the Calf* and had finally noticed what a painful wound the 1965 fiasco had represented to me—how the ruin of the unfinished *Gulag Archipelago* and of the history of 1917 would have meant the destruction of an entire lifetime of effort. But all he wants to know is why I did nothing to work out a common tactical response to the Blagov investigation. If Zilberberg was so incapable of understanding either the magnitude of my burden or the scale of the enterprise, what was the point of responding? No writer can avoid being struck by the hoof of a donkey on occasion. I was right in not responding at the time of his publication: the answer makes sense only here, in the context of my Invisible Allies.

It would be far better if Zilberberg explained why, instead of publishing the study he received from Teush, he has shelved it—this, despite viewing Teush's friendship as "the greatest gift of fate," which came to him "like an outpouring of grace." Teush, he writes, was a "kindred spirit," after whose death "a new stage of life began—life without V. L." All this notwithstanding, Zilberberg has evidently decided that the study of his mentor must not see the light of day. (1986 note)

4

The Estonians

In *Ivan Denisovich* I let my protagonist give voice to my thought that I'd never met a bad Estonian. This is of course an exaggeration. After all, there were some Estonians who helped drive their country into Communism; others had helped keep it there; still others had worked in the early Cheka; and some had contributed to the defeat of the Whites at Livny in 1919 (whatever possessed them to meddle?).* But my overall impression of Estonians was decidedly positive and was rooted in my prison-camp experience: all the Estonians I had met there were decent, honest, peaceable people. (If in 1919 General Yudenich had had the courage to tell them that independence was theirs to take, might they not have liberated

Petrograd for him?) My opinion of Estonians also sprang from our collective Russian guilt in regard to them, from observing these hundreds and hundreds of strangers speaking an unfamiliar tongue and getting to know only one of them closely, a bright point of light at the head of this long line of strangers: Arnold Juhanovich Susi, my cellmate in the Lubyanka prison in 1945. Afterward I lost sight of him and thought he had disappeared forever, though I had heard the rumor that he was an invalid in the Spasskaya section of the Steplag prison camp. Later, in Ekibastuz, I briefly met the heroic and picturesque Georg Tenno, but he was a Petersburg Estonian, quite Russified and a former Soviet naval officer. (There are many pages devoted to each of these men* in *The Gulag Archipelago*.)

When *Ivan Denisovich* appeared in *Novy Mir* and I was in Moscow, sitting like an idiot in the Moskva Hotel on the former Okhotny Ryad, Tenno was among the first to call me, out of the blue, and to drop by. We had not known each other well in prison camp, but now, sure of each other by virtue of our common past, we quickly became friends. An athlete and gymnast, Tenno was engaged in popularizing *kulturizm* (the clumsy word used for bodybuilding) by lecturing and giving lessons. This was his way of remaining true to his former self: if we cannot be free of our chains at this time, we can at least prepare our bodies for the future attempt. His entire circle of friends consisted of former zeks, and it was he who introduced me to Alexander Dolgun* (who regarded Tenno as a model for emulation in his attitude toward prison camp and toward life). Tenno's wife, Natasha, a Petersburg native of Finnish extraction, at one time a flaxen-haired, fragile young woman, was now also a seasoned zek, having "pulled a tenner" like her husband. She had the same philosophy of life as the rest of us—namely, that the really immutable things are the camps, the prisons, the struggle, and the Communist hangmen, while life "outside" is just an odd and temporary anomaly. (In *The Gulag Archipelago* I noted that the Tennos' chairs were so rickety you could hardly sit on them. "We're just living between prison sentences," they would say.) Because of this spiritual kinship, we hit it off immediately; none of us needed to persuade the other of anything, and all of us were ready to leap to the others' defense in time of danger.

Among the flood of letters I received after the publication of *Ivan Denisovich*, I was particularly gratified by the one from Arnold Susi. He told me that his whole family had spent time in Siberian exile and that they had only recently been allowed to return, but they did not have permission to settle in a city. They lived on a farm near Tartu, and Susi's wife had died of cancer.

In the summer of 1963 we met in Tartu, a charming medieval university town with numerous Latin inscriptions and a hillside park in the city center. Arnold Juhanovich looked at me in the same grave and unambiguous manner as he had in our Lubyanka prison days long ago, peering through the same kind of severe horn-rimmed glasses, but his physical strength had visibly declined, his head had become grayer and his whiskers were quite grizzled. His wife was dead; he had come down from the farm to meet me. His son Arno was then struggling along somehow in Tartu without an apartment to his name; his daughter Heli had arrived from Tallinn where she had procured a residence permit through an oversight of the powers-that-be. I had heard about Susi's children (Arno was now married and Heli had a small son) in the Lubyanka prison cell, and only his older brother Heino was missing—he had retreated with the Germans and now lived in the United States. The scattered and disrupted Susi family was in fact one of the fortunate ones. Others sentenced in connection with the same hopeless cause of trying to establish an independent Estonia were still—twenty years later—not allowed to return to their country; many exiled families remained in Siberia. Among these people, into this small country, the translation of *Ivan Denisovich* fell like a spark. It was the first translation in the U.S.S.R. published in a cheap mass edition, in a run that allowed for one copy for every four or five families, an incomparably greater proportion than was the case with the Russian edition. Virtually everyone in Estonia had read the book, and I felt very much at home there, engulfed by an atmosphere of cordiality that I had never experienced in the Soviet world. Of course the weak manifestation of the Soviet spirit was precisely what made Estonia so attractive at the time. (In the Russian part of the Soviet Union, this spirit will need years and years to die out.) I felt psychologically at ease and realized that a part of me would forever remain in this place.

The following summer, in 1964, my wife and I acquired a Moskvich car and, after loading it to the limit, drove to Estonia for a summer of work. It so happened that a new and very active helper from Leningrad, Elizaveta Voronyanskaya, also spent every summer in Estonia; she had already rented a place on a farm near Võru, in the beautiful lake-covered countryside. This is where the three of us settled down to work. In the farmhouse the women worked in shifts, typing out a version of *The First Circle* (with eighty-seven chapters) that pulled fewer political punches, while I stayed on a pine-covered hillside a little ways off. A worktable had been set into the ground, there was a trail that led to the spot, a tent for protection from the rain, and through the silent forest, access to a mysterious lake. This was the first summer in my life that was not filled with constant disruptions, yet was not a vacation and not a time consumed by urgent trips to and fro. It was a summer completely open to work, and in my mind this period became associated with Estonia and increased my affection for the country. I was going over the text of *The First Circle* as well as inserting the newly received testimony of witnesses into an early draft of *The Gulag Archipelago*. The overall structure of the complete *Gulag Archipelago* was conceived on this hillside near Võru, along with the methodology that allowed me, in an orderly fashion, to incorporate all the chaotic materials in my possession.

My soul was so much at ease in Estonia that my thoughts could not help but turn to the future: could I not find a securely hidden location somewhere in these parts—not a place for rent but a home *with friends, just in case*? Caution and intuition were pushing me to look for a Hiding Place. A person with regular employment in the Soviet Union could not go off to a secret location, but I—liberated from teaching by my official status as a writer—could do just that. So we set off to visit friends, keeping an eye out for possible sites.

Haava, the farm near Tartu where Susi had lived after returning from exile, belonged to Marta Martynovna Port, the widow of a learned biologist. A broad-shouldered woman with a wide and resolute face, she was remarkable for the firmness and truthfulness of her character. Her late husband's work had been apolitical and entirely loyal to the Soviet regime; her sons were building successful careers in the same mold (one of them was the chief architect of Tallinn), and their whole family had been shown favor by the Soviets. As a result, both her maternal instinct and a desire for her own self-preservation should have suggested to her that it would be simpler not to offer support to illegals. Nevertheless, she provided shelter for Susi's politically stigmatized family, she did the same for other compatriots who had been ruined by exile, and now she unhesitatingly offered me the chance to come to Haava secretly and work there as long as I wished. It was a wonderful place—four spacious rooms with high ceilings, enormous windows, old-fashioned stoves, and a supply of firewood. I could imagine how cozy it would be in the winter. In summer there was a shallow river nearby and a small wooded area. I accepted gratefully, keeping it in mind for the future and not suspecting how soon I would need to use it.

We then traveled to Pärnu, where Tenno and his wife were visiting Lembit Aasalo, another zek and Tenno's young campmate in post-Stalin times at Andzyuba, a Siberian prison camp for "incorrigibles." Lembit had been named after the hero of an Estonian national epic, and I think he will be worthy of the name. At the time he was probably not yet thirty, but he exhibited a striking combination of camp-acquired self-discipline, resolute self-control, an excellent grasp of politics, a love for Estonia, a commitment to restore its history and natural way of life, and an extraordinary capacity for hard work. He was a soil scientist about to get his diploma, after which he planned to study history at Tartu University, all the while continuing to work for a living. On top of this he personally kept up the last farmstead in Rae, commuting the eighty kilometers from Tartu; he was heartsick to see rural Estonia dying as the young people left for the cities. In whatever "leisure" time he had, he collected books and read the whole night through. He was the model of an intellectual who worked the land—strong in body, intelligent, and widely educated—one who had been conditioned for all this in prison camp after his arrest as a teenager. I was certain that he would be one of the outstanding citizens of the future free Estonia, unless, God forbid, the Soviet regime took a close interest in him before that time. I did not show my wife the way to his farm in order to avoid giving her unnecessary information: as a condition for accompanying me, she had to lie on the back seat and not watch the road. That same summer, Lembit visited us near Võru and had supper with us. Elizaveta Voronyanskaya was also present, and even here I took the precaution of introducing him under a false name.

On another trip to this more remote hiding place, I took along a table and folding cot, but the journey was not without incident. Lembit, his wife Eevi, and a stove-setter were heading to the farm to reset the stove. We went in my car, and Tenno was with us. We rolled merrily along the highway before turning off onto a muddy dirt road near the farm. But I failed to slow down enough on the turn, and the car started to skid. Inexperienced as I was, I did not take my foot off the accelerator fast enough and the car slid down an incline toward a little lake. We would certainly have gone to the bottom if the chassis had not caught on the stump of a felled tree covered with thick new growths sturdy enough to suspend the vehicle in their embrace but not stiff enough to wreck the drivetrain. At least we were unhurt, thank God. The car had to be pulled out by tractor and needed repairs. At the garage a lanky and uncharacteristically careless Estonian lowered the massive steel frame of the repair ramp onto Tenno's and my heads, nearly smashing Tenno's shoulder and adding another scar to the bridge of my nose. But since I had developed a soft spot for Estonians, I wasn't going to take offense at this one either.

That autumn Khrushchev was deposed and my situation became more uncertain. In the early spring of 1965 we again traveled to Estonia, staying some ten days at Marta's farmhouse. Once I adjusted to the place, I found it an excellent spot for work. I was able to produce the final edition of my play *Tanks Know the Truth* there, and I decided to leave my favorite Rheinmetall typewriter at the farm in case it might come in handy. (I had tapped out all my secret writings on this typewriter by myself, several times over, in a format more compact than even single-spacing could achieve: with each new line I would disengage the spacing control and bring the lines slightly closer together by hand. This typewriter is today serving out its last years in exile.)

The whole Estonian support system was so sturdy that on September 13, 1965, when I learned that the storm had broken over my head and my papers had been seized from Teush—I was at that time surrounded by drafts and preparatory materials bearing on *The Gulag Archipelago*, with everything except the "Katorga" section still in fragmentary form—I had no hesitation about where I should store my treasure and where I would go to continue working on it if I survived: Estonia, naturally. I was then staying openly in Rozhdestvo, expecting arrest or a search at any time, while that evening in Moscow, Tenno was waiting for my wife at Nadya Levitskaya's apartment on Bolshaya Pirogovka Street. In the elevator, unobserved, she handed him everything that then existed of *The Gulag Archipelago*. (If that had been lost, I am sure I would never have written the book. I simply wouldn't have had the patience or the ability to restore it: a loss of that magnitude is just too destructive and too painful. But in all my years of exhausting effort, God has preserved me from major losses involving years of work.) Tenno had thought through the whole operation brilliantly, and on the next day he was on his way to Estonia, certain that he was not being tailed. A day later everything was hidden away on Lembit's farm. Through Susi's daughter Heli (whom I had introduced to Tenno), he then passed the word that I might come to Marta's farmhouse in the winter, and indeed everything was meticulously prepared for my arrival.

I lived through the bleak autumn of 1965 without being arrested. On the evening of December 2, I walked from the offices of *Novy Mir* to the Chukovskys' Moscow apartment, shaved off my beard, and descended with two suitcases to the street, where Lyusha had a taxi waiting for me. (The courtyard of the Chukovskys' apartment building was under surveillance, and the KGB post disguised as an Agitprop branch office across from the main entrance was probably in operation by then. Shaving off my beard should not have been much help, then, but perhaps the KGB had not instituted an around-the-clock watch. The hesitation of the security people during that autumn remains a mystery to me; no doubt it will all become clear someday.) In the train to Tallinn I sat among Estonians and tried to stay silent, using only simple Estonian phrases with the conductor. In prison camp, the Estonians had told me that I looked like one of them. I had noticed this myself on my trips to the country, and now it proved useful.

I arrived in my beloved Tartu on a snowy and frost-covered morning when the medieval features of the university town were particularly prominent, and the whole city seemed to be a part of Europe, entirely beyond Soviet borders. The effect was magnified by the fact that the Russian language was avoided here, and I, clutching a little phrase book, did not force it on anyone. My accent gave me away, of course, but a Russian trying to master Estonian is such a rarity that he is always greeted warmly. I left my suitcases with Arno Susi and spent the day strolling about the town, buying myself enough groceries to last four weeks or so. For the first time in my life I felt as if I were safely abroad, as though I had left the U.S.S.R. and broken away from the accursed surveillance of the KGB. This feeling calmed me and helped me to begin my work.

The young Susis marveled that I had this impression. They knew only too well that the police kept an eye on everything and that there were the usual informers. They pointed out, furthermore, that because I stood out among Estonians, I could bring surveillance onto Arno's apartment—though, thank heaven, this did not happen. Despite the risk, Arno did not hesitate to offer me hospitality and help. He was no longer very young—over thirty-five and balding. He had experienced more than seven years of arduous Siberian exile during which he had to take care of his grandmother, mother, and sister. Then he faced the humiliation and restrictions imposed on all those considered to be politically unreliable: difficulties in getting an education, obstacles to acquiring a residence permit, limits on his choice of work. His life was one continuous struggle to be free of oppression—no wonder he was losing his hair. He had an outstanding gift for economic analysis, and he could have had a career as a scholar or at the very least as a businessman or manager, but he was happy to become a deputy director in some insignificant construction office doing hackwork because, as a result, he was issued an apartment in a noisy, cold, and poorly constructed high-rise building—three rooms, one of them no bigger than a closet. There were four people living in the place, including Arno's three-year-old daughter and a ten-year-old village girl they were bringing up out of compassion. Arnold Juhanovich would stay for a month at a time—having no residence permit, he shuttled back and forth between his son in Tartu and his daughter in Tallinn—and for two winters they occasionally had to put up with me as well during my arrivals and departures, my trips for food, and some overnight stays. I was always in a rush, Arno was harried by work, and there was little opportunity for conversation, but I remember his incisive comments on Western society. (Some years later he bought a spacious farmhouse, one of the many being abandoned, and how happy he was!)

In the early morning darkness of the next day, Arno took me to Haava in a taxi, keeping up small talk with the driver while I kept quiet. That was the beginning of my stay at the Hiding Place where I worked two winters in a row, 1965-66 and 1966-67, completely out of sight of the KGB and out of range of any rumor. Marta Port did not tell her sons either then or later that I was living in her farmhouse.

The two winters were so similar in terms of my daily routine that they have merged in my memory. During the first winter I spent sixty-five days there; during the second it was eighty-one. In the course of these two seasons, the pile of preparatory materials and drafts of early chapters of *The Gulag Archipelago* was turned into a finished typescript, seventy author's sheets* long, not counting Part Six. During those 146 days at the Hiding Place, I worked as I never have in my whole life. It even seemed as if it was no longer I who was writing; rather, I was swept along, my hand was being moved by an outside force, and I was only the firing pin attached to a spring that had been compressed for half a century and was now uncoiling. I read nothing, except perhaps, before going to sleep, an occasional page from my notes on the *Dahl Dictionary*,* every word of which seemed like a delicious drop of dew. I listened to Western radio broadcasts only when I ate, did household chores, or fired up the stove. By seven P.M. I would be exhausted and would call it a day. I would wake up after one A.M. quite refreshed, and would immediately resume work, all lamps ablaze. By the time full daylight had arrived, at some point after nine A.M., I would usually have completed the work of one full day, and I would proceed directly to the allotment for the next day, wrapping it up in time for a six o'clock dinner. During the second winter, when the temperature outside was thirty degrees below, I caught a bad cold, with chills and gnawing body aches. But although I ran a fever, I continued to split logs for firewood, stoke up the stove, and do part of my writing standing up (with my back pressed to the hot mirror-smooth tiles of the stove in lieu of mustard plasters), while the rest of the time I wrote lying in bed under a blanket; in this way I produced my only humorous chapter ("The Zeks as a Nation"). During the second winter I mostly typed, introducing many small revisions and producing an author's sheet a day. Such rapid progress could only have been achieved with a soul unencumbered by anxiety, a condition impossible to attain in those parts of the Soviet Union where the security boys might barge in and discover my work at any moment.

During the early weeks of my first winter I was not completely at ease in Haava either; I had not yet recovered from the fiasco of losing my papers (I wrote down three prayers that came to me in the midst of this depressed mental state). I allowed myself no links with the outside world—for all I knew, there could have been a raid on my house; the Western radio was then less quick and thorough in its reports on persecutions in the U.S.S.R. In fact, however, what was happening in the outside world could in no way concern me: I had merged with my cherished material, far from the rest of the world, and my single and ultimate goal was that this union should give birth to *The Gulag Archipelago*, even if it should cost me my life. Heli Susi, who came by from time to time, said that she had the impression that I no longer belonged to anything or anyone in this world and that I seemed to be moving all by myself in an unknown direction. Shortly after that I had to take a trip across Estonia to Lembit's home in Pärnu in order to deposit some of my manuscripts and pick up some others; for security reasons I did not keep everything with me. The trip involved a night ride in a bus, several hours long and with almost no stops along the way. The cabin lights were turned off, the passengers were dozing in their reclining seats, no one talked, no radio was on, and I seemed to be alone in the darkened bus as it raced through the emptiness of night, engine growling and headlights sweeping across patches of snow on the road ahead. It was just as Heli had said: an empty bus was carrying me through the darkness across the whole world ("Across the Neva, the Nile, the Seine"*), or even out of this world entirely. I was ready for anything as long as I could finish *The Gulag Archipelago* and was even prepared to accept death if need be upon my return to the outside world. Those weeks represent the highest point in my feelings of victory and of isolation from the world.

But then again, how can I speak about being alone with all those loyal friends helping and guarding me?

While in exile, Heli had married a fellow Estonian, an artist who made a name for himself after they were allowed to return. He then deserted her, leaving Heli to bring up their son Juhan. Her excellent knowledge of German allowed her to keep her head above water, teaching at the Tallinn Conservatory and living outside the city in a drafty old house she shared with relatives, where water had to be lugged up to the second floor in buckets, slops had to be taken down by the same means, and heating was provided by a wood stove. Her arduous life, however, was warmed by an exemplary son: he was a hardworking, obedient, serious-minded boy, an excellent student in school, imbued with a passion for national and political ideals from an early age, and always ready to help. (He was fourteen when I suggested microfilming to him, and he immediately began to help me prepare the microfilm of *The Gulag Archipelago*, soon handling the operation entirely by himself.) And three of Heli's friends—Ello, Erika, and Rutt—together with Heli herself offered to safeguard my drafts, typed versions, and preparatory materials, a hefty stack that must still exist somewhere today. Lembit kept the most important documents separately. During the second winter he enrolled in correspondence courses at Tartu University; we met in the city when he came to take his exams, and in his satchel he brought the missing parts of *The Gulag Archipelago*. I introduced him to the Susis, father and son, and I recall the joy and sense of friendship that enveloped my soul like a soft flame.

During those two winters Arnold Juhanovich was completing his memoirs in Estonian on the life of the intellectual elite in Tallinn before World War II; on the country's existence during the war, squeezed between the German and Soviet juggernauts; on the weak attempts to set up an Estonian government at the end of 1944; and on the camps, camps, and more camps that followed. In *The Gulag Archipelago* I used some of his recollections of life in prison camp, which he passed along to me in response to a questionnaire that I had devised to address those issues where my own information was spotty. He was particularly helpful in the terrifying chapter on juveniles ("The Kids," Part Three, Chapter Seventeen). Arno and Heli, in turn, vied with each other in relating their experiences in Siberian exile. Both father and daughter would sometimes read one of my chapters as it was being produced. Heli had a well-developed aesthetic sensibility and offered a number of valuable comments. I even spent one Christmas with the whole family—as a rule, Estonians gather only with their family members for this holiday and don't include outsiders.

My first winter in the Hiding Place was cut short prematurely and painfully. I was planning to spend about a week longer—and once you're up to speed, a week represents a very significant period of time, one that can be more productive than a whole month under other circumstances—when I suddenly beheld poor seventy-year-old Arnold Juhanovich struggling through the deep snow toward me in his low-cut shoes (a city man, he owned no boots). A telegram had arrived at their Tartu address from Ryazan: "Come immediately. Ada." The message was clearly from my wife, but why "Ada"? We had made no agreement involving that name, it had not come up in any context whatever. And in any case there was no need to sign the telegram, the source was obvious anyway. Could this "Ada" be a hint at some kind of *ad*versity? Had our *ad*versaries launched a major assault? Whatever did she mean? Something had happened that was serious and demanded immediate attention, this much was clear. My sheltered existence, my intense work—everything had to be abandoned at an hour's notice, wrapped up helter-skelter. My mental peace was gone now anyway; continuing to write was out of the question. Farewell, cherished manuscripts, perhaps I will not be able to return to you from the outside world. But they still needed to be hidden away securely—a difficult task without previously agreed-upon trips, meeting times, and places. The manuscripts would therefore have to stay in Arno's apartment, a place where I had frequently been seen and that was protected only by a flimsy lock. Night train to Moscow, from there a call to Ryazan. "Come quickly! Hurry!" Finally I arrive in Ryazan, with my beard shaved off and in plain view of the security people. What in the world has happened? Well, nothing, really. You've spent almost no time in Ryazan since fall, I'm constantly alone. I simply couldn't wait any longer. (Over the past year and a half our marriage had come apart completely.) Besides, we need to get a new apartment in Ryazan, but the city council is not responding. . . . But why "Ada"? Well, there had to be some signature, and a non-Russian name seemed better for Estonia; Ada was the first thing that came to mind.

Since the preceding autumn she had come to hate *The Gulag Archipelago*. She would not have been afraid of typing it if she had been with me, but if I departed for its sake and could not even write home, then it could go to hell, this *Archipelago*! (I later had a chance to listen to a taped interview that Reshetovskaya gave to *Le Figaro* in 1974, right after the appearance of *The Gulag Archipelago*. She was accompanied by K. Semyonov, a journalist assigned by APN* to help her put together a book against me. She stated on that occasion that *The Gulag Archipelago* was merely a collection of camp folklore, an unscholarly study of a narrow theme blown out of all proportion in the West, and that I had made use only of facts that supported my preconceived notions.)

My next Haava winter was a period of greater mental tranquility. I was no longer haunted by the fear of being arrested and having my manuscript stashes raided and ransacked. I felt ever more secure amid these now familiar walls, the large frost-covered windows, the old-fashioned stove with its intricate cast-iron latch, the antique sideboard, and the group portrait of Estonian fishermen on the wall. I would now fearlessly undertake cross-country ski runs in the area—the neighbors knew that a "professor from Moscow" lived there, that he was not aloof, and that he tried to speak Estonian. On moonlit evenings I would sometimes step out to stroll back and forth, prisoner style, on the packed snow of the grounds, blinded by the joy of contemplating the nearly finished book that had by now grown into an imposing structure. That winter I did not shave my beard. They never did track us down there; the state security boys do not deserve high marks. (In the winter of 1974-75 there were some arrests in Estonia, some individuals were dragged in for inter-rogation, but the Susis were not bothered, nor were Heli's friends.)[1]

That second winter my thoughts grew increasingly combative. As I warmed my ailing back on the stove in mid January, I hatched the idea of a letter to the Congress of Soviet Writers;* at the time it seemed an audacious, even earth-shattering step. I finished my work and set off for Tallinn to see the Susi family and to microfilm the entire *Gulag Archipelago*. As Arnold Juhanovich said good-bye to me, he gave his blessing to my idea about the letter. My Estonian friends, to say nothing of Estonians in general, found it difficult to believe, as I did, that their liberation could only begin in Moscow, that the shake-up would have to proceed from the center. At the beginning of 1967 this did not seem a likely scenario, but the truth of it became obvious to me when I emerged from twenty years of

[1]They have not been touched to this day. (1978 note)

underground writing into open confrontation. Estonians unthinkingly viewed all Russians as oppressors; to them, I was just a strange exception to this rule.

The following summer I made another trip to my Hiding Place, this time by car and accompanied by my wife. I packed up my typewriter, said good-bye for the last time (as it turned out) to Marta Martynovna and Arnold Juhanovich, and on the way back took Heli along to see the sights in Leningrad. This last detail may seem unremarkable enough, but a conspirator must foresee all the links that are formed by each of his moves and must know which ones to avoid. I wanted to introduce Heli to Voronyanskaya—they lived so close to each other, I reasoned, and it would establish an extra line of communication. Fortunately I didn't go through with it. Thus Heli's (or Lembit's!) name did not end up in Voronyanskaya's fatal diary,* and during her five-day-long interrogation she was not able to name any of my Estonian friends. True, she knew and, I hope, concealed that "some Estonians" had helped me (that unnecessary information was my fault), but she had no knowledge of specific names or places.

That same spring, in the Saint Petersburg he loved so well, Tenno suddenly fell ill. It looked like food poisoning—from eating sausage, he suspected. He tried the hunger treatment and during our six-hour train ride back to Moscow he merrily recounted many episodes from his life. Several days later that May he was to become the most active of those who helped place copies of my letter to the Congress of Soviet Writers in mailboxes throughout Moscow—he was still unaware of the nature of his illness. But it was cancer, and it devoured him within five months. Hero, fighter, and athlete, Tenno was the strongest and most audacious—even reckless—of all those who are named in this chapter. He was in the prime of life and seemed to be in flourishing health—yet he was the first to die. Like many bold, strong zeks, he was laid low by the petty but nerve-racking aggravations of "free" Soviet existence; he had allowed himself to be sucked into that way of life. As one of the main heroes of *The Gulag Archipelago*, he had looked forward to its appearance more than most, but he did not even live to see the final typed version, to say nothing of the triumph to come. I last visited him on September 22, 1967, an hour before I had to confront the secretariat of the Writers' Union.* Good God! Nothing but a spindly frame remained of this former Hercules, and over it his cherished striped sailor's jersey was loosely draped. His dark gray face had shriveled down to a deathly skull. Pain was twisting his tortured body. His wild plan to assassinate Molotov* had come to naught—the Soviet hangman still strolled the tree-lined paths of Zhukovka like a gray louse, but Tenno's arms could no longer reach him. My friend still had enough fighting spirit left in him to appreciate the battle I would have to face, and his eyes even flashed for a moment—but he did not have the courage to acknowledge the nature of his disease or his impending death. His wife signaled that I was to take part in the lie that the problem was a temporary stomach blockage and that he would recover as soon as this was set straight.

I think that one reason I fought such a good fight on that day was that I confronted the fat-faced literary bullies having just come from the deathbed of a zek.

A year later at Christmas I made my last visit to Tallinn. Following Estonian custom, Heli, Lembit, and I lit candles and placed them on the graves of Arnold Susi and Georg Tenno. They are not far from each other, by the Pirita.*

Ah, my dear Estonians! Do you know how much you have done for our common cause? Part of my heart will remain forever with you.

And how many of you have departed this life one by one, zek friends and comrades in my secret struggle? There are mines still primed and waiting to explode. Lord, grant that none of those still living should perish in their blast.

The seizure of *The Gulag Archipelago* in 1973 in a certain sense repeated the misfortune that had befallen my papers in 1965. Yet everything was different. I now had strength and confidence, and instead of being stunned into inaction or driven into hiding, I lit a fuse that led all the way to Paris.* But the sudden flurries of chaotic activity, the whirl of urgent meetings and alarms that both episodes engendered did indeed suggest a similarity. It was imperative that I warn the Estonians and that we decide what to do with the materials that were hidden, and with *The Gulag Archipelago* as a whole.

Fortunately Heli had just arrived in Moscow to begin a two-month-long course of studies. I met three times with her and with Tenno's widow in the very room where Georg had suffered and died. (His widow had been unable to move because of the residence rules imposed by the Soviet system and was forced to recover from her loss in the same surroundings. But she had shifted the furniture around in ways that made one forgot the former scene of death.) Visibly aged, exhausted, and smoking ceaselessly, Natasha Tenno had a hectic job in the detested APN agency, a job she needed to hold until her retirement. "Nata," I said to her, "I'll be publishing *The Gulag Archipelago*. Maybe I should remove the part about Georg's plan to assassinate Molotov?" Her still lively eyes flashed: "No, leave it in!"

But how was I able to continue meeting with her after the discovery of *The Gulag Archipelago*, now that all the eyes and claws of the Moscow security apparatus had unquestionably been mobilized against me? I'll reveal the secret. If you need to go to an address that must not be traced, it is best to set out at five in the morning, without turning on the light in your window. No matter how closely your apartment is being watched by the KGB at eleven P.M., one A.M., or three A.M., by five they get groggy and no one works conscientiously (the KGB has long ago ceased working conscientiously in general). Their electronic equipment may start blinking, but there will be no one to notice. You go out on the street at five in the morning, and there will be neither pedestrians nor cars for a whole block in any direction—you can satisfy yourself that the security people are not watching. You take the first trolley bus, sharing the vehicle with the driver and perhaps one other passenger who is entirely above suspicion, and you get off alone, making it simple to figure out if you are being tailed. As soon as the subway opens its doors, you go in with only a few others who are all genuine, absolutely "natural" citizens and from any one of whom you could in any case separate yourself easily.

Thus, stepping lightly as I passed the early morning street sweepers, I would enter the huge and still empty courtyard and quietly ascend the stairs—avoiding the elevator—to the apartment where Nata Tenno would silently open the door before I could ring the bell. (The apartment was a communal one, and the neighbors must not see or hear anything.) I had set the time of the first meeting by means of a call from a telephone booth; subsequent meetings were arranged "like the last time" or "half an hour earlier." Heli would also be there in expectation of the visit.

The first time I rushed to their apartment, I was beside myself: to protect the custodians of my papers, everything hidden in Estonia must be burned! On my second visit I was calmer: delay the bonfire until I give the signal. By the third visit I had regained confidence: instead of burning the text, start translating it into Estonian; we'll soon begin to circulate it privately!

However you look at it, history is moving our way.

5

Elizaveta Denisovna Voronyanskaya

After the publication of *Ivan Denisovich* in 1962 the flood of correspondence addressed to me became so enormous and so insistent that if I had responded to every single letter, I would have had no time for anything else. In short, it would have spelled the end of me as a writer. Only by maintaining my sense of purpose was I able to avoid this danger. But at the same time I tried not to overlook anything valuable that these letters might contain, some of them smuggled out of camp or scribbled in light pencil on sixteen well-worn sheets of paper. A number of the letters I received also sounded a note that I appreciated greatly: a disinterested offer of help. In the immediate wake of Khrushchev's "miracle,"* Soviet citizens could, without fear, send me their expressions of sympathy, praise, or gratitude, as well as their offers of help, and among the hundreds of superficial, haphazard, and occasionally insincere letters, some stood out by their purity of tone. This is how I discovered several of my future Invisible Allies, Elizaveta Denisovna among them.

Voronyanskaya's very first letter—she was a brilliant letter writer—expressed the intensity of her remorse for the past, the contrition of a soul that had not tasted of the prison camps. In the preceding fifty-six years she had led an entirely conventional Soviet existence, without participating in Soviet iniquities but also doing nothing to resist them. She obediently voted whenever this was required, sometimes conscious of the deceit thanks to her sardonic cast of mind, at other times not recognizing it as she let herself be carried along by the general public apathy. She had no political ax to grind, and the waves of terror had passed her by, but the Twenty-second Party Congress and my *Ivan Denisovich* (her "brother" by virtue of a shared patronymic!) acted upon her tempestuous nature to produce a stormy crisis of remorse concerning the people (even though she herself was the first in her family to receive an education), together with a loss of respect for the Party and a hatred for the KGB. She was not the kind of person who shapes history; on the contrary, she was the type that is shaped *by* history, but for her this process took on a profound and passionate form.

Even though the whole of society was then undergoing a shift in orientation, many individuals went no further than halfway, while others marked time or pulled back. Voronyanskaya, in contrast, never once deviated from the direction she adopted in 1962. There were simply no bounds to her indignation at those who had ordered acts of repression and at the ideological Founding Fathers,* too, as she learned more and more—to a significant extent from my books. In letters sent via private channels, she tended to express herself more harshly than any of us; keeping these notes would have been dangerous. (In any case, we had a firm rule that any letter not sent through the regular mails should be burned right away.) She was tireless in copying out various insidiously scandalous passages from the Founding Fathers, distributing them among her friends, and sending copies to me. In her adamant protests against an era that had stalled and was now beginning to re-Stalinize, she was moved more by emotion than by intellectual concerns. One of her favorite quotes came from a poem:

> If it be love, let reason set no limit,
> If sword be raised, then slash with all your might.*

It was precisely this kind of resolute spirit that marked both her enthusiasms and her revulsions.

The emotional force with which she offered to help—nay, to serve—immediately set her letter apart. I answered, and an exchange of letters ensued. In the summer of 1963 we had our first meeting, one marked from the start by expansive gestures and impassioned tonalities. During the winter that followed I asked her to look over some rare publications from the 1920s with an eye to events or traits typical of the period, items that could be used in *R-17*, my projected work on the revolution. (In my haste I had set extraordinarily ambitious plans for this new book and was then engaged in gathering data for each of the twenty projected "knots" or volumes; I did not realize that I would never have time for an undertaking of such scope.) Voronyanskaya handled this task rather well, sifting through a huge number of printed texts in search of characteristic tidbits. She had a fine aesthetic sensibility and a particularly well-developed feeling for the anecdotal. By the following summer she was already working with us, helping to type out *The First Circle* at a farm near Võru. Earlier, she had been the director of a geological library in downtown Leningrad. To meet my needs she quickly and easily mastered typing, a skill she had not needed before. This brought her into the samizdat distribution network, and one of her early projects was the release of my "Prose Miniatures," to which she decided on her own to add my "Prayer," a text I had lent to her for reading only. By virtue of Elizaveta Denisovna's act, the "Prayer" slipped out into worldwide publication. It was the first warning I received, but one I did not heed.

According to E. D., her irritable nature had led to an unhappy life; she had not married the man she loved and had always lived alone. Her protruding chin and sharp nose were also rather unattractive, but her sparkling conversation, sharp wit, the flashes of humor or anger, the wholehearted plunges into vigorous activity or genial hospitality more than offset her appearance and made her look younger than her years. Above all else she adored music and managed to obtain tickets to all the best concerts in Leningrad. She thought nothing of chasing all over town in search of a second-rate movie theater showing a film in which von Karajan had conducted the score. She could write without exaggeration that "music and worthy individuals are the mainstays of my life. After hearing good music I feel as though my heart is freed of scar tissue." (By a coincidence shading into premonition, E. D. supplied my wife and me with tickets to a performance of Mozart's *Requiem* at the Capella concert hall. She sat next to us, listening to the music in tears. She later gave us a recording of Verdi's *Requiem*.) Her attitude toward Shostakovich was literally worshipful ("If he would allow it, I would scrub his floors and clean his overshoes"), but now she divided this feeling between him and me, all the while jealously defending her attachment to him and expressing pain at reports of the abject social stance her idol had assumed. ("Shostakovich and I are like Ivan Karamazov and the devil—I can't sort it all out. The point is that while he has indeed *given in* to them, he at the same time remains the only one who has cursed them in musical terms.") She was an avid reader of English-language books, even though she had to depend on the help of a dictionary, and she thought nothing of alternating between Agatha Christie and James Joyce. She loved to read the utterances of wise men through the ages and to copy out aphorisms for herself. In fact, she would tirelessly copy entire paragraphs into her letters to friends. "To explain the creation of the world by chance alone is as naive as to suggest that the symphonies of Beethoven are a purely accidental collection of marks on paper," she might write, although this in no way suggested that she had begun to believe in God. She was an ardent admirer of Nabokov, defending him against any and all criticism. The witty aphorisms she cited would always be generously interspersed with her own pithy statements. Before ill health set in, E. D.'s letters were lighthearted, cheerful, even sparkling. In our little circle we began to refer to her as "Queen Elizabeth," or "Q" for short.

It is clear enough that if one were seeking an employee under normal circumstances, in a free country and using standard professional criteria, one would avoid hiring anyone as intense and volatile as Q. But I had one foot in the underground and did not hire employees. I accepted them as friends and enthusiastic volunteers, and I could not avoid entrusting Q with a great deal. (Nor would I have any regrets about this to this day if it were not for her horrible death.) To be very strict and selective would have meant to remain essentially on my own.

Q lived on Romenskaya Street near the Razyezzhaya thoroughfare, but the house had to be seen to be believed. The stairwell alone, with its peeling dingy gray paint, its filth, and its dim lighting, seemed a holdover from the Petersburg of Dostoyevsky. Instead of the standard electric bell operated by a white push button, a heavy wire loop protruded, nooselike, from an opening hewn out of the dark door. A yank on the loop produced a jangling somewhere in the depths of the apartment, and a heavy serrated bolt had to be pulled aside for the door to be opened. And whether I would be let in by E. D. herself (who might be expecting me at a particular time) or by one of her neighbors, there would always be other elongated, squinting, unfriendly faces peering out of other doors. "Neanderthals" and "troglodytes" were the terms Q used to refer to the other inhabitants of her communal apartment, a flat consisting of four small rooms facing a narrow, irregularly shaped windowless hallway that reeked of the kerosene heaters stored there, as well as of a poorly kept-up kitchen and the sewer. The whole place resembled nothing so much as a Neanderthal cave, and only after closing the door of Q's unnaturally narrow room—with its single window at the end and with a side mirror that never failed to startle by the illusion of depth it produced—and then choosing one of Q's wonderful records for the phonograph could one put some distance between oneself and the "Neanderthals" audible through the thin walls.

Yet despite all this I liked coming to this crevice of a room after surveying the streets of revolutionary Petrograd;* I liked sinking into a tired old armchair, listening to fine music while having tea and a bite to eat, looking over the materials E. D. had prepared, and relishing her rapid-fire shifts between rapture and rage on a variety of topics. The dark and gloomy nature of the house, stairwell, and apartment did not strike me as any sort of ill omen; I was quite used to all kinds of dingy rookeries, but I don't know how Q felt about it.

Q introduced me to Irina Medvedeva-Tomashevskaya (see Chapter Fourteen), the widow of the literary scholar Boris Tomashevsky; they had been friends in their student days at Leningrad's Institute of the History of the Arts. For my part I introduced Q to Ekaterina and Efim Etkind. Ekaterina Fyodorovna was especially kind to Q, visiting her frequently when she became ill, arranging for treatment with the doctors, and letting Q stay at the Etkinds' summer house. I also acquainted Q with my former Ryazan pupil Liza Shipovalnikova, with whom she became fast friends. (Whenever Liza travelled to Moscow or Ryazan she would carry messages between us.) Through me, too, Q got to know L. A. Samutin; the firm friendship that developed between them, however, eventually brought misfortune to both.

Q was wholeheartedly loyal to all her friends, and to me most of all. Her impulsive nature prompted her to begin keeping a diary (we knew nothing of this at the time) in which she recorded the people she met, what she did, and what messages she had received by private means—messages that needed to be burned! It was something like *a conspirator's diary*, for heaven's sake. The same extravagant romanticism—the desire to be a custodian in the service of history, keeping safe what would otherwise perish and be forgotten—would later prompt Q's fateful decision not to burn the draft of *The Gulag Archipelago* that was in her possession, as she was supposed to do.

On my way from Estonia in 1967 I left Q one of the two extant copies of my densely typed version of *Gulag* with the request that she retype the text in a way that would leave space for entering corrections and emendations. And tap out the whole fifteen hundred pages she did, without incident and in three copies, working at the only available table in her cramped quarters, hemmed in by wardrobes and walls in a hostile communal apartment where she could be seized on the least suspicion. (She was retired by now and spent most of her time in her room.) I later used one of these copies in the preparation of the final text.

Q was mesmerized by *The Gulag Archipelago* from her first acquaintance with this book; she regarded it with a mixture of adoration and horror, seeming to sense her own fatal link with it, and she distinguished it sharply from all my other works. But it was precisely the superlatives she used to describe this book that induced her to share her knowledge of it, along with several pages, with some of her close friends. Only very, very few, mind you, just one or two. But the world, or at least the world of the Russian intelligentsia, is an amazingly small place, and this leak to two Leningrad ladies became instantly known (via Nina Pakhtusova) to a person in Moscow who happened to be a close friend of ours, the wonderful "Princess" (Natalya Vladimirovna Kind). She reported the news to us, and Q's indiscretion was nipped in the bud before the manuscript, or any word of it, could reach a wider audience.

Yet even this lesson did not serve as a serious warning to me, and I limited myself to a few superficially stern reproaches, since the whole thing had ended so painlessly, so neatly, and one might even say amusingly. In our circle we did not even ask ourselves whether Q should be excluded from future work or cut off from access to our secret plans.

Despite what seemed like fairly broad (although diminishing) sympathy for me on the part of society at large, there were never more than ten of us working together, with Lyusha (Elena) Chukovskaya (see Chapter Eight) acting as the coordinator. The volume of work was huge and exhausting and involved constant games of hide-and-seek: there were times when you could not deliver texts, places you could not leave them, telephones you must not use, and ceilings beneath which you were not supposed to speak. You could not keep the typed texts in your apartment, the used carbon paper had to be burned, and for all correspondence you had to depend on direct delivery by friends, since the regular mails were out of the question. Heartfelt devotion to the cause seemed to be the paramount quality under these circumstances—what was the point of quibbling about minor shortcomings?

In the spring of 1968, when I was feeling the pressure of the imminent Western publication of both *The First Circle* and *Cancer Ward* and when the final editing of *The Gulag Archipelago* was about to be completed, we decided to speed things up by having three typists— Q, Lyusha, and my first wife Natasha—meet in Rozhdestvo in order to finish the job in one big push. We did it in thirty-five days: before the summer-cottage crowd gathered in Rozhdestvo in early June, we were able to produce the final copy of *The Gulag Archipelago* without once opening the windows during the day for fear that the clatter of typewriters would attract attention. (On the very day we finished, N. I. Stolyarova rushed in to report that a Russian edition of *The First Circle* had appeared in the West; she also whispered in my ear that a way had been found to take a microfilm of the *Gulag* text abroad on Pentecost, in a week's time. Our hour was striking, high up on an invisible bell tower.)

After our blitz of that May my collaboration with Q began to taper off for perfectly natural reasons: I had completed all the texts that needed voluminous typing or urgent duplication and was turning my attention to *The Red Wheel*. The lines of communication with my Leningrad collaborators also grew less reliable in this period. Once I had taken up residence in Rostropovich's dacha, I traveled to Leningrad only infrequently, and these visits were brief since they no longer entailed library study or systematic peregrinations in the city as before; I now came only for quick second looks at certain Petrograd locales relevant to *March 1917* or for high-priority meetings with individuals who had special knowledge of those events. Meanwhile Q was eagerly pressing me for more and more work. After her retirement the typing skills she had acquired became a partial source of income. But her increasing lameness deprived her of mobility, and day upon dark Leningrad day she was confined to her crevice of a room in that Neanderthal apartment where, with plenty of time on her hands, she now clamored for "work for the soul." And in fact she had time to accomplish a great deal, including making extra copies of the ninety-six-chapter *First Circle* and of *August 1914*. She also typed chapters from Irina Tomashevskaya's manuscript* on *The Quiet Don*. At that point Lyusha and Q conceived the idea of saving an intermediate typed version of *The Gulag Archipelago*, a project that entailed inserting the numerous emendations that appear in the final version, including some entire chapters. It was an overambitious undertaking from the start, apart from the fact that we now had a shortage of places to keep all these texts, yet at the same time it seemed a pity to destroy the intermediate versions. Three new copies would be produced, and who knows when they might come in handy. Q did complete part of the job, but it soon became obvious that it was unmanageable, and we decided to destroy all extant copies of this version so that no divergent readings might remain. But as it happened, each of the individuals holding these texts dithered and resisted. One copy had been hidden with the help of O. A. L., another was buried near Efim Etkind's dacha, and Q's own copy was at L. A. Samutin's dacha, also purportedly buried. In March of 1972 I was in Leningrad for the last time before my expulsion, and I was able to receive assurances about the destruction of only the first of these copies. The second and third still remained intact, despite my repeated requests that they be burned. At the time I was ready to dig them up and burn them myself, but the ground was frozen and the job had to wait for warmer weather. Etkind, for all the good judgment and caution that he normally exhibited, was given to an occasional burst of recklessness, and this made him run the unnecessary risk of keeping the manuscript for an extra winter. He assured me that he burned it that spring. But Q had not yielded to my request even by summer, pleading with me in her letters to preserve the text, and it was already autumn 1972 before she sent me a dramatically vivid account of how she and Samutin had lit a bonfire, and then, with crimson and yellow foliage falling around them and to the accompaniment of her sobs, they had burned the priceless manuscript to the last page. In reality nothing had been burned; she had lied to me. But it was impossible to doubt Q's dramatic report, and to console her I wrote that I would soon present her with a real book version of the text. At that time I envisioned publishing *Gulag* in the spring of 1975, but events were already beginning to move according to a different schedule.

The letters Q wrote to me in her last years provide glimpses of a presentiment that went unnoticed by either of us at the time but that is obvious in retrospect. "I pray to God that I don't collapse and become bedridden. I am preparing myself for a different kind of end and I keep repeating Shakespeare's Sonnet 66 ('. . . for restful death I cry')"; "No, I don't want to end up in the jaws of a hyena"; "A couple of days ago I *took a stroll* to the Big House.* Fortunately it concerned the case of a certain geologist. It was a *cozy* place, with *nice* people . . . " (Could that have been their way of getting a close look at her?)

Because I had not involved Q in any major conspiratorial projects for some time and saw her rarely, I was not overly concerned about the degree of caution she exercised in her dealings with the world at large. Meanwhile, her extravagant nature allowed her to switch from fear to extreme carelessness and to begin sending Lyusha Chukovskaya very witty letters through the regular mails, letters that contained playful hints and bore mysterious signatures like "Vorozheikina,"* with a different pseudonym each time. Lyusha's address on a letter was pretty much the same as mine as far as the security boys were concerned; her mail was thoroughly scrutinized, and Q's provocative hints could not have failed to attract attention.

After I received the Nobel Prize in 1970 it became possible for me to help some of my friends, and at one point I arranged for a money transfer to Voronyanskaya from France, though we had to invent a fictitious sender, since she could not suggest any real names. Perhaps this unusual transaction also raised suspicions. And there was an episode involving Liza Shipovalnikova, whose meetings with Q had evidently been noted and whose neighbors were now questioned about Voronyanskaya by the KGB. (This particular line of inquiry seemed to have no follow-up, however.) But even without any of these leads, which, in hindsight, add up to an obvious pattern, my former collaborators could also have been identified thanks to the close friendship that my first wife Natalya Reshetovskaya had now formed with the people from the Novosti Press Agency who now had full access to her papers as well as to those of mine that Reshetovskaya had refused to return to me. (She soon gave the APN my letters to her, and they were put on sale in the West.) She had photographs of Q and of other helpers, but fortunately she had not become acquainted with any of the collaborators who had come into the picture during the last several years. Reshetovskaya had also met with Samutin several times (he had passionately sided with her in our marital dispute), and he was by now under the watchful eye of the KGB.

The KGB could have struck any of a number of people. They chose Q for starters because she was on the periphery, lacked any renown or defenses, and appeared to have the type of personality that would buckle from a sudden blow and methodical pressure. Still, if Q had not preserved the typescript she had allegedly destroyed and had not kept a diary, they would have gotten nothing out of her arrest.

Voronyanskaya had retained a high degree of mobility, sprightliness, and pure spunk well-nigh to the age of sixty, and like many others who had experienced virtually no illness in their lives, she assumed that this would not change. But in 1965 she took a vacation on the Caucasian shore of the Black Sea and, in the midst of her cheerful gambols, suddenly broke her leg. Her entire life dimmed from that moment on. She returned to Leningrad with the fracture; all the torments of sloppy, uncaring, but "free" Soviet treatment followed. She was laid up for six months; then came two years of limping in constant pain and the stiffening of a joint deformed by poor treatment. The leg eventually did regain some strength, but by now edema had developed, together with cardiac arrhythmia and shortness of breath. "The treatment I am receiving causes me to lose weight and makes me feel like I am an attic where my internal organs have been hung out on a line like laundry. Whenever I look in the mirror I get the urge to don a Muslim veil." Yet despite all her ailments and her unsound leg, she undertook a trip to the Crimea during her last summer (1973) with her friend Nina Pakhtusova and there clambered over the slopes "all swollen and gasping for air." She loved the Crimea and seemed to sense that she was saying good-bye to it forever. During the last couple of weeks of their vacation the two ladies had the oversolicitous company of a shady character who introduced himself as "Genrikh Moiseyevich Gudyakov, an unpublished poet from Moscow." He kept spouting verse by Gumilyov and by himself, and Q invited him to visit her for a reading of *The First Circle*, *Cancer Ward*, and Avtorkhanov.* Nina Pakhtusova thought the man suspicious, but Q argued heatedly that one must not go through life constantly distrusting everyone. Indeed, later that summer she was planning to use the same approach in order to enlighten a retired prosecutor, no less, the unexpected "uncle" of an unexpected new neighbor in her communal apartment. The situation was pretty remarkable: the Neanderthal proletarians had been moved from their ghastly, crumbling nineteenth-century apartment into better quarters, while the niece of a prosecutor had been eager to move in there! (There had been yet another warning that we did not heed at the time: that spring, before Q's trip to the Crimea, two young women came to see her about a private typing job but only took away samples of her typeface and never returned.)

Both Q and Pakhtusova were arrested in Leningrad's Moskovski Station as they were alighting from their train on August 4. They were separated: Pakhtusova was taken to her apartment to be present while a search was conducted; Q's place had probably already been ransacked. From that moment on we know nothing further from Q directly, except for one last statement reported by Pakhtusova. During her unremitting five-day-long interrogation (August 4 to 9, with Elizaveta Denisovna's ordeal perhaps being longer still, who knows?), Pakhtusova was allowed to bump into Q once, in the toilet. Haggard, with inflamed lips and feverish eyes, Q whispered to her, "Don't resist. I've told them everything."

Nina Pakhtusova was a person of great loyalty and firm principles who in the course of her geological expeditions had often found herself in the vicinity of various islands in the "archipelago" of prison camps. In fact she had attempted to compile a map of the camps for us, and this unfinished project now also landed on the desks of the KGB. Pakhtusova did not yield an inch, despite the relentless five-day-long interrogation, but Q's diaries as well as the letters Q had preserved were all seized in Pakhtusova's apartment.

One can only imagine Q's terror during the interrogation process. Not only was she old, in ill health, and with precious little strength to resist; not only did the circumstances represent a new experience for her personally, even though she was, from reading *The Gulag Archipelago*, only too familiar with what to expect; not only must she have been weighed down by the recognition of her mistakes, by self-blame, and by the thought that others would suffer because of her; but it must have been especially tormenting to realize that her diary was right there on the interrogator's desk, so that silence or denials were no longer possible, and she could only twist and turn, desperately inventing explanations and mitigating circumstances. It must have been impossible for her to avoid giving some kind of testimony about Etkind; it was inevitable that she had to name Lyusha Chukovskaya; and Irina Tomashevskaya and her study on the authorship of *The Quiet Don* may also have been implicated. But most painful and inevitable of all was turning in *The Gulag Archipelago* and pointing to Samutin as the manuscript's current holder.

Leonid Aleksandrovich Samutin, a former Vlasovite* and anti-Communist journalist who by some miracle had escaped being shot at the end of the war, had served out a "tenner" in the Vorkuta camps and then spent fifteen more years of forced residence in the area; finally, well into retirement age, he had managed to finagle his way into Leningrad. He was the most vulnerable of all the individuals affected by the KGB raid. He later passed the word to me that he could not have refused to point out the hiding place to the KGB men since, so he claimed, other things were buried elsewhere on the premises. His explanation was superfluous: I understood perfectly well that there was no way he could have resisted.

There is one very curious aspect to this episode, though. The KGB had information about the buried manuscript for at least three weeks before going after it. Surely this was not due to a fear that their action might have explosive consequences—they have never had brains enough for that kind of consideration. Why then?[1]

About Voronyanskaya's subsequent fate in August we have no reliable information. The only report we do have comes from her suspicious new neighbor in the communal apartment, the nurse whose uncle was a prosecutor. According to her, Voronyanskaya was permitted to return home after five days of interrogation, where she remained in her room in a terrible state of agitation, repeating over and over that she was a "Judas" who had betrayed innocent people. (I do not doubt that the psychological toll must indeed have been devastating, with the worst of it being not the threats of the "Big House" but the terror of a crushingly lonely life, with friends who by now might have perished and with a priceless book, a memorial to millions, now lost forever.) Later, so the account continues, Voronyanskaya was hospitalized with a cardiac condition (the same neighbor took her to the clinic). She was discharged a week later and soon thereafter, presumably at the end of August, she hanged herself in that crooked, dark, fetid, Dostoyevskian hallway.

[1] After Samutin's death, his account of "How *The Gulag Archipelago* Was Seized" appeared in the samizdat network. From this text I learned with great astonishment that Samutin (who, it turns out, had long been aware of my instructions to burn the typescript but had joined Voronyanskaya in deceiving me) had not buried the text at all but had simply kept it in the attic of his dacha along with a copy of the ninety-six-chapter *First Circle*, a still-secret text at the time. Such carelessness was beyond anything I could have imagined.

Several months later, yet another version of Samutin's reminiscences appeared. According to Samutin's widow and daughter, this new text had been virtually dictated to Samutin by the security people; it seems possible that it then underwent still further doctoring by the KGB. (1990 note)

(But the same nurse gave a different version when she had a drink too many at the wake for Voronyanskaya. The body, she now said, had knife wounds and blood—hardly something consistent with suicide by hanging.)[2]

Voronyanskaya was forbidden to make any attempt to notify us; this is obvious both from standard KGB operating procedure and from the similar prohibition announced to Nina Pakhtusova. But did Voronyanskaya submit to this injunction? Could she have tried to reach us and been killed for this attempt? It is horrible to imagine the scene of this foul murder in that gloomy cave of an apartment.

That August Nina Pakhtusova made a point of walking down Romenskaya Street several times, but the windows of Voronyanskaya's apartment were always dark. Screwing up her courage, she climbed the stairs and yanked on the wire noose: the sinister little bell tinkled inside, but no one came to the door. (The apartment had no telephone.) Had everyone been moved out? There were no more witnesses, and the very place had in a sense ceased to exist: no one lived there anymore.

But it turned out that Voronyanskaya had an illiterate relative living in Leningrad, a second cousin of sorts named Dusya, a woman who knew none of us and of whom we were not aware. Dusya also happened to be the only person who was informed of Voronyanskaya's death—and this information came not from the militia, mind you, but from the KGB. Voronyanskaya, Dusya was told, had been brought to her death by the intelligentsia. Such an explanation must have seemed safe enough, given Dusya's illiteracy and lack of contact with any of us. She was not shown the body but was told when the burial would take place.

[2]Many years later Y. Vinkovetsky wrote me that soon after Voronyanskaya's death, a colleague at his geological institute was interrogated by an investigator who boasted that "people have hanged themselves after being grilled by me." (1986 note)

People from the village, even when they move to big towns, retain something of the intuition and sharp eye needed in the field and forest. At some point years earlier Dusya had accompanied Voronyanskaya on her way to Samutin's apartment house; she knew that he was a good friend and remembered the entryway Voronyanskaya had taken. The house and entryway were easy enough to recognize, but what to do next in a large apartment building? Her solution was to knock on every apartment door and ask whether anyone knew Elizaveta Denisovna Voronyanskaya. Samutin's apartment happened to be one of the first Dusya tried, and he also happened to be at home. Thus did an illiterate woman outwit the KGB and fasten the first link in the chain that would set off the explosion of *The Gulag Archipelago*.

Samutin was meanwhile still unaware of what had taken place, but he had been wondering why Voronyanskaya, always so friendly, was not writing, calling, or coming by: shouldn't she have returned from her Crimean vacation by this time? And now the news of her sudden death! The burial was to take place the next day, August 30; the body was presently in the Botkin barracks. Of Voronyanskaya's arrest and the whole KGB operation Dusya of course said nothing to him, since she had no knowledge of it. Samutin promised to be there.

Samutin's first thought was to inform the Etkinds, since from his conversations with Voronyanskaya he had heard that they could easily get in touch with me. They lived near the Alexander Nevsky monastery, not far from the Botkin barracks. That same day (August 29) he called the Etkinds:

"Did you know a woman by the name of Voronyanskaya? She has passed away. This is a friend of hers calling. She'll be buried tomorrow; departure from the morgue is scheduled for 2:30 P.M. No, I don't know the cause of death. . . . Please notify *our common acquaintances* [that is, me]. . . . "

Etkind's phone went dead for two hours immediately thereafter.

Needless to say, all means of communication were being monitored by this time, but the KGB had blundered by not cutting off the conversation immediately.

At this time Lev Kopelev happened to be visiting Leningrad, and the Etkinds asked him to pass the word to me. But Kopelev had no idea that this death might be closely connected to our whole conspiracy, so without any attempt to deliver a private message, he simply called Alya in Moscow and asked her to tell me that my typist Elizaveta Denisovna had died.

The KGB people must have been as astonished as they were furious: the whole operation was top secret, no outsiders were supposed to know, yet the accursed intelligentsia had already gotten wind of it, and in three hours' time I could conceivably be on the day train from Moscow, arriving in Leningrad by evening. They had known for three weeks where the *Gulag* text was to be found, but they had delayed making their move. What if I were now to arrive on the scene and pick up the text myself? Kopelev's phone call sent the fire further down the fuse and sped up the course of events.[3]

By 2:30 on the afternoon of August 30, the group gathered at the Botkin barracks consisted of Samutin, the Etkinds, Zoya Toma-

---

[3]The authentic version of Samutin's reminiscences allows us to determine that he was arrested *within hours* of that call on August 29. He was taken to the "Big House" and immediately agreed to hand over *The Gulag Archipelago*. (One thing amazes me: that a veteran prison-camp inmate like Samutin, a former Vlasovite who had found his way into Leningrad by unorthodox means and whose overall position was so shaky, should have had a notebook filled with the addresses of people who could now be pulled in and that he should have been afraid that the numerous samizdat texts he had collected would be discovered—as though they compared in danger to *The Gulag Archipelago*!—and above all that he should have feared that a KGB search of the premises would traumatize his wife and children. . . . As it turned out, he was not even subjected to a search of his person.) That night the KGB took possession of the *Gulag* text at his dacha. It is clear that they forced him to vow complete silence—he must not utter a word to anyone. But on the morning of August 30 they suddenly realized that they needed a statement to the effect that he had turned over the text *voluntarily* and they hauled him in for one more meeting at the Evropeiskaya Hotel. (1990 note)

shevskaya (the daughter of Irina Tomashevskaya), and Zoya's friend Galya, who happened to be visiting Zoya at the time. They were now informed that the body had been taken away two hours earlier. "How is that possible?" "Oh, we had a free vehicle."

But where was Dusya? It turned out that following the village custom, she had come early just in case and had left for the cemetery with the hearse.

Etkind had the presence of mind to ask for the official record at the morgue: what was the cause of death? The attendant obliged readily; the entry read "asphyxiation by mechanical means," which, he explained, meant suicide by hanging. "Impossible! An error, maybe?" "As if you didn't know yourself," the attendant muttered, no doubt wondering what kind of relatives these were.

There was another character loitering around the morgue, making real conversation impossible.

All five now got into Etkind's car and set off for Yuzhnoe cemetery, a long drive beyond the city limits toward the Pulkov hills. Yuzhnoe cemetery is a veritable city of the dead serving the capital; a place for those who cannot manage to be buried in a better spot, a dumping ground for an overpopulated city. Conversation en route was stormy. What could have happened? Someone remembered the hard-currency vouchers that Voronyanskaya had received: might her Neanderthal neighbors have killed her for them? Samutin disposed of that: "They've all moved out. A decent-looking nurse lives there now." Etkind's wife Ekaterina Fyodorovna spoke up: "Suicide is simply out of the question. I knew her well enough to be able to say that." "Then it must be political murder!" someone shouted.

The cemetery is a vision of depressing uniformity, a huge churned-up vacant field with the type of clay that clings to your shoes when it rains. There is not a tree in sight, and the whole area is divided into rectangular sections, each containing thirty-six rows with twenty-four graves per row. Crosses or enclosures are prohibited, and each grave resembles a concrete tub with an oarlike protrusion at the head; to this is attached a small blue panel bearing the name of the deceased and the years of birth and death (more specific dates are not allowed). The "tubs" are topped over with earth, and flowers may be planted there. Motorized carts distribute the coffins smartly along the passageways, and the mourners try to keep up as best they can. A socialist cemetery, no mistake about it. À la Fourier, perhaps?

The five arrivals were directed to Voronyanskaya's grave site, which still lacked a mound of earth; nothing but a stick marked the spot. (The grave was unmarked even a year later when Lyusha came by with Zoya Tomashevskaya.)

Q's death was looking more and more like foul play. But the people present hardly knew each other, and Etkind very gingerly asked Samutin whether something might have been confiscated from Voronyanskaya.[4]

Zoya Tomashevskaya's friend Galya had the bad luck to be present as this affair unfolded. But since she was entirely free of any previous involvement and since Dusya had given Samutin the address where she planned to hold a wake that day, the question formed itself: "Galya, would you mind going? Perhaps you could find out something new?" She was agreeable and managed to arrive in time. Dusya's friends from the village were there, along with the nurse Lida. It was there that Lida gave the version of events referred to earlier.

If it had indeed been a suicide, how could the physically ex-

---

[4]Samutin, who throughout this trip had not revealed to the others that *Gulag* had been seized, writes that he responded by telling Etkind that "*they* have everything" and that Voronyanskaya's death was directly connected to this fact. But the Etkinds had no way of knowing what "everything" referred to and had no idea that the manuscript had been kept in contradiction to my orders. They thought that he must have been referring to some kind of archive Voronyanskaya had been keeping. (1990 note)

hausted Voronyanskaya have found the strength for a hook and a rope?

As for Samutin, would he, after turning in *Gulag*, now conceal this fact and keep silent? What must the veteran zek have felt?

"Ceilings" were being bugged, his apartment was under surveillance, his every step was being watched. The KGB was compensating for its earlier oversight and making absolutely sure that no further leaks would occur.

But would it be all right for his wife to go to work? . . . To work, you say? Certainly, no problem.

Yet in fact nothing more was needed! That's the "grapevine effect" of large cities for you: at the Mining Institute where she worked, Samutin's wife tells the story to only one person, her colleague Arshanskaya, whose husband, she knows, is friends with Kopelev. (And the latter happens to be in Leningrad at this very time; Etkind has mentioned it earlier in the day.) She speaks to no one but Arshanskaya, during working hours and safely beneath the ceiling of her office.

Simple?[5]

In any case, Arshanskaya simply goes home and repeats the account to her husband, who was planning to meet with Kopelev anyway. He does so rather late that evening.

It is after eleven o'clock that night when Kopelev places a call to Etkind, and in his suavest voice invites him to come by if at all possible.

It is now the late evening of August 31, a day after the funeral. The

---

[5]We learned about these circumstances immediately from the Kopelev-Etkind circle, yet Samutin himself does not mention them in his reminiscences. Perhaps this was his attempt to keep his wife clear of the whole thing? It would nevertheless seem that between August 30 and 31 his conscience convinced him that it was impossible to remain silent, that the author had to be warned about what had happened to *Gulag*. But then again, could not Samutin's wife have acted on her own initiative without telling him? (1990 note)

KGB has plugged all possible leaks, and yet everything is known!

The jolt reaches Etkind even through the telephone receiver; no ordinary invitations are issued at this time of night. He sets off. A meeting with Arshansky follows. There is still time to catch the night train to Moscow, and it would look entirely above suspicion if Sergei Maslov, Kopelev's host in Leningrad and a man with no involvement in any of our affairs, simply passed the following message: "Tell him that Arkhip has been taken." (Those of us who knew about the existence of *The Gulag Archipelago* sometimes referred to the book that way.)

It seemed simple, but only at first sight. Etkind awoke later that night, struck by the thought that a gross blunder had been made. Maslov had no idea what the message meant; passed mouth to mouth, "Arkhi*p*" could turn into "arkhi*v*" [that is, archive]. This would make the message meaningless and a nuisance to untangle.

On the morning of September 1, Maslov arrives in Moscow and delivers the message to "Koma" (Viacheslav) Ivanov, who interprets it exactly as Etkind had feared: an archive has been seized. By the end of that day, Ivanov, accompanied by Lyusha (still weak from injuries sustained in a car accident), brings the message to me in Firsanovka. My reaction is immediate doubt: is *arkhiv* or *Arkhip* meant? And then, what archive could Q have possibly been holding? And was not *Arkhip* disposed of long ago?

In our nervousness Lyusha and I make a false move. We want, we *need* to know right away and with absolute certainty just what it is that has been seized. And she asks Alyosha Shipovalnikov, who is acquainted with Samutin through his sister Liza, to look up Samutin and ask him point-blank.

Wrong move. Wrong because we are placing the boy in danger without having any clear understanding of how much room Samutin has to maneuver. But Alyosha consents manfully and pays a visit to the beleaguered apartment. What would have been the point of writing the answer on a piece of paper (and then burning it immediately) if the boy were seized on the way out? And keeping his bugged ceiling in mind, Samutin responds as follows: "Yes, they've seized *The First Circle*." Quite so: he could not have said more below those ceilings.

On the evening of September 1, Etkind sets off for Moscow with a single-letter clarification. He comes to Lyusha in Peredelkino, whereupon she, as weak and ailing as before, hires a taxi for the ride to Moscow, through the entire city, and up north to Firsanovka to deliver that one letter of the alphabet to me by the evening of September 2. Now it was beyond doubt: *The Gulag Archipelago* had been seized.

On September 3, I go to Moscow to see Alya. She is in the company of our two small children and is expecting our third, Stephan, any day now. "We'll have to detonate it, don't you think?" I ask her. "Let's do it!" is her fearless reply.

On the morning of September 4, I arrange an evening meeting with the correspondent Stig Fredrikson (see Chapter Thirteen) by means of a call (in prearranged code) from an out-of-town phone booth. At this meeting I make a statement for the Western media, spelling out the fact that *Gulag* has been seized and including a secret instruction that it should be published as soon as possible.

The KGB, meanwhile, is certain that everything has been tightly battened down, but on the morning of September 5 the Western radio hits them over the head with a nasty surprise.

At that point they direct Samutin to give some kind of despicable interview for Western consumption, but it turns out to be of little value to them. (I never did get to read it.)

Q used to chide me in her letters after each of my sharply worded statements: "What's the point of getting involved in a bullfight on such unequal terms? Why do you insist on hastening events?"

The fact is that no one hastened them more than she did. This elderly, ailing, lonely woman, gripped by fear and without meaning to do so, set the mighty boulder of *The Gulag Archipelago* rumbling into the world, headed toward our country and toward international communism.[6]

---

[6]Verdi's *Requiem*, given to me by Q, is with me in Vermont, and I play it every year at the end of August in her memory. (1978 note)

In November 1985 I received a letter from a Swiss follower of Rudolf Steiner by the name of Johanna Fischer, a lady previously unknown to me. Elizaveta Voronyanskaya, she wrote, a person with whom she had not been acquainted before, had begun to "visit" her frequently, begging Johanna to let me know that she is in urgent need of my help in her current circumstances. She appears to Johanna as a far-off shadow.

Of course I pray for her, it goes without saying. . . . (1986 note)

6

Natalya Milyevna Anichkova and Nadya Levitskaya

Like Q, Natalya Milyevna first came to my attention by means of a letter. She wrote to express the gratitude that she and her adopted daughter (former zeks both) felt after reading *One Day in the Life of Ivan Denisovich* and to offer to help in any way they could. As a further enticement, to increase the chances that I would respond, she added a note to the effect that the painter Pavel Korin* was their neighbor and that a meeting could be arranged. She also mentioned that she and her daughter enjoyed hiking in isolated northern regions, and she enclosed some striking photographs taken there.

The phrase "former zek" was like a password for me: letters from those who had been prison-camp inmates made up the most treasured folder of the correspondence that I saved; this folder already contained several hundred items. However I might treat letters from others, these I never passed over, finding information worth jotting down in virtually every one of them and later meeting with many of their authors. And it was this that made me set off for Bolshaya Pirogovka Street where the Anichkovs lived. They turned out to be exactly as they had presented themselves in their letter: "eternal zeks" still vigorous in spirit, who in their unsettled way of life seem to be in perpetual transit and who would not be surprised if state security should pay them a visit tomorrow. Every summer they took lengthy trips, highly risky ones for the sixty-five-year-old and ailing Anichkova, trekking to the kind of godforsaken areas that would give pause to hikers half her age. Their determination not to burden themselves with worldly goods, their cheerful uncertainty about the morrow, and their ardent loyalty to those who had shared their past misfortune all contributed to bringing us together. It was simply natural for us to become fast friends. At our first meeting I made an effort not to reveal too much, but by the second time we met I no longer restrained myself. As best I can remember, every single visit, from first to last, included my request to undertake some kind of task for our common cause, a task they would always joyfully take upon themselves as their foremost priority.

This zek spirit and their common prison-camp past bound the two of them into a family, even though they were entirely dissimilar in other respects: the short, plump, jovial Anichkova, whose lively—even capricious—disposition belied her years, was a striking contrast to the tall, gaunt, uncommonly reserved, ever-busy, efficient, and circumspect Nadya. While Anichkova was serving her sentence in prison camp, she happened at one point to be put in charge of bread distribution and was able to save the starving orphan Nadya by offering her extra food and maternal encouragement. This had united them forever like mother and daughter.

Natalya Anichkova came from an ancient aristocratic family, her grandfather having been a high-ranking member of the palace administration. She had gone to the Tagantsev lycée, and her childhood friends had been young Saint Petersburg aristocrats—all of them dispersed, shot, or forced to flee in the wake of the revolution. The five Soviet decades that followed had continued to scatter her relatives, friends, and loved ones; now no one was left.

Nadya Levitskaya had a more modest background, although her father, the biologist Grigori Levitsky, had been a close collaborator of Vavilov and had perished as a result of the Lysenko campaign.* The whole family had been arrested, with each of the four members (father, mother, Nadya, and a brother) hauled off and charged separately. Nadya's parents had died in camp, but she had been saved by Anichkova, and in gratitude she had attached herself to the older woman forever. The most remarkable aspect of their life together was their attitude—shared by the Zubovs, by Tenno, and no doubt by many other zek families—of regarding their present existence as an unexpected gift, a sort of illicit addendum to the years spent as zeks and understandable only in the light of that experience. Every fifth of March, the anniversary of Stalin's death, they would express this way of looking at their life through a symbolic act: rearranging their tiny rooms in museum fashion, they would put out as many photographs as they could find of those who were shot or who had perished in camp, put on somber music, and for several hours would let friends and former zeks file through.

When Anichkova was young, her volatile character had only magnified the chaos that war and revolution had produced in her life, with the result that her life had proceeded in topsy-turvy fashion, in the end leaving her with neither family nor profession. Nadya, on the other hand, had known German from childhood and now depended on this skill in her job at the Library of Foreign Literature. (During the war, while Nadya was still a very young girl,

she could have easily withdrawn with the Germans when they retreated from the Pskov area, but she decided against it—and was re-
warded with prison camp. Still, she always maintained that she
never regretted having stayed in Russia.)

Thus it was only natural that the help Nadya gave me primarily
involved translation. She translated a multitude of texts for me, including newspaper articles, reviews, and later, entire books that I
would otherwise never have had the time to work through in the
German original. The quality of her work was exemplary. With her
fine understanding of how I worked and of where my interests lay,
Nadya never translated a book in its entirety; this, after all, would
still have left me with the task of reading a large tome. Instead, she
prepared outlines that she then grouped according to the themes I
needed, providing each with a clear title and recording them on paper of specific sizes. I recall with particular gratitude how Nadya,
pressed though she was by her own affairs and often forced to work
during her commuting time on trains and subways, handled General
von François's book on the beginning of World War I, as well as the
memoirs of General Gurko (neither work is available in Russian).
She also translated Zeman's study on the links between Lenin and
the German Ministry of Foreign Affairs.*

Anichkova's talents lay elsewhere: she had a gift for striking up
friendships with a multitude of extraordinarily diverse individuals.
Generally speaking, this is hardly the kind of talent appropriate for
a conspirator, but in Anichkova's case it proved most fortuitous;
whatever unexpected new need I might articulate, she would mull
it over for a bit and would then invariably find the right person to
whom I should turn. When I urgently needed to find a new place
to keep the manuscripts rescued from Teush, for example, I dashed
off to the NNs (we referred to them collectively in this way, com-
bining the initial letters of their first names), and they unflinchingly
took the texts from me. But their own apartment was insecure:
there were always people milling around, and besides, the place was

under suspicion. After some thought Anichkova suggested the eminent geologist Boris Abramovich Petrushevsky, a man who had clearance for foreign travel yet who agreed to safeguard the texts when Anichkova turned to him and did so for three or four years; at one point, he even held several copies of *The Gulag Archipelago*. (For security reasons I did not see him at the time and even tried to put his name and address out of my mind. I didn't meet him later either, but I am profoundly grateful.) Was there nowhere to stow a copy of the final version of *Gulag*? Anichkova would ponder the question, come up with an answer, and take away the text. On the other hand, there were also some occasional fumbles. She once took a copy of *Gulag* to the Vesyegonsk nature sanctuary, a long trip entailing transfers and travel by riverboat—to a man she considered noble and dependable, but he took fright and so did his wife, leaving Anichkova with no choice but to lug back the twenty-odd pounds of manuscript-laden phonograph, not something she should have had to do at her age. She then took the text to Leningrad, where she was to deliver it into the supposedly secure hands of her cousin —only to be met with an anguished request to take it away: "We can't keep this awful thing here!" A further search, now confined to Leningrad, finally yielded results, and one copy of *Gulag* remains buried there to this day. Neither the name nor the address of the person who hid the text is known to me, and I am aware only that it is buried "beneath an apple tree."[1]

Or perhaps I needed a typist, someone very proficient and at the same time reliable enough to be given access to the most dangerous texts (and one, moreover, for whom enthusiasm would be payment enough, since there were no funds to draw on). And wouldn't it be wonderful if I could also find a trustworthy secret bookbinder so as to keep all those typed pages in proper order? Anichkova gave the

---

[1] *Gulag*, together with the play *Tanks Know the Truth*, was preserved for two decades by the high-minded and fearless Aleksei Liverovsky. The texts have now been unearthed. (1989 note)

matter some thought and found both individuals in the same place: Olga Konstantinovna Kryzhanovskaya, a typist whom I also never met and to whom I am deeply indebted for her extensive labors and the safekeeping of a multitude of texts, and her husband Andrei Ivanovich, a career military man (a colonel in the engineering branch) who, though barely on his feet after a heart attack, bound all the samizdat copies of the *The Gulag Archipelago* and *The Oak and the Calf*, as well as a number of copies of the ninety-six-chapter *First Circle*. I wrote him thank-you notes but had no chance to shake his hand before he died.

Given Anichkova's wide circle of acquaintances and the constant coming and going of the intelligentsia in Nadya's library, releasing texts for samizdat distribution became a natural thing to do. Over the years, whenever I chose to release a text, Lyusha Chukovskaya and I would always count off from one to five copies for the NNs. (Lyusha and Nadya had worked out an efficient system of meeting in subway stations: the place and exact time would be set in advance, they would pick a station that was convenient for both of them on the way to work or back, the only signal needed would be a brief phone call. The two women resembled each other in terms of punctuality and dependability.) The compilation* "How People Read Ivan Denisovich" was assembled in its entirety by the NNs in the spring of 1968; they typed it up and launched its samizdat distribution.

Anichkova considered it a matter of honor to disseminate samizdat writings beyond Moscow, with special emphasis on the provincial cities, including Ekaterinburg. I made a serious miscalculation with my ninety-six-chapter *First Circle*, thinking that we were about to distribute it widely and that we should therefore prepare as many copies of the text as possible. Carried away by this idea, we typed up four batches (twenty copies) of the text, and then had nowhere to store it all. More than once the novel came close to being seized because of the sheer number of copies. A hefty pile kept in one safe house had to be burned. I carelessly allowed the NNs to have one copy delivered to Ekaterinburg, but the recipient, Sergei Ivanovich Osyonnov, turned out to be someone they knew very slightly. During a summer vacation trip, the adventurous Anichkova had become acquainted with him in the course of an argument over *Ivan Denisovich*, of all things. He had criticized the work harshly, but she had succeeded in changing his mind and had then accorded him the status of friend and confidant; after that she began supplying him with samizdat materials, including the ninety-six-chapter *First Circle*. To be fair, Osyonnov did not betray us, and in fact he remained very firm indeed. (In the main part of *The Oak and the Calf*, this episode was related in a deliberately distorted way so as to protect his identity. Passing through Novocherkassk in 1971, A. A. Ugrimov and I met with Osyonnov in the apartment of some other friends of Anichkova.) But he was suddenly endangered from a direction he could not have foreseen. His nephew, who had landed a soft job in the army involving radio jamming or radio interception, had returned home after his tour of duty and wished to work in a similar capacity as a civilian in Ekaterinburg. But this required filing a lot of papers and naming all his relatives, each of whom would then be examined in great detail by the security agencies. This, in turn, brought to light a report that Osyonnov had lent out a copy of *Cancer Ward* for reading. In the Russian provinces, this was deemed a dangerous act, a veritable bomb, and in their impatience to pounce, the security boys did not institute surveillance (in any case, they could not imagine that anything could be worse than *Cancer Ward*) but they simply showed up at the door of our safe-keeper, several men strong. At the time, the actual typescript of *First Circle* was in Osyonnov's summer cottage, which stood empty and unprotected during the winter; certain samizdat materials were in his apartment as well, and at the very moment the KGB arrived, he was chatting with an acquaintance who had come to borrow a copy of *August 1914* and had just slipped it into his bag. The quick-witted friend took one look at the visitors and said, "Listen, I have to be off!" The provincial gumshoes seemed only too pleased to be rid of a witness and made no effort to detain him. Moreover the dolts did not even search the premises; instead, they took Osyonnov to their headquarters and only there asked him to admit that he had a copy of *Cancer Ward*. By this point the poor devil understood clearly that confession was indeed the best course. "Bring it, then," was the command, and he did as instructed, after which the KGB seemed to leave him alone. But how was he to know whether he had been placed under surveillance? And what should he do with the *First Circle* text? In an excess of zeal, Anichkova had charged him to guard it with his life. And guard it he did, even though after the summons to the KGB this had become a desperately dangerous thing to do. Meanwhile his opportunities for communicating with us were rare. One couldn't say much in a letter, traveling in person was not an option because of the possibility of surveillance, and he had no one whom he could send as a messenger. We did get word that he was being watched and that he had had "visitors," but there was no way we could cry out to him that he should burn the typescript immediately. As a result, the ninety-six-chapter *First Circle* loomed ominously over his head and ours for several months, until a natural way of passing the message presented itself. It was spring 1973 before Osyonnov was persuaded that the instructions were authentic and finally burned the text.

At one point Anichkova, by then already long retired, had become active in the society for the preservation of Russian historical monuments. In due time she recognized how the whole enterprise shaded into hackneyed conventionalism, and in any case her deteriorating health was forcing her to spend more time at home. But her volcanic energy would not allow her to sit back, and she kept thinking up new individuals and novel sources of information I must get to know, even though I might not have been looking for anything of the sort. Moreover she would often persuade me that such an acquaintance was indeed necessary, and I would follow up on her suggestion. As I think about it now, this involved an astonishing profusion of individuals, too many to remember. It was Anichkova who introduced me to Dmitri Petrovich Vitkovsky, a veteran of the White Sea Canal construction project.* It was she, too, who acquainted me with A. V. Khrabrovitsky, the son-in-law of Vladimir Korolenko.* Khrabrovitsky was devoted to archival research and, on his own initiative, brought me a huge volume of data, some of it useful, some not. (At one point we relaxed our rules out of gratitude, allowing him a brief in-house glance through a volume of *Gulag*, with the result that word about this book began to spread through Moscow and even surfaced abroad. The efforts needed to quash these rumors and to counteract the anxiety they produced were incalculable.) Through Anichkova, I also found traces of the long-dead Pyotr Palchinsky:* she discovered a living relative of Palchinsky's wife from whom I was able to gather a great deal of information, allowing me to bring Palchinsky into *August 1914* and *October 1916*. Did I need reliable information about General Svechin* from his family, for example? Anichkova would produce it, even though this might involve spending months corresponding, making inquiries, and arranging trips for intermediaries. Did I wish to receive information about Tambov?* She found Y. Shmarov, the only specialist in heraldry in all of Moscow who happened to have been born and raised in Tambov and had witnessed the uprising there. Though reticent about his own life, Shmarov proved to be a gold mine of information about the region as a whole. Did I need someone to visit the actual sites of the rebellion on my behalf, asking questions in a discreet but systematic fashion? Anichkova came up with Valentina Pavlovna Kholodova, a biologist who had crisscrossed central Russia many times over and who agreed to travel to Tambov at my request. Could I use some help in the Historical Library? Anichkova would point out the staff members who were willing to lend a hand. And would I like to see some important secret materials bearing on the Don region? She also introduced me to Pavel Korin, as originally promised, and I had the good fortune of meeting this remarkable individual and seeing the portrait studies that make up his *Vanishing Russia* series. And then there was a find I could never have expected and certainly could not have asked for: following a scent, Anichkova learned that a Cossack woman living in Leningrad held the papers of Fyodor Kryukov, including a notebook of prerevolutionary vintage filled with his writing and containing the first part of *The Quiet Don*!* This, of course, was not only utterly unrelated to my work but represented a major distraction, yet how could I possibly refuse? Whose pulse would not begin racing at such an opportunity?

I couldn't help but notice, and soon grew convinced enough to mention it to Anichkova repeatedly: she had a lucky touch.

Of course I also saddled Anichkova with various chores myself. Perhaps there was a promising individual, for instance, but no time whatever to deal with him. What to do? Let him contact the NNs, of course! This was the case with Nikolai Pavlovich Ivanov, the grandson of a priest and a man endowed with remarkable clarity of mind, one who had attained intellectual independence after a painful struggle through the thickets of Soviet obfuscation. Ivanov had plans of breathtaking scope yet was never able to achieve anything substantial; he also proved of little help to me. He envisioned running off *The Gulag Archipelago* on a mimeograph machine, but the project turned out to be impossible. He did undertake a useful trip to the Tambov region at my request, bringing back some archival data and arranging a meeting with the sister of Pyotr Tokmakov, one of the rebellion's leaders. The NNs got involved in trying to find a suitable woman for him to marry, but with no success. (Because of the many links to us, Ivanov came close to being locked up in a madhouse; he was in fact held for a time by psychiatrists in Ryazan.) I also linked the NNs up with Margarita Sheffer, another example of a devastated Russian life, about whom more later (Chapter Ten).

As long as the NN's apartment was assumed to be microphone-free, the two women also verified texts for us, reading, among other things, copies of *The Gulag Archipelago* against the original. In 1966 and 1967 they stayed in our summer place at Rozhdestvo when it was unoccupied. They had grown to be such good friends and the relationship between us—former zeks all—was so easy and down-to-earth, with its informality and in-jokes, that it was only natural to invite them to stay in our favorite spot. There Anichkova planted the seedlings of a rare black-berried type of mountain ash imported from a Yaroslavl nature preserve.

When Anichkova stayed in Rozhdestvo, Nadya, who showed more concern for Natalya Milyevna than most daughters do for their own mothers, spent two hours daily commuting from Moscow after work and two hours each morning traveling in the opposite direction—not counting the long walk to and from the Bakshino station—in order to be with her. Nadya was a great walker, crisscrossing all my favorite haunts in the region even more frequently than I. Indeed, her figure now seems an organic part of the landscape of forests and clearings that I see in my mind's eye. When, in May 1968, we were typing the final version of *The Gulag Archipelago* on two typewriters, Nadya came up from Moscow every third day to take away the completed pages as a precaution. (She then had the task of distributing the five copies to separate depositories.) She was also involved in saving the manuscript of the beginning chapters of *Gulag* in September 1965 when she took part in Tenno's rescue operation.*

I had barely settled into a wing of Rostropovich's Zhukovka dacha in the fall of 1969 when the main house suddenly became vacant: Rostropovich and his wife were unexpectedly and hastily departing for a lengthy foreign tour and had no time to look for lodgers. We suggested the NNs; Rostropovich dashed off to see the Anichkovs in his inimitable style and tempo: overwhelming and charming them, he brought them to his house several hours later.

They lived there for two winters, occupying the main house while I stayed in the wing, generally by myself, with the only other creature on the premises being a shaggy black Newfoundland in the front yard, to whom the NNs became intensely attached, and he to them. In effect, three zeks were occupying a piece of terrain in a restricted zone, next to the property of the vice-chairman of the Council of Ministers of the U.S.S.R. And a very satisfying time it was for us all. I shoveled snow off the walks and tended the boiler room, Nadya carried privately delivered mail to and from Moscow, and I would occasionally drop in on the NNs to chat, but the workload did not leave much time for that. The NNs, meanwhile, used the spacious Rostropovich home to set up an entire samizdat industry, typing and verifying texts. They also helped me as much as they could, and it was a novel luxury for me to be able to hand over texts without fuss or travel. It was also here, in the "tavern" under the roof and in the company of the NNs and Lyusha Chukovskaya (but without Rostropovich, who was abroad) that we celebrated the presentation of the Nobel Prize. Anichkova was there, too, when the militiamen came to evict me from Zhukovka.*

In the years that followed, we were never again able to meet with such frequency. Caught in the whirl of ever-intensifying events in Moscow, I rarely made my way to their place, but our relationship remained unshakably simple and straightforward, a classic bond among zeks sharing common memories of a portion of black bread, unwiped tables, and a bowl of watery soup. Not many family relationships could have been as direct and as natural.

In the last winter before my exile, Anichkova was laid up with a lengthy illness. I promised to visit them at Christmastime, and she tried her best to sound cheerful. On the very day I had planned to go, just before I set off, two advance copies of the published *Gulag Archipelago* were privately delivered to me from Paris. They were the first copies to reach the U.S.S.R., and commercial copies were not yet available to the KGB and the Central Committee. With no time even to glance through the book, I left one copy with Alya and dashed off to the NNs with the other.

So it was that I first opened the book in their apartment. We flipped through the pages together at the table where we had made our acquaintance ten years earlier, when our common path was still entirely before us. Together we turned to the page showing six individuals who had been shot;* all six photographs had been supplied by Anichkova following her March exhibit—one was a portrait of a man dear to her long ago.

Over the course of those years, Anichkova had put her entire life into my work; now, through these photographs of her loved ones, she became a part of *The Gulag Archipelago*, forever, in all its editions and in all languages.

———

But the earthquake had by now already begun, and I was expelled. Alya was getting ready for departure. During those six turbulent weeks she was surrounded by local and foreign sympathizers, but Nadya did not come by—it would have spelled the end of her vulnerable job. But there was a phone call just before the family departed, and a person who did not name herself spoke in a familiar voice punctuated by sobs. "Tell *him* that those were the happiest years and that they will never return."

———

A year later we learned that Anichkova had passed away. She had suffered from various ailments for many years, often severely enough to be bedridden, and each time I would tell her that she just had to live long enough to see *The Gulag Archipelago* published, long enough to witness our common triumph. And indeed she recovered every time.

In January 1975 she suffered a heart attack. The doctor tried to persuade her to check into a hospital. Sitting in her bed, Anichkova responded, "Why the hospital? It's better to die at home!" At these words a greenish blue shadow passed over her face; she lurched to the side and started to fall over. The doctor immediately gave her artificial respiration, a resuscitation unit was summoned, but she was gone.

———

When we heard of Anichkova's death, we wrote to Nadya from Zurich, inviting her to move in with us and share our life and work. Her answer was no, she would never leave Russia.

7

Mirra Gennadyevna Petrova

While she remained outside our close-knit circle and its underground enterprises, Mirra Petrova was my active and invaluable collaborator for four years. Her role was always different, and she did not become acquainted with any of the others because her path and theirs simply did not intersect. We all carry within us a vague hope of meeting a person of this caliber, but such individuals are precisely the kind who never advertise themselves, and the searching gaze invariably passes over them to stop on others.

I had established some links with the people at TsGALI, the Moscow depository of archival materials related to literature and art. They had made the error of nominating me for the Lenin Prize in literature and had suffered a severe dressing-down as a result. At a difficult moment I had asked them to safeguard a copy of *The First Circle* for me; at a later point I came to TsGALI to give a reading of several chapters of *Cancer Ward*, after which I asked Miralda Kozlova, an extraordinarily energetic member of TsGALI's acquisition staff, to collect any written comments that other staffers might wish to make. There were about ten such responses, and I was delighted and astounded by one that focused on Kostoglotov's fate, his hapless love, and all that had perished in it. The comments were set forth with such poignancy that you would have thought their author had been a doctor at the clinic I had depicted, or else had written the work with me; no outsider could have been expected to respond this way. Moreover, the remarks showed a level of literary perception that was beyond anything critics could provide; it belonged, once again, in the realm normally accessible only to writers themselves.

When I voiced my desire to meet the author, it turned out that she no longer worked at TsGALI. A professionally trained literary historian and textual critic, she had found employment more appropriate to her talents in Moscow's Institute of World Literature. Miralda Kozlova nevertheless willingly arranged a meeting at Mirra's place on Vorotnikovsky Lane.

I asked Mirra to lay out her views in some detail. Specifically, what would she suggest amending or correcting in *Cancer Ward*, which at the time (the fall of 1966) could still absorb changes? In response she boldly advanced her judgments, comments, and even advice. (In general she was a fearless, radically independent, even brusque person, in contrast to her small stature and generally quiet demeanor, which changed only when she was stirred up.) I was struck by the literary cogency of her evaluation, as well as by the specifically feminine point of view that I knew I lacked—a deficiency that in fact I had first perceived in this particular work. Her comments were like a whirlwind for the ever-shifting point of view they seemed to demonstrate, ranging as they did from disapproval of insufficiently high-minded depictions of women to objections that the portrayal was inadequately sensuous. She was precisely the kind of person—a woman closely attuned to my work—whom I had never had the good fortune to meet in all the years of my literary activity in camp, in exile, and outside of Moscow. But then, the subject matter I had dealt with up to that time had been focused on the prison-camp theme and had thus been closely familiar to me, while now I was reorienting my work toward different areas. It became clear to me that I would return many times to Vorotnikovsky Lane. And in fact I had barely left when I began to feel a nagging desire to continue the conversation.

I did return to Mirra's place many dozens of times in subsequent years.

Mirra's parents were Old Bolsheviks,* but her own views were far removed from the Bolshevik line—a sign of the times and a phenomenon not infrequent in our days. Her father had been shot; her mother was still alive but was so difficult to get along with that Mirra had long ago moved out, even though she was unmarried. She had a dark room on Domnikovka, a street roaring with traffic; Soviet circumstances made it well-nigh impossible to exchange it through official channels, and rather than suffer there, she had abandoned the place, with its library and rickety furniture, and made private arrangements to rent one and a half rooms from a former star of the Maly Theater who lived in actors' housing. These quarters were bright, quiet, cramped, and cozy; an especially warm aura emanated from an elaborate old secretary that, according to legend, had come from an estate along the Smolensk highway where Napoleon had spent a night and where he was alleged to have worked at this very writing table. Now we put in many hours at it, with very substantial results indeed.

Mirra had given a great deal of thought to the color scheme of her room—she was a passionate admirer of Van Gogh and was horrified by any clash in hue. She paid homage to several other cultural icons with a devotion that was as unquestioning and reverential as she was independent in other respects. Her pantheon included Thomas Mann (with Böll added later), Chekhov, Tsvetaeva, and . . . Ehrenburg, of all people. Portraits of the two last-named writers stood in her glass-front bookcase. (I teased her for a long time about Ehrenburg, arguing that he had no right to be in such company. She yielded by degrees and finally removed his portrait, but Ehrenburg's death shortly thereafter produced a jolt of superstitious dismay in her, and his photograph reappeared in its former place.) It goes without saying that Mirra's choice of idols expressed not only her own tastes but also the general orientation of the contemporary intellectual elite. For all the striking independence of her personal opinions, she remained well within the mainstream of familiar "democratic intelligentsia" values, which are perhaps better labeled "late Kadetism."* Apart from the characteristic overstatements of this viewpoint (seeing Chekhov as the greatest Russian writer, for instance, more significant than Tolstoy or Dostoyevsky), Mirra was so gifted in terms of literary sensibility that she could easily replace ten or twenty readers for me. This was an invaluable boon to an underground writer like myself, since it was enough to test any new chapter or page on her alone. It is simply a fact that in circumstances where so much effort is expended on concealment and camouflage and where one is hemmed in on all sides by the rigid time constraints associated with a clandestine organization, the writer runs the danger of failing to pause for an unhurried aesthetic contemplation of his work in all of its details. That is precisely what Mirra would not infrequently remind me of, and that is why she came to occupy a position unconnected to any of my clandestine activities. In a sense, she became the guardian of a special retreat, a space where I was not a conspirator but simply a writer. Of all my books, therefore, *The Gulag Archipelago* was the only one that did not pass through her hands; I did not ask her to look it over, nor did she request to do so. In that inexorable and spontaneous outpouring of our history, even her diligent hands could find nothing to modify. And when I brought all three volumes to her for a five-day-long stint of reading, this was the only book about which she had nothing to say. For this work had shaped *itself*; it had not emerged from the workshops of art, but remained oblivious to any of art's commandments, heedless of a single rule.

In other respects Mirra was an irreplaceable contributor to my all-too-harsh mode of work during the three or four years that followed the confiscation of my archive. She was also my first critic in the sense that I would never discuss my work in progress with anyone before I had broached it with her (this role was later assumed by my wife Alya). At times this included even preliminary plans that had not yet taken textual shape. Discussions of this type are chancy things, capable of destroying an entire literary conception if the interlocutor happens to have a cast of mind incompatible with your own rather than being a version of yourself. The conversations proceeded in a sort of multidimensional literary space beyond the pressure of time (in contrast to the rest of my life); they were not the kind that call for pencil and paper and note taking. Instead, they consisted of an unhurried and deliberate scrutiny of basic approach and structure from a variety of viewpoints. Such discussions could bring to light and hence prevent a misguided undertaking that might otherwise consume years of work.

But her role went beyond these conversations. The tireless and ever active Mirra was always prepared to take on other lengthy, burdensome, painstaking tasks, even at some cost to her official duties where, fortunately, she could keep her own hours. She helped me complete a number of projects that the intense rate of my work and the perpetual need for concealment had left in a disheveled state. Bringing to bear her professional training in textual criticism, she undertook a comparative study of the numerous extant versions of my texts—the original version, the redaction "softened" for the benefit of censorship, and the ones redone later—in order to discover what might have been lost or distorted in the process of revision. In this way she helped me produce the final versions of *Ivan Denisovich* and of all the short stories. This was an undertaking I could not have tackled by myself at the time, but she did 80 percent of the work, reducing my part to making the final choices. She also retyped some of my longer works (*Cancer Ward* and the ninety-six-chapter *First Circle*) and undertook the painstaking labor of verifying copies against originals, comparing editions, and correcting misprints. Of all my collaborators she was the only one with genuine expertise on prerevolutionary Russia (this was, after all, her line of work), and she could quickly locate all the quotes and references I needed, especially when they concerned the better-known members of the intelligentsia, or the Kadets, or general history. She could hunt down any other reference as well, since much of her life was spent in the reading room of the Lenin Library.

Mirra was also a great devotee of the theater and of dramatic readings; in this respect, she was like many women who, while not actively involved in the theater, view it as an outlet for appreciation, discernment, and increased understanding. As a way of getting her assessment, I read some chapters of my novels into a tape recorder in her room. (These recordings were later erased by Soviet customs officials when my family was leaving Moscow, although it is possible that copies were made at the time.)

Mirra kept in close touch with the best work being done for our stage and screen, and thanks to her I was able to stay informed for several years in a way that would have been impossible for me without residing in Moscow. She was an ardent partisan of *Novy Mir*, and in all my conflicts with Tvardovsky she always took his side; Tvardovsky had no inkling of the ally he had.

As fate would have it, Mirra's aesthetic paradise was situated a mere five-minute walk from the offices of *Novy Mir*, and I could set up a meeting as soon as I could get through to her (the phone was much used by the actors). I would arrive at Mirra's place with fresh impressions, hastily prepared emendations, sometimes a headache, fatigue, and hunger. There I could collect my thoughts in silence or talk things over. Living as I did outside of Moscow, with my heavy schedule of travel to points scattered throughout the capital—I might have seven places to visit in the course of a single day—getting a bite to eat and stopping to catch my breath could become a top priority; without this respite, there might well have been times when I would have collapsed under the strain. Mirra would proudly and with great conviction quote Tsvetaeva (I think) to the effect that a poet needs not only appreciation for his verse but also dinner. And she tended to go far beyond the bare essentials in this regard, quizzing a woman who had been a cook in a well-to-do home before the revolution about the kind of meals prepared in those days and then serving up fare like grouse in mulled wine "in order to make such things easier to write about."

At one point in 1969 I had reason to suspect that I had been followed on my way to Mirra's (I was carrying an important package from an important location). As a result, we worked out a detailed plan whereby I would leave via several courtyards while she would watch and signal. She took part in this (successful) operation with considerable relish, cutting an attractive figure as she turned and held her purse in the agreed-upon manner. The venture suited her, even though she had never before participated in anything of the sort. She had always tried to talk me out of making combative public statements, arguing that I should focus my energy on the central concerns of art. (But at the same time she approved of my letter to the Union of Soviet Writers, typed some of the copies, had all the envelopes stuffed in her room, and personally dropped many of the letters into mailboxes.) Yet she did not share my growing conviction that it was wrong to call for a new revolution. This small and fragile-looking woman, most of whose literary idols were paragons of moderation and even passivity, had a distinctly anarchistic streak in her, and if the right call were to be sounded in the streets tomorrow, she would no doubt join in from her window. Her sympathies now lay with the February Revolution, and she imagined that something similar would be a desirable way out of the present morass. In this respect, as in many others, Mirra expressed the dominant mood of the contemporary intelligentsia: the powers-that-be deserved a good wallop of the sort dealt to the Romanovs (but one that of course should not affect *us*).

I made a point of never calling Mirra from telephones that were likely to be tapped, nor did I place any calls from her residence to suspect numbers. And not many women would have been capable of being as discreet as she was. But of course the KGB had not relaxed its surveillance of me, and it is clear that Mirra's place was duly noted by the security people.[1]

Mirra was also tremendously dedicated to her regular job, and I doubt that even a trained and seasoned Ph.D. could match her accomplishments in terms of quality and quantity. (Her work required her to hold a high opinion of Gorky; otherwise all her endeavors at the institute would have lost meaning. This view was not easy to sustain, given Mirra's aesthetic sensibilities, and to prop it up she fell back on contrived arguments such as the universal admiration that Gorky had enjoyed before the revolution or the remark by her beloved Tsvetaeva that Gorky had deserved the Nobel Prize more than Bunin.)* She was then working on a chronological listing* of turn-of-the-century Russian literary events, and this immersion in the prerevolutionary press made her a convinced champion of the Kadet party. The drift of my *August 1914* aroused her suspicions, and some of the polemical comments she wrote out for me opened my eyes to the meaning of "neo-Kadetism," to the

[1]Some years later I learned that the KGB operatives had badgered her from the end of 1974 until 1979, refusing to admit defeat for all those years. They read her the incriminating evidence they had concocted (all of it wide of the mark) in their attempt to persuade her to issue a statement against me through the Novosti Press Agency, but she withstood the pressure without wavering. (1990 note)

strength of this orientation among the contemporary intelligentsia, to the influence it is likely to have on future Russian events, and to the fact that it is entirely alien to me.

The last piece of my writing that Mirra reviewed in its preliminary form was a batch of trial chapters drawn from *August 1914* that I had distributed to several readers in the fall of 1969. She reacted with great hostility to the Tomchak family, as well as to Orya, a character she found uncongenial and quite incomprehensible. From that time on we met rarely, for reasons unrelated to external circumstances. But she did read *August 1914* in its virtually complete form in 1970 and made a number of valuable comments. She liked the structure of the military chapters and the depiction of Samsonov.

This habit of discussing a manuscript was difficult to give up for both of us, but during the next two years we hardly saw each other. Only in 1973 did it seem that our friendship or at least the possibility of looking at as-yet-unfinished manuscripts might again be on the rise. I paid several visits to her new apartment by Preobrazhenskaya Gate with parts of *October 1916*. But the quick mutual understanding and spontaneous agreement that had marked our earlier relations were now gone, and the differences between us could no longer be ignored. She was horrified by the "rightist" and anti-Kadet drift of *The Red Wheel*, and it was with particular irritation —almost personal pique—that she objected to chapters with a religious theme. She kept pointing to the antireligious stories of Vasili Shukshin,* a writer of whom she had a deservedly high opinion, for a contrary model. (Shukshin appears to have been much agitated by the question of religion, and at the time he was making a strenuous effort to justify himself in a way that seemed specifically hostile to religion yet was not without inner concessions to it. Shukshin did not suspect that these stories were destined to be among the last things he wrote before his sudden death.) As we were discovering, our former unity of vision had in fact been less than that.

But even while Mirra was angrily rapping the manuscript of *October 1916* with her finger in that last summer before my expulsion and while I disagreed with her entirely, I had no thought of responding with acrimony, but I accepted this outpouring of wrath with attentiveness and gratitude.

8

Elena Tsezarevna Chukovskaya

From the end of 1965 for a period of almost five years, Lyusha Chukovskaya stood in the eye of the storm, at the heart of the vortex that engulfed me. During those years she was the point of intersection for every strand, every contact, for everything that needed asking, answering, or transmitting. Then, for a further three years, right up to the moment of my exile, a good many of our communications continued to be routed through her. In this book, whenever I write "we decided," "we did it," "we overlooked," "we never thought," that "we," for several years on end, meant Lyusha and me. Everyone in our immediate circle was aware of this, even those who were not part of the conspiracy, and if Lyusha telephoned someone unexpectedly insisting that they come and see her, or suddenly and unceremoniously invited herself round to their home, then everyone understood at once that it was either I who was inviting them or who was coming to see them, or else that Lyusha was coming on urgent business from me. She was in effect my chief of staff—or, rather, my whole staff rolled into one (as the KGB, alas, gradually came to understand full well). One particular reason was that at this time I was living sometimes in Ryazan and sometimes just outside Moscow but never in the capital itself—yet it was in Moscow, where she lived, that things were constantly happening, and it was there that they needed to be resolved.

Lyusha was the granddaughter of the writer Kornei Ivanovich Chukovsky.* There were four other grandchildren, but Lyusha was his favorite. She was utterly devoted to his work and helped him a great deal. She specialized in chemistry and after her postgraduate studies was awarded an advanced degree, whereupon she began a successful scientific career. There too she distinguished herself with her capacity for hard work, her thoroughness and accuracy, her love of order, and her inability to leave any job half done. (It is the same the whole world over: the irresponsible ones can never get down to their work, it rolls off them like water off a duck's back, while the conscientious few get to do the work of several people and are forever taking on extra chores.) As if this were not enough, Lyusha had for many years been compensating for the unfulfilling nature of her work at the institute by spending the weekends out at Peredelkino, acting as a secretary for her grandfather. Flinging herself into the task of helping with his correspondence and putting his files in order, she transformed these gloomy days of rest into the most energetic and constructive time of all, gladdening the heart of her grandfather, who was a hardworking man himself. (How well I understand and share his feelings.)

This work was interrupted when Lyusha, by now thirty-three years old, suffered a tragic loss, a devastating crisis that left her family fearing for her life—and which indeed she barely survived. In the autumn of 1965, while she was still convalescing, she returned from the Crimea and on her first trip out to Peredelkino learned that Kornei Ivanovich had offered me shelter after the seizure of my literary archive. This was a time when I, too, was in the depths of despondency. (With this gesture he helped me through the weeks of unrelieved danger and dejection.) From time to time he would take advantage of his standing as the virtual dean of Soviet literature in order to come to the defense of persecuted individuals or even of those under arrest; he would sign petitions on their behalf or make a phone call to someone "upstairs," but these were essentially personal interventions and he did not let himself be drawn into public polemics. Moreover, Chukovsky never lost his sense of the Russian literary heritage and its universal scale of values. Dejected though I was, facing imminent arrest and with it the end of all my literary plans, he would have none of it: "I can't understand what you are worrying about when you've already established yourself as second only to Tolstoy." He took me out to a raised wooden platform on a remote part of his land and put into my head the idea of concealing my secret manuscripts under it. He had read the stories of mine that had appeared in *Novy Mir*, but had never read anything else, despite his words about my being "second only to Tolstoy." He did not finish *Cancer Ward*, perhaps due to his squeamishness about illness, but what about *The First Circle*? Was this so that he would be able to deny any knowledge of my more extreme views? Or was it to avoid exposing himself to these alarming subversive rumblings? On one of the evenings I spent with him and his daughter, Lidia Korneyevna, I recited my *Prussian Nights* from memory, not knowing whether it would ever reach a wider audience or whether I would even succeed in preserving the manuscript.

Thus Lyusha and I became acquainted at the worst and most precarious of times for both of us, when we were both struggling to stay on an even keel—she had barely recovered her will to live, while I was holed up in my room like a wounded animal, not even bothering to switch on the light in the evenings as I could not muster the strength to read. One night I was summoned to supper by Kornei Chukovsky's cautious knock at my door, and emerging from my darkened room, I met the lively, attentive gaze of his granddaughter and instantly sensed that help was at hand. (Later she told me that she had been expecting to see a broken and dispirited man but in fact had been amazed at how unbowed I seemed; my breaking point was evidently set quite high. Later still, she recalled how our friendship had helped her to face life with new resolve and had so changed her outlook that she would never again experience that crisis of despair.)

With her frail constitution, poor appetite, and constant unflagging activity, the only thing that sustained Lyusha, even at the best of times, was her intensity of spirit, and this was all the more true in times of adversity. Though by no means a tiny, ethereal figure, she nevertheless appeared to defy the normal balance of physical forces, and this made her all the more reliant upon the driving force of her own spirit and upon a sense of conviction, if not a genuine conviction.

It was within the same time period (and in the same dining room in Chukovsky's house) that my differences with my first wife came to a head; she declared that she would rather see me arrested than hiding away and "deliberately choosing not to live with my family." From that instant I knew I could no longer depend on her. What was worse, I would have to keep up the arrangements that she was party to, while at the same time establishing a whole new secret system that would have to be kept hidden from her as from a hostile outsider.

During those few short weeks, with the danger still threatening to strike, Lyusha was soon coming up with one helpful suggestion after another. First of all she offered me the use of the town apartment that she shared with her mother, Lidia Korneyevna—not just as a place where I could stay overnight and meet people but as a place to work (living in the provinces, I sorely missed having a pied-à-terre like this in Moscow); soon afterward, she offered her services as secretary, organizing my affairs, typing my work, meeting people on my behalf—whatever needed to be done. For me this was something new and unfamiliar—a real load off my shoulders. Help so sudden and on such a huge scale made it easier for me to keep my peace of mind during those grim months. Then, when I went off to my Hiding Place in Estonia, who was it but Lyusha who organized my departure, watching wide-eyed while I shaved off my beard in her kitchen, and who but her, of all my Moscow friends, should I entrust with Susi's address in Estonia in case of emergency?

In the spring of 1966, when I had just completed Part One of *Cancer Ward* out at Rozhdestvo, I was about to start typing it up myself as I always did. (In fact, this was a useful way of making a third or fourth revision of the text.) But Lyusha was so persistent in offering to do the typing for me that I was sorely tempted. It seemed unthinkable not to do it myself, yet, hard-pressed as I was, the gift of two whole weeks—so much time, so much breathing space!—was almost irresistible. Despite my misgivings, I agreed. Back I went to Rozhdestvo that May—and it was like a birthday present, two weeks out of the blue! Lyusha went about her task with amazing speed and dedication, and it never so much as occurred to me that this was her first experience of typing on such a scale. (Another area where she was short of experience was proofreading. For tactical reasons there was not a moment to lose in getting the text into samizdat distribution, so all seven copies were snatched from her high-impact typewriter the moment they were finished, and sped on their way.)

That was when I learned just how quickly books could be launched into samizdat—a lot faster than you can get them written! While Lyusha was tapping away at the first part, I was quickly writing the second; the work went like wildfire. The Chukovskys' posi-

tion at the very hub of Moscow literary life greatly eased the problem of distribution (we did not know, nor could anyone know,
whether something as big as a whole novel would take off in samizdat), and the entire task of distributing the copies, getting them to
the next typist, retrieving them when the agreed time was up and
remembering who still had what—this, too, Lyusha took upon
herself. She did so much to relieve the pressure on me that my
strength and my time were virtually doubled, and in the course of
that summer, writing at full speed, I was able to finish the second
part of *Cancer Ward*—and there was Lyusha already tapping out the
final version before it, too, set off to brave the fields of samizdat.

After the debacle of 1965, it was Lyusha who helped me trans-
form the whole pace of my life and go irrevocably on the attack. I
thought of her as my closest collaborator in all my practical plans
and actions; we would go over everything carefully together (turning increasingly to the seclusion of nature as the threat of bugged
apartments grew). Lyusha was in on the secret of *Gulag* from the
first and knew all the details of its development. That was when she
first started gathering information and making inquiries; she spent a
lot of time on the scheme to map all the camps in the Gulag system.
(Two qualified geographers, Nina Pakhtusova and Natalya Kind,
were working on it; indeed, they had finished much of it and had
even photocopied their map, but it turned out too amateurish, with
too many areas left incomplete, and I decided against using it.) I had
barely finished drafting Part One of *Gulag* and begun to type some
of it up before Lyusha was already hard at work making the final
copy. By now the KGB had a pretty good idea that she was helping
me, and the Moscow apartment began to look increasingly dangerous, since it was often left unattended when Lidia Korneyevna was
out at Peredelkino and Lyusha was at work. So Lyusha avoided doing the typing in small batches; instead, knowing in advance when
there would be an upsurge of work, she would save up the vacation
that was due to her and take it all at once when a period of intensive

work was called for. Spring of 1968 was a case in point: typing away in Moscow all April she managed to finish the entire first volume of *Gulag*. Then at Easter Q arrived and we all met up at Rozhdestvo, whereupon Lyusha went at it and had the whole of the second volume typed up by the end of May. (Q was so impressed with her speed that she dubbed her "the Paganini of the typewriter.") With the third volume, Lyusha helped not just Q but my wife, too, even though there was not much love lost between the two of them. Lyusha just gritted her teeth, plunged into the work, not setting foot outside her damp room for a month, and kept the pressure on. Lyusha was the only one of the three who knew the route, the courier, and the destination of the microfilmed copy of *Gulag*, and she alone was involved in every twist and turn of that eventful Pentecost when we smuggled it abroad. I remember her coming out to Rozhdestvo from Peredelkino one dull and windswept day to pick up the capsule of film and take it to Eva (as described in Chapter Nine). I don't know whether it was the malevolent driving wind that gave me such gloomy premonitions at the time. But then, two days later, on the eve of Pentecost Sunday itself, Lyusha suddenly turned up back at Rozhdestvo to tell me that there had been a snag with the handoff and that the "youngster" (Sasha Andreyev, see Chapter Nine) had been tailed. It seemed that all our presentiments were coming true! If I look at it quite soberly, she ought not to have come out to fetch me: Sasha was not due to fly back until Sunday, and the capsule was to follow on Monday; I could have stayed at Rozhdestvo for another forty-eight hours without any risk. But Lyusha came hurtling to the rescue, bent on getting me out of harm's way. Once I heard about the surveillance, my little plot of land at the forest's edge amid the waving crowns of the birch trees could no longer hold any joy for me. Her sense of imminent danger communicated itself to me, and I gave in and made up my mind to disappear from Rozhdestvo, spending these critical days in a place where I could not be followed; if everything went wrong, perhaps I would head back to my Hiding Place to spend a few more months at liberty and at least get something done. Half an hour's notice to leave the ordered world of my beloved little dacha and drop out of sight! I told my wife not to come and see me in my temporary refuge, in case she should be tailed. On the way to catch the train I explained to Lyusha where I would be staying, and we parted at the station, leaving her relieved that I had made a clean getaway. But then I spent three days locked away in utter misery. Lyusha was supposed to come and tell me if there was any news at all, but she did not come; she was languishing at home, waiting in vain for word to get through. It was not until the evening of the second day, when I was already asleep, that she burst in, bearing preliminary glad tidings: at least the "youngster" had been allowed to leave the Soviet Union without being detained. But we had to wait till the fourth day to learn of the happy outcome—the capsule had arrived without incident, and everyone and everything had got away safely!

With that threat lifted, I immediately got down to the final revision of the ninety-six-chapter *First Circle*. For her part, Lyusha, who had already used up her "vacation" typing *Gulag*, was back at the institute trying to catch up not just with her work but with her chores for Granddad too; Kornei Chukovsky had long since noticed that she was not the assistant she had once been, and he was understandably jealous that so much of her energy was being diverted away from him. It was autumn when Lyusha picked up *First Circle* from me—and finished the whole text in one great spurt of typing. And that winter, during one of our forest walks at Peredelkino, she put her plan to me: in order to save our "American friends" (that was how we thought of the Carlisles* at the time) from having to redo the translation and hunt out the variants between the original and revised version of *First Circle*, she would retype the entire novel specially for them, highlighting all the changes. Then all they had to do was translate the new passages (we called this our "cosmetic" edition). It was a grueling, painstaking task, yet Lyusha managed it in a few months that winter, dashing home from the institute each evening to get back to it. (In the summer of 1975, when she was burning all the papers Alya and I had left behind, this typescript went into the flames unused. Years and years of work would vanish without a trace this way.)

There was no limit to Lyusha's appetite for work and the amount she could get done. In the course of the three years of our acquaintanceship, she typed up no less than five hefty books of mine. (And don't forget that in the Soviet Union, finding all those reams of uniform, high-quality paper was no laughing matter; sometimes you could not buy it for love or money. Then there was all the carbon paper as well.) And apart from working directly on these and other ventures, she was party to all my tactical moves and precautionary measures.

In 1966 I made my first explicit ventures into the public arena, beginning with readings, then my letter to the Congress of the Writers' Union, then the feud with the union's secretariat. Not one of those steps ever enjoyed Lyusha's direct support. Never did I hear her say, "Yes! Now's the time to strike!" Rather, she would shake her head in anxious disapproval or even try to talk me out of it, as she did with my statement about Zhores Medvedev.* I always felt uncomfortable and unhappy about this: my immediate plans were known to only a handful of people, so the advice of any one of them was bound to carry great weight. And I was so tied up with my work and the fight I was waging that it only gradually dawned on me that Lyusha's focus was not on the issues as a whole, not on the strategy or principles involved. She was just afraid each time that something would happen to me, that the claws would snap shut on my latest sortie. Yet even though she disapproved of my letter to the Writers' Union, she helped type out more than a hundred copies of it, and it was the same with all the "open letters" and "declarations" that followed. Fifty copies of the lengthy "Record" of my meeting with the Writers' Union secretariat went out thanks solely to her. I could rest assured that she would make the right number of copies and have them ready to launch at what we calculated to be the moment of maximum impact. Then she would deliver them to our principal springboards (to Nadya Levitskaya at the Library of Foreign Literature and Anna Berzer at *Novy Mir*, to various apartments in the Aeroport* district of Moscow and out to Peredelkino to an intermediary who would ferry them to Leningrad). After that they would circulate automatically.

About this time Lyusha got to know others who were helping me, and she naturally assumed responsibility for our frequent meetings, communications, and related business. Her apartment quickly became the focal point for my connections with Leningrad—that is, with Q; the Etkinds; the "First *Infantes*," a group of young people who emerged in Leningrad at that time and wanted to help me (I got as far as planning to use them to make copies of *Gulag*, but our collaboration came to nothing); and with the "Second *Infantes*" (the Kuklins). All my "unofficial" communications bound for Leningrad would be kept at Lyusha's apartment and picked up by couriers traveling that way, while everything that came in from Leningrad would go to her, too, and visitors from there would stop by. (Lidia Korneyevna was a Leningrader by birth, and Lyusha, too, had been born there, so their links with the city were still active.) Before long there were several trusted acquaintances who knew the addresses of our Leningrad contacts and would take things directly to them. In addition, there were people from the provinces whom I had no wish to rebuff but whom circumstances prevented me from meeting in person; they would be given Lyusha's address, and she would provide the books they needed, pass on letters, and hold talks with them on my behalf. Since she was in the heart of Moscow and I was only there on the occasional flying visit, it made life much simpler to put my contacts with certain specific groups of my acquaintances entirely in her hands. This applied to Tenno's widow, for instance, and various visiting Estonians, as well as to the Kobozev and Teush families. At one point I even gave the Zubovs her address to use when they wrote to me. And then there were the monthly parcels to be sent to my Aunt Irina,* another task that was entrusted to her, to say nothing of all kinds of meetings with my Aeroport contacts; they were literary people so Lyusha was, of course, in her element. In their scores they passed through Lyusha's hands—too many, indeed, to list in these pages, even if I could confidently call them all to mind.

The arrival of a Dictaphone opened up new possibilities for Lyusha's work: she could take the lists of questions I had prepared and interview various eyewitnesses about the events of the revolution (a sister-in-law of Palchinsky, a nephew of Guchkov, the engineer K. M. Polivanov,* and so on), then type up their recorded answers so that they reached me on neatly organized sheets. As my representative, Lyusha found herself at the center of a very considerable circle of contacts. The amount of time and effort she saved me by acting in this way I could not even begin to estimate. In all that she did for me she was never once the cause of delay; everything ran more smoothly in her hands, and this gave me far greater freedom of movement. How can I measure the energy she expended? Such concentrated effort exceeded the powers of a single person and could only be achieved thanks to her unfailingly buoyant spirit.

———

In the autumn of 1969 Kornei Ivanovich lay close to death, and love and duty combined to keep his favorite granddaughter at his bedside. (Besides, the fate of his unpublished writings and any hopes for their posthumous publication rested squarely on her shoulders.) And then, suddenly, danger threatened from afar: in Rostov-on-Don a complete set of the full text of *Gulag* was somehow left dangling in the hands of people we did not know. And Lyusha tore herself away from her grandfather and went racing off to Rostov to try and save it. (Coming back on the train, she put the bag containing it into the luggage space under the lower berth—

safer that way! This meant that two old ladies had to make do with the upper bunks, try as they might to persuade her to give up the lower one. But how could you leave a bombshell like this lying around unattended? So she had to make up a story about recovering from an operation.)

Inevitably, the efforts that stick in one's mind are those that yielded tangible results. But what of the countless efforts that proved fruitless, what of all those abortive dry runs? It was Rostropovich who sent us up one such dead end. When our paths crossed, it was a long time before he could appreciate just how dangerous and delicate things were. In autumn 1968, on his way back from Western Europe, he wondered what to give me for my fiftieth birthday. And what should he buy and gaily set off with (indeed, he actually got it through customs, since they did not check him at that time)? A *whirly-printer!* We did not know its proper name, but in fact this was a duplicating machine that could turn out multiple copies from a single typed stencil. Rostropovich thought he was opening up marvelous new possibilities for me to publish my own things inside the Soviet Union! And indeed, Lyusha and I really got involved with this new toy: we experimented with it, planned how we might use it to run off one or two hundred copies of *Gulag.* (The idea at the time was that we would publish it all within Russia by ourselves.) We stocked up on paper, ordered other things we needed from Rostropovich, who brought them back from the West with him. But eventually we realized that there was no way we could cope with a task like this. And then we were at a loss about what to do with this whirly-thing of ours and had to think of someone we could give it to for printing leaflets.

Lyusha took the initiative in making good the opportunities I missed, arranging meetings, contacts, consultations, and sources of assistance. She was so absorbed in my work and the public response to it that in 1968 she thought up, compiled, and published in samizdat a collection of essays and public statements entitled *The*

Word Can Smash Concrete. And all this she did single-handed.

Shifting more and more of the organization onto Lyusha purely for reasons of convenience, I also handed over to her the task of meeting and talking with Y. A. Stefanov, an expert on the Don region and the tsarist army. This was a man so alien to her and the circles in which she moved that their paths would never otherwise have crossed, and they would never have had a chance to talk. In the thick of the fray, organizational considerations dictated our actions, and I tended to forget that Lyusha had sprung from quite different soil and was not to be uprooted from it. On the face of it, the Don was a theme altogether remote from Lyusha's background and interests, but it began to impinge on our lives from various directions and in various ways. Now it took the form of Kryukov's posthumous papers, now of I. N. Tomashevskaya's study of Sholokhov. Or it suddenly turned up in the person of an artist from the Don region who wanted to present me (through Lyusha's agency, as ever) with copies of *Donskaya volna*, the magazine Kryukov had published in Novocherkassk between 1918 and 1919. And once we were brought maps of the Don region, so detailed that they showed every farmstead, and Lyusha was the one who organized the copying. Then there were the Don Cossack materials provided by S. Starikov, which had to be processed as a matter of urgency—and yet again, who should come to the rescue but Lyusha? (The Don Cossack theme is discussed in Chapter Fourteen.)

So selfless, effective, and indispensable was Lyusha that at the beginning of 1968, when my thoughts were turning more and more often to the prospect of my sudden demise and I was wondering how to ensure that my work would carry on after I was gone and my writings survive into the future, I began to weigh whether I should make Lyusha my literary executor, and we both asked lawyers we knew what steps we could take, even under Soviet conditions and given the official hostility toward me. This turned out to be far from simple and dragged on for some time; under Soviet law the state could "compulsorily purchase" (that is, confiscate) the copyright of a deceased citizen.

And not once in those first four years of working together did we clarify the basic questions (who needs clarification when things are going well?), such as how she understood my work as a whole, whether she saw it as I did, and exactly why she was doing all this. I saw things my way and she hers, yet our work together went smoothly, harmoniously, without a hitch. In those years we were under such inhuman pressure from all sides that we never had a chance to talk about anything but the matter at hand. Once, though—I don't know what prompted it—I asked her outright and with belatedly dawning amazement, You must surely be doing all this for the *cause*? For that great Goal (which, incidentally, neither of us had ever named)? She answered with a frank "no." She was just doing it for me, to help me—although she was, it is true, much taken with the idea that books can plow furrows in the minds of men.

And for years Lyusha was content with such justifications, for they allowed her to turn a blind eye to my long-term aims. But for me this was a disheartening revelation.

It is simply a fact that an understanding of the large picture never comes easily to us. Swept up as we are in an unceasing flow of events, we are inevitably slow to grasp their overall significance. Thus, not only Lyusha but I, too, for a long time failed to see the true nature of my position in society. After five years of Khrushchev's shilly-shallying in the shadow of Stalin's mausoleum,* an irrepressible cry of impatience was forming in the land: there was a limit to marking time. To paraphrase Pushkin, the country was waiting for anyone at all.* That is when my *Ivan Denisovich* made its appearance, at first in samizdat form. But this was decidedly not what the educated part of society had hungered for; they had yearned for a different protagonist and a different realm of experience. (I think, incidentally, that this explains why a samizdat copy of *Ivan Deniso-*

vich did not immediately find its way abroad, as Tvardovsky had feared would happen in 1962. The work was too peasant-oriented, too Russian, and hence, as it were, encoded. If Western correspondents did read the samizdat version at the time, they probably judged it to have limited appeal to Western tastes.) Indeed, before the publication in *Novy Mir*, there was some instinctive hesitation among the cultural elite as they wondered whether there might be a certain "anti-intelligentsia" bias in my work. It seemed the better part of wisdom not to overdo the praises of *Ivan Denisovich*. But the forces released could not be contained, and it was precisely the intelligentsia in the widest sense of the word that did the mos for the dissemination and recognition of my peasant tale. None of us could foresee the future, and we all lacked understanding. Thus I recall wondering for years why it was that writers are supposed to have enemies and envious detractors, whereas I had *not a single one*. (Needless to say, I was wrong, but I was in too much of a rush to notice.) The desire to lambaste the powers-that-be was so universal that I received unanimous support from every unofficial quarter, even from individuals or groups whose orientation I could not share. For several years I rode the crest of this wave, with no one but the KGB persecuting me while I enjoyed the solid backing of society as a whole. (This type of thing had happened a number of times in tsarist Russia, too—for instance, when Tolstoy was championed by people who had no sympathy for his teaching but who supported him solely to express their opposition to the state.) Throughout this time I simply did not realize that the support I received from "progressive society" was but a passing phase based on a misunderstanding. And neither I nor my closest associate, Lyusha, had any grounds at first for exploring the dissimilarities that existed between her view of the world and mine. At the time, things were undifferentiated to such a degree that even my "Prose Miniatures"* were warmly greeted by the cultural elite. Russian Orthodoxy might have been looked down upon by them, but it had become fashionable to acknowledge the aesthetic worth of icons and even to recognize the lyrical beauty of a church in a landscape.

The first question that revealed a glimpse of the gap between Lyusha and myself concerned the Vlasov movement, an issue that came to the fore when Lyusha read my play *Prisoners*. The work was alarmingly alien to her. Deeply upset, she tried in vain to find an explanation, ultimately falling back on a makeshift formula to the effect that she "could not accept certain parts of the text."

Lyusha's reaction really had to be expected. For without lengthy and patient elucidation, how could one possibly communicate the nation's experience at the front and in prison to a person like Lyusha, who had been a teenage Muscovite in the wartime Soviet Union? Beyond that, her reaction also reflected the essential split in public attitudes toward Vlasov: the cultural elite judged it quite unforgivable that during the war with Hitler the Vlasovites could have spared a thought for anything else that lay ahead—the future of Russia, for instance. (The Vlasov theme was even more jarring to Lyusha in *Gulag*, a work for which she was literally risking her life. She loved this book, helping to draw it forward, to carry its burden, and to bring it to completion, all the while without fully approving of its explosive potential.)

Although the cultural milieu to which the Chukovskys belonged had long since lost all sympathy for the Soviet regime in its present form, they were nevertheless psychologically wedded to the nonreligious traditions of the Russian nineteenth-century liberation movement with its special brand of populism. (Thus, Lyusha's mother, Lidia Korneyevna, virtually idolized Alexander Herzen.)* For this reason the Chukovskys were incapable of connecting their repudiation of the present state of affairs with what had been the decisive product of the liberation movement—the events of 1917 leading up to October. What's more, the very way of life in the Moscow of the 1920s and 1930s was such that educated society was quite sincerely unaware of the suffering visited upon the Russian national spirit. At one point—this was in the context of the collection *From Under the Rubble*—Lidia Korneyevna voiced perplexity as to when slights to the Russian national consciousness could have occurred or become acute. She simply had not noticed. Educated society had a clear awareness only of slights directed against the Jews and to a lesser degree of those directed against some other nationalities.

In any case, Lyusha and I were always so caught up in the whirlwind of our conspiratorial enterprise that I had little chance to make detailed inquiries about her view of my writings. I didn't always have the time even to savor the charmingly apt sense of humor she displayed in some of the lighter moments. And her unfailingly noble dignity and tact were blessings I took very much for granted. Meanwhile Lyusha was probably trying to account for my remoteness in purely human terms, settling on the explanation offered by many others: that I was overwhelmed by the double burdens of work and struggle and that this had caused ordinary human feelings and attentive kindness toward others to atrophy in me.

But of course no loss of feeling was involved here—only the relentless press of duty, as well as the desperate shortness of time. I could not have carried my burden to the end if I had acted otherwise. What is more, the full picture was never clear to persons close to me, for beyond the immediate struggle with the Communist state loomed a greater challenge still: the Russian spirit lay comatose, as if crushed beneath a mighty rock, and this vast tombstone—even less visible at the time than any of my invisible allies—must somehow be raised, overturned, and sent crashing downhill.

Lyusha was still hopeful when she picked up a bundle of handwritten notebooks containing my *August 1914*. She was always fond of these moments and of her role as the first person to convert my text into typewritten form. But what was this? Chapter after chapter simply dismayed her: "The purpose of writing all this is utterly beyond me." (This was a judgment I heard from many members of the same cultural milieu, including even E. Zvorykina.* What was the point of stirring up the past, the events of 1914, the tsarist era? Who needs all that?) But when it came to surveying the selected responses of "test readers," Lyusha carried out the whole operation with dispatch. The texts needed to be distributed, collected, and passed along to others, in each case rapidly and secretly. The delight of many of these readers served to reconcile Lyusha somewhat with *August*, and one of the results of this process, carried through with her characteristic energy, was a collection of samizdat essays* on *August 1914*. This compilation seems to have been intended in part as a polemical response to me, the thought being that the bulk of the essays would confirm Lyusha's view of my book.

But when I asked her to type up my "Lenten Letter to Patriarch Pimen"* in February 1972, she flatly refused—for the first time in the course of our long collaboration—and at that moment became true to herself by shaking off the spell. After more than six years of working together, it became apparent that we did not think alike.

What did this mean? What was it specifically that had caused Lyusha to protest so vehemently? In what way had my open letter given such offense to educated society? It could hardly have been the accusatory tone, since my readers had gotten used to that. And surely it was not a question of resenting criticism directed at the high office of Patriarch. What rankled, I suspect, was the fact that my "Lenten Letter" did not address some abstract spiritual issues but had called upon Russian Orthodoxy—with all its traditions and rituals—to begin participating in the real world. That was going much too far: enlightened society simply could not accept Orthodoxy in such doses. It was clearly *August 1914* and my "Lenten Letter" that destroyed the wholehearted support of society that I had so undeservedly enjoyed until then. After the appearance of these texts, only a small minority remained on my side; this faction will grow only with the slow development of new generations and social strata.

Lyusha was tormented by split loyalties. She could not escape the influence of the milieu that had shaped her entire life, but she also cherished the forward movement of our common task and felt certain of its significance and value. And in the final analysis it was not a question of philosophical opinion: Lyusha was the kind of dedicated and psychologically whole individual who had no need to light every step of her way with an ideological lantern. After her "revolt" over my open letter to the Patriarch, she resumed lending a hand in every way she could. But it is also true that the areas in which we worked together had begun to shrink some years earlier, with several new projects (such as the planning for the collection *From Under the Rubble*) coordinated outside her immediate circle. Nor did I return to the unfinished business of making her my formal literary executor.

Meanwhile my work on *October 1916* kept raising a multitude of questions that could not have been foreseen when I wrote *August 1914*. It was only now that it became clear to me that besides researching World War I, I also needed to take a close look at early twentieth-century Russian social currents, at a large number of public figures ranging from monarchists to Mensheviks, at the Russian governmental structure at the time, at the workers' movement, and even at the list of factories in Saint Petersburg, with the exact location of each marked on a map of the city. Many of the queries relating to these issues, as well as numerous other tasks, such as the transmission of messages, now fell on Lyusha's shoulders. Sometimes I put her in touch with those who could supply specific information, such as Professor P. A. Zaionchkovsky,* but usually it was Lyusha herself who sought out informants or consultants appropriate to my inquiries. (I didn't even learn the names of these individuals and don't know whom to thank.) Lidia Korneyevna's right to take out books from the Lenin Library—she was still a member of the Writers' Union at the time—was also pressed into service here, and a steady supply of books, all clearly intended for my use, now flowed from the library to the politically tainted wing of Rostropovich's house in Zhukovka under the very nose of the KGB. Indeed, we made no secret of it and discussed it openly on the telephone.

Lyusha's prominent role in my struggle finally became too much for the KGB to bear, and the flames of danger flared up at her feet. Toward the end of 1972 she was attacked by an "unknown" assailant in the lobby of her apartment building. The man knocked her to the concrete floor and began choking her. (A doorman-cum-informer normally sat there, but he was suspiciously absent at that time.) Lyusha was so startled that she did not cry out, but she managed to fight free and the attacker fled. Friends thought that this could have been some genuinely sick individual; the courtyard, however, was under constant surveillance, and the KGB had an office a mere twenty yards off. All of the Chukovskys' dissident acquaintances were as well known to the security people as Lyusha was, having been observed many times. The militia seems to have made a halfhearted attempt to investigate the incident, but nothing came of it.

Then, on June 20, 1973, just when my family was being bombarded with anonymous threats through the mail,* a truck traveling beside the taxi in which Lyusha was riding on a major Moscow street suddenly made an inexplicable ninety-degree turn out of its lane and crashed into the right side of the vehicle Lyusha was sitting in. The force of the collision should have killed her; Lyusha's survival, after lengthy medical treatment, was thus unexpected. Once again there was no direct proof that it had been a deliberate assassination attempt. (And who can ever gather such proof against the KGB in the land of the Soviets?) But in the multiple-lane traffic of Sadovoye Ring Road, where the crash happened, not even a lunatic would dare make such a turn, a maneuver for which a driver would earn a prison term even if no accident were involved. Lyusha attended the trial with the naive purpose of defending the driver so that he would not be jailed (he had two children), but the court was quick to set this suspicious motorized bandit free in any case on the grounds that he was a member of a "special" military unit.

In the weeks that followed, the attacks on me continued, Voronyanskaya was arrested, and a typescript of *Gulag* was seized. In this context, the crash seems a calculated blow planned by the KGB.

When Lyusha was riding in that taxi, she had with her some things that had to be kept out of the hands of the security people, as well as the keys to her apartment where many other items were stored. From the scene of the accident she was removed to the Sklifosovsky Clinic, where all her things were taken from her in accordance with hospital regulations. Badly injured though she was, Lyusha still had the presence of mind to call Natalya Stolyarova, who lived nearby. Stolyarova rushed over to take possession of Lyusha's belongings and, with the assertiveness of a camp veteran, overcame the hospital's resistance and saved everything.

Though conclusive evidence is lacking, I am virtually certain that the blow that fell on Lyusha was delivered on my account.

Nor was this the first serious traffic accident in which Lyusha had been involved. Several years earlier she had crashed on her motorcycle and had vowed never to drive again. This time she suffered a major concussion with lingering aftereffects. For some time she could not even walk by herself. She needed bed rest and could neither read nor think properly. Medicines were urgently brought in from abroad; fortunately, this was something that we could do at the time. Lyusha, meanwhile, did not always seem aware of her actions, of the way she became excited, could not stop talking, and jumped from topic to topic. In August she returned from a period of convalescence on the Baltic Sea, and in a forest clearing near Peredelkino I told her about my plan of attack: a major interview with Western correspondents.* In the past she had always made impassioned attempts to dissuade me from such actions, but this time she listened with what seemed like befogged indifference—another symptom of her injuries that manifested itself at times. I asked her whether I could mention the attempt on her life in the interview, but she forbade it.

But the battle that had now been joined did not seem to require Lyusha's participation. Sitting there in the tranquility of a forest clearing, I thought that she would now have the chance to recover peacefully, quite free of any tasks on my behalf. But in fact an "encounter battle"* was shaping up, with Q going through her torments at KGB headquarters in Leningrad, though this was still unknown to us. Two weeks later the news of Voronyanskaya's death and the seizure of *Gulag* hit Lyusha like the stroke of a lash, setting back her recovery and almost blocking it for good. On two consecutive days she traveled to Firsanovka to bring me the news that first the "archive" [arkhi*v*] and then Arkhi*p* had been seized. She regressed to the confused and agitated state she had been in after the accident, while the situation demanded calm deliberation, with numerous matters hanging in the balance along with various caches of texts that had been stored by or through her. Lamara (see Chapter Ten) held a particularly significant collection, but every move to warn her posed deadly risks, while not warning her was also out of the question. Lyusha, her mind clouded by her injuries, now needed to solve increasingly complex problems, with the dark mystery of Q's death tormenting her like a beak hammering on her vulnerable head. She tried to put together the contradictory pieces of evidence, quite plausibly expecting to share Q's fate, and in this state of extreme stress she really needed to meet with me for several hours a day in order to talk things over. It was a genuine need, and I had an obligation to her, yet precisely because of the extreme danger, this was a period when I could not spare a minute for meetings and conversation as I scrambled to take countermeasures and to salvage manuscripts. The only joint action that Lyusha and I undertook at the time was to send Alyosha Shipovalnikov to meet with Samutin in Leningrad—a false move (see Chapter Five). For years

Lyusha had helped maintain that relentless momentum without which we could never hope to succeed. But now, during the weeks of her convalescence, it worked to her disadvantage. What she required at this time were extensive sympathy, help in everyday affairs, and words of encouragement. With all this in short supply, Lyusha was overcome by a feeling of abandonment, abandonment in a hostile world.

However, no further blow fell on our circle, precisely because the furious counterattack had proved to be the best defense of all. The caches of texts were safe. With time, Lyusha's recovery resumed, permitting her to worry about Irina Tomashevskaya, who had fallen seriously ill in the Crimea. October brought the news of Tomashevskaya's sudden death (Chapter Fourteen). This was another blow to a mind not yet fully recovered, and it brought a new round of urgent concerns.

That autumn I had left Firsanovka for the season, had not lived in Rostropovich's house since spring, and was barred by the militia from settling in Moscow with my family. In November Lidia Korneyevna once again invited me to spend the winter in the Chukovsky home in Peredelkino. This did not lead to more frequent meetings with Lyusha, however. The pace of events was now brutally harsh as I tried to finish what I could—my introduction to *Troubled Waters of the Quiet Don* and especially my essays for the collection *From Under the Rubble*. Though I understood fully that both Lidia Korneyevna and Lyusha would find these essays distasteful and difficult to accept, I nevertheless decided to let them sample these writings. Lidia Korneyevna read my "Letter to the Soviet Leaders" and, to my great surprise, voiced her approval. (Her ultimate test was always a comparison with Alexander Herzen, and he had addressed a letter to Tsar Alexander II.) She also read two of my essays for *From Under the Rubble*, finding them somewhat remote from her interests but nothing to get angry about. (She tends to take a broad view of things.)

With Lyusha it was a different story altogether. The "Letter to the Soviet Leaders" was the first text she had read without prior knowledge: it had been finished several months before and by now was already on its way to the leaders in question, as well as to the West. And on top of that came the three essays intended for *From Under the Rubble*. It was all too much, quite intolerable! She erupted like a volcano, with a particularly impassioned protest against Orthodoxy and patriotism. As she read the texts, Lyusha practically cursed. She tried to take notes, but her impatience got the better of her, and she decided to record her anger on a Dictaphone so as not to forget her most caustic comments, dropping all trace of the intellectual restraint and sobriety typical of her. She then used the recording to prepare written comments in which she denounced me in terms more bitter than anything that had ever been said between us. Although these written remarks were still rather disorderly, Lyusha rushed over to Peredelkino to spill them out to me herself. A certain degree of emotional substitution was involved here, no doubt, as can happen in arguments with women, where annoyance in one sphere is transferred to an entirely unrelated one. But there was also a pitiless revelation of a misgiving with which she could hardly come to terms: could she have sacrificed so many years and her best efforts in the service of this? Would it not have been infinitely more appropriate and more loyal to have helped her grandfather in the last years of his life? And now to help her mother, who was going blind and whose work had become a constant struggle?

I walked into the dining area from the same room I had occupied eight years earlier. Then I had come out into the softly illuminated room in order to meet Lyusha for the first time; now I stepped out into the dim January light for a painful confrontation. Looking pale and drawn, not yet fully recovered—one had to wonder what was keeping body and soul together—Lyusha launched into a passionate tirade against my unspeakably shameful Orthodox-cum-patriotic orientation in *From Under the Rubble*. And, she added, now she understood that it was not for nothing that she had some Jewish blood in her veins.

My defense was halfhearted at best. This was not the time for persuasion—that should have been started long ago, and in any case arguments are not much use against emotions. On top of it all, this was taking place in January 1974, a less-than-propitious moment for quarrels. All of Lyusha's strength had gone into her monologue— afterward, she needed to lie down and catch her breath. For my part, I was grieved by the realization that all too much had been neglected over the years and that it was now far too late to set it straight.

But even in the course of these months and after this conversation, Lyusha asked for work. She no longer had control over the course of events, yet she asked for work and wanted to help! At the time I did not happen to have that much to suggest, and I asked her to work on a chronological "mesh" of the February Revolution, focusing on particular fragments among the mass of revolutionary events as well as on background information about specific individuals. And work she did, to her everlasting credit! Her stance toward the regime was also irreproachable both before and after my expulsion from the country. My own view of the world was emerging more clearly and, alien though it must have seemed to her, she gave it full support. Disregarding her own background, her upbringing and outlook on life, she bent her back to the task I had set myself and forged ever onward.

During this period Lidia Korneyevna was also expelled from the Writers' Union. (In response she let loose a fine broadside against the literary bureaucrats.)*

Soon thereafter I was deported, and Lyusha now became a frequent visitor to our besieged and disrupted Moscow apartment, where my wife Alya had her hands full with the task of coordinating the evacuation of my effects. Lyusha would come by every evening after work and sit at my writing table, sorting drafts and preparatory

138 — Invisible Allies

materials, many of which she knew or had even typed. She helped
put together my papers for shipment to the West, even though it was
not yet certain that Alya would succeed in bringing this off.

The first months after my expulsion were a difficult time for the
Chukovskys. Both mother and daughter were bombarded with
anonymous letters, some in verse, some filled with obscenities,
some informing them that "the lion has been killed" or "will be
killed." Among the visitors to their Peredelkino dacha—it was open
to all in the manner of a museum—there were now spies and inso-
lent agents provocateurs. The informer-doorman in the lobby of
their Moscow apartment building would now stop their guests on
the grounds that they had not greeted him politely enough (one visitor thus treated was seventy-five years old). Lidia Korneyevna's
near blindness made it possible for her to write only with black
marker pens brought in from abroad, but these would be deliberately mangled at customs or else filled with useless pink fluid. These
were some of the ways in which the state played its untraceable dirty
tricks, many of them so petty that it seemed almost embarrassing to
make a public fuss about them and hardly worth the trouble.

On the eve of my first birthday in exile, Lyusha, in an act of de-
fiance against the powers-that-be, sent a congratulatory telegram to
Zurich—a message of admiration addressed to Public Enemy
Number One. This proved to be more than the security people
could swallow. Early the next morning her phone rang, and the following characteristic dialogue ensued.

"Elena Tsezarevna, this is so-and-so from the KGB. I hope that
does not frighten you."

"No, why should it?"

True enough, it was no longer the 1930s, and the name of the
agency did not make one's blood run cold; the KGB had even been
mocked.

"I'm happy to hear that. I take it, then, that you could come by
to see us sometime after lunch."

"Sorry, I can't make it."

"When would be a convenient time for you?"

"To tell the truth, it would be inconvenient to come to see you at any time."

"In that case we'll come and see you."

"That would be highly undesirable."

"So what do you suggest?"

"Send me a summons."

"You mean to say that you admit your guilt and want us to begin formal *proceedings* against you?"

Thrust and parry have their limits. . . .

"No, I didn't mean that, but isn't that the accepted procedure?"

"Look, I'm trying to be polite with you as you're a woman."

"Do you mean to say that you're not polite with men?"

The voice at the other end grew sterner. "I am calling to request that you come here."

By now Lyusha was angry, and she, too, was getting worked up. "I am not an ambulance, and I don't rush out in response to telephone calls."

"When will you be at work?"

"I have no intention of informing you."

"Then we'll pick you up on the street."

"I'll scream for help."

"But you don't always scream, do you?" (An allusion to the incident in the lobby of her apartment house some time ago. A confirmation from the horse's mouth that *they* were responsible.)

"But this time I most certainly will scream."

"There's really no need to talk this way. After all *we're with you all the time*."

"I see. You're just like the good Lord, I suppose."

"No, the good Lord is with your friend."

"What friend? I have many friends."

"The one you address with a capital F." (Had they intercepted a letter sent via private channels?) "In any case we would very much like to have an unofficial talk with you."

By now Lyusha had lost all patience. "Get it into your heads that I shall have no unofficial talks with you whatever, only official ones!"

And she slammed down the receiver.

They never did come, and she was not touched.

With these people one has to exhibit an uncompromising firmness of spirit—this was a point Lyusha had assimilated in the course of our common struggle. But it could not have been an easy lesson to absorb for a single woman confronting a well-fed system smugly conscious of its long arms and many heads.

There followed a long series of crank calls: "Expect the Bedouins to arrive today." "The camels have set off."

All of this seemed straight out of the satirical novels of Ilf and Petrov, but then again, could one always shrug off such things lightly?

After several quiet months Lyusha rejoiced to think that the hounds had been called off. But at that very point there was a break-in at her apartment, and the place was ransacked.

The KGB also took revenge on Kornei Chukovsky's books. His *Chukokkala*,* any new editions of his children's books, and even studies about him were all blocked by the vengeful agency.

Although the most dangerous period is now behind her—since Lyusha is no longer closely linked to affairs that were deemed unlawful—it is of course impossible to predict what the future may bring. Not long ago she could not refrain from defending me at a meeting in her institute. And some recently interrogated individuals report that she was referred to as the "head of Solzhenitsyn's counterintelligence service."

In case of arrest, Lyusha plans to follow a very simple course of action: she won't deny anything or entangle herself in complicated statements but will simply admit that she gave help to Russian literature and make it clear that she has no intention of saying anything else.

For a number of years after my expulsion, Lyusha helped to support an old aunt of mine in Georgievsk. And she wrote to me in Zurich using unofficial channels, supplying me with many important materials.

———

My meeting with Lyusha in that far-off autumn helped her emerge from a state of dejection. It led to her participation in a furious struggle. But that struggle consumed years of her life, took possession of her soul, and dragged her—at least in part against her will—into a tragic and uncharted orbit.[1]

[1]With the advent of Gorbachev's *glasnost*, Lyusha was the first to raise her voice in the press (in *Knizhnoe obozrenie*) about me and about the need to permit my return to Russia, though in the process she tended to present me in terms of Soviet virtues. The journal received a mass of positive responses, as well as some letters expressing indignation. The readers probably thought that Lyusha's statement had been a disinterested appeal: none of them knew how much energy, time, and heart she had given to this author. (1990 note)

9

Natalya Ivanovna Stolyarova ("Eva")

In 1906 a group of revolutionaries attempted to assassinate Prime Minister Stolypin and his family by blowing up their dacha on Saint Petersburg's Aptekarsky Island. As it turned out, almost thirty visitors were killed and two or three dozen more, including children, were seriously injured, while Stolypin himself escaped untouched. One of the leading figures in the attempted assassination, the so-called lady in the carriage, was Natalya Sergeyevna Klimova, a twenty-two-year-old member of the Maximalist faction of the Socialist Revolutionary Party and the daughter of a prominent Ryazan family. Natalya was arrested and sentenced to death together with her co-conspirators. She did not beg for clemency herself, but her father—a member of the State Council, no less— appealed on her behalf. Acceding to his petition, the tsar spared the lives of the two women conspirators, Natalya and a merchant's daughter by the name of Varvara Terentyeva. Their sentences were commuted to life imprisonment with hard labor. (While awaiting execution, Natalya had sent a valedictory letter from prison, which was subsequently published, prompting a response in print from Semyon Frank:* her letter, he wrote, "shows that the divine power of the human spirit is capable of overcoming" even the anguish of impending violent death; "the ethical value of these six pages is greater than that of all the weighty volumes of contemporary philosophy and tragic literature put together.") Natalya Klimova served the first part of her sentence in Novinsk prison in Moscow, and with her charm and forceful personality won over her wardress and used her help to organize the renowned breakout by the "Novinsk Thirteen," all of them women. (In the Soviet period, this incident inspired a film scenario, but production was banned since there had not been a single Bolshevik among the escapees.) Once the women were free, friends were ready and waiting. Natalya was immediately taken by night to the home of a liberal lawyer, where she spent a month in comparative safety, while the police were keeping watch at her parents' estate and at their home in Ryazan. Then, veiled as if in deep mourning, she was escorted by the lawyer to a train bound for Siberia. After making her way across to Japan, Natalya set sail for London, where Savinkov was waiting to welcome her back into the ranks of the organization's militant (that is, "terrorist") wing. The "Amazons' dacha" near Genoa was a place where the Novinsk escapees and other political convicts could regroup, and there she met and married Ivan Stolyarov, an émigré revolutionary, by whom she had two daughters. In 1917 he forged ahead into the maelstrom of revolutionary Petrograd, leaving his wife pregnant with their third daughter. But the little girl died of the Spanish flu almost as soon as she was born. Natalya managed to nurse her two elder daughters— Natasha and Katerina—through the illness before she herself succumbed and died.

At that time the whole of revolutionary Russia was converging on Paris, and a tightly knit community of political émigrés grew up, including, as it turned out, the Menshevik son of Judge Shilovsky, the Klimovs' next-door neighbor in Ryazan. The young Shilovsky adopted Natasha and her younger sister and brought them up in Paris. Although they say the heart has room for but a single great love, Natasha's heart proved large enough to embrace both an unreserved affection for France and an ardent devotion to Russia (but not to the revolution her mother had served). At the beginning of the 1920s, the eleven-year-old Natasha went to visit her father in Petrograd. (Although her parents had belonged to non-Bolshevik parties, such trips were still possible for a time; indeed, not far from the family home in the center of Ryazan there was then a little public garden still named in honor of Natasha's mother.) While she was there, Natasha contemplated her future and resolved that when she was twenty, she would return to Russia, come what may. According to her sister Katya, who stayed behind in France, Natasha inherited her mother's vivacious personality, her high principles, breadth of vision, and generous spirit—but she also had her mother's impetuosity and physical daring. Nothing was allowed to stand in the way of her planned return to Russia, and she ignored the sober admonitions of her émigré friends, who were justifiably concerned for her safety; after all, it was December 1934, Kirov had just been assassinated, and it was patently insane to think of going back now.* (Nor has she ever regretted her decision, not even from the depths of the Gulag inferno and certainly not today, when she is making her own direct contribution to the spiritual renaissance of her country. Perhaps if millions of others had pressed forward as she did through fire and danger, our history would have progressed more rapidly than it did.)

By the time she reached Russia and was reunited with her father, he had already been exiled, along with other Socialist Revolutionaries, to a place near Bukhara and had only been extricated thanks to the efforts of E. P. Peshkova,* herself a former Socialist Revolutionary. His final arrest and execution did not come until after Natasha's own arrest. She was granted two years to experience not the Russia of her dreams but freedom Soviet-style. Then in 1937 they came for her. (So she came back of her own free will, did she? Obviously a spy. Or just put her down for counterrevolutionary activity.) And in her very first cell at the Lubyanka prison, whom should she meet but one of the women who had broken out of Novinsk prison with her mother!

Natasha trod the same bitter path as so many others, and the experience did not fade from her memory; her soul was indelibly seared. Especially grim were the years following her "premature" release in 1946: for a zek actually to be allowed back into society after finishing his or her sentence in camp or exile was virtually unprecedented, and the "free" Soviet public was not yet ready to cope with anything so bizarre. In 1953, after a series of misfortunes and only thanks to the intercession of Ilya Ehrenburg and other influential figures, she managed to secure permission to reside under administrative surveillance in her hometown of Ryazan—whence, not many years before, her mother had gaily sallied forth to join the revolutionaries. Here Natasha passed her time working as a French teacher and coping with the vicissitudes of a turbulent personal life, scarcely suspecting that one day she would find herself involved in subversive anti-Soviet activity.

Later, when the political climate relaxed, Natalya Ivanovna could afford to lower her guard. In 1956 she moved to Moscow, where Ehrenburg's daughter, who had been at school with her in Paris, persuaded her father to take Natalya on as his private secretary. As a famous writer and public figure, Ehrenburg received a steady flow of letters and visits from people seeking his help, many of them former zeks, and here Natalya was in her element. (In fact, she went on working for Ehrenburg right up to his death.)

When I went looking for the former Klimov Gardens in Ryazan, I found them lying in the menacing shadow of the Party's regional committee building, uncared for and shunned by the townsfolk. The nameplate was gone, and Natalya's mother might as well have never existed. I learned the whole story from Natalya when she revealed that we were compatriots twice over: we had common roots in Ryazan—and in the Gulag.

Natalya contrived our first meeting in the spring of 1962 with a characteristic display of audacity and harmless guile. She sent a message via Lev Kopelev informing me that she had something important to tell me. In fact, she simply wanted to meet me. (I knew from Kopelev that she was a former zek.) Around this time typescript copies of my *Ivan Denisovich* were circulating quietly, and it was no secret that Ehrenburg was one of the influential figures who had read it.

But nobody knew at the time how Ehrenburg had managed to be among its first readers, when he was the last person Tvardovsky would have chosen to show it to. In fact it had been Natalya's idea. When she got wind of the story, she went to the *Novy Mir* editorial office and asked in Ehrenburg's name for a copy of the manuscript. Boris Zaks* hemmed and hawed but could not bring himself to say no to someone of Ehrenburg's stature. Natalya took one look at the story and was struck to see on the first page the name "A. Ryazansky,"* a pseudonym devised at the *Novy Mir* offices. She took it directly to Vadim Afanasyev, a photographer friend of hers, for copying. (We called him "Leather Jacket"; he was married to her cousin, and later he did occasional jobs for us as well.) Only when Afanasyev had finished did Natalya deliver the story to Ehrenburg. Poor Tvardovsky underestimated the power of modern technology, and he was bewildered and alarmed when samizdat copies of *Ivan Denisovich* began circulating like wildfire. My own initial reaction was one of idiotic delight: I did not realize that this development put the whole future of the story in the gravest jeopardy.

Then along came Natalya Stolyarova's message asking to see me. I took it for granted that she must be wanting to report on how efforts to publish *Ivan Denisovich* were progressing or to let me know what the high and mighty thought of the story. So, somewhat reluctantly, I did as she asked and phoned her at Ehrenburg's number, where-upon she invited me over to Ehrenburg's apartment and would not take no for an answer. (Her manner was so animated and insistent that although she did not say as much, it was easy to conclude that her boss must be sitting next to her, just dying to see me.)

When I reached the apartment, it emerged that Ehrenburg (who, in any case, had hated *Ivan Denisovich*) was abroad and knew nothing about this meeting. Nevertheless, we sat and talked together in his office. Natalya scraped together some sort of news to tell me, but it was obviously too insubstantial to justify my visit. (I imagine she was just trying to boost the morale of the author of *Ivan Denisovich*.) Had it been anyone else I would have lost my temper there and then, but how could I be angry with a Gulag veteran whose memory still bore the imprint of our archipelago and whose sympathy for the lost tribe of zeks was as keen as ever? Besides, she had not asked to see me sim-ply out of idle curiosity but rather to test me, to find out how res-olutely I would keep to my chosen path. Was I ready for the trials that lay ahead? Would I let "them" butter me up and turn me from my chosen path? Far from confining ourselves to literary matters, we were soon talking simply and directly, as one zek to another, so much so that I inadvertently strayed beyond the bounds of caution: news travels fast in all walks of Soviet life, and nowhere more so than in the thin-walled world of literature. We touched on the uprisings in the Special camps. "You've just got to write it down and tell it the way it was!" she exclaimed, and rather than simply shrugging and keeping quiet, I half-confided in her: "It's already written!"* And I saw her face light up with joy. At the front door she lowered her voice so that none of Ehrenburg's people should overhear, and with her parting words urged me to keep my nerve in the months ahead and not let fame turn my head. "Don't worry. It won't!" I assured her categorically. (Later she confided, "That was what made me so committed to you. And I seemed to have developed a sixth sense: I would come out of my apartment and set off down the stairs, then suddenly I'd feel myself drawn back again. What could I have forgotten? As soon as I was back inside, the phone would ring, and it would turn out to be you. That happened quite a few times.") On one score I was adamant: fame would never win me over. I was inching my way up the wall of Soviet literature like a man weighed down with a load of mortar, straining every fiber not to spill it. But what about today? Had I spilled it after all, by letting my tongue run away with me? My heart told me that I hadn't, that she was one of us. And so it turned out to be.

After this rapport was established, we saw each other only occasionally and quite fleetingly at that. Nothing of substance was discussed, yet my confidence in her grew stronger. Hers was an odd combination of qualities: her thoroughly muddled sense of world affairs was coupled with an unshakable loathing of the Soviet regime; the chaotic feminine logic of her speech and behavior would vanish the instant our cherished cause was at stake, giving way to dogged single-mindedness, clarity of thought, and a decisiveness that was as audacious as it was unerring. (As the years passed I became more clearly aware of these qualities.) She was a woman of excellent education, always tactful and unassuming, and with an easy manner. Yet in her dealings with the secret police she would become haughty and unbending. (Years later she would undergo a second round of interrogation in the Lubyanka prison, but they never got near the heart of our conspiracy.)

A year or so after our first meeting Natalya suddenly visited her old hometown with a group of friends, and while they were in Ryazan they looked me up. I do not know what prompted me to ask her help in sending microfilm copies of my works to the West. I knew that sooner or later it would have to be done, but there was no particular urgency: Khrushchev was still in power, and I enjoyed some degree of protection, however precarious. Nevertheless, acting on the spur of the moment, I took Natalya to one side and asked whether at some point she would be prepared to take something like this on. She agreed without a moment's hesitation, stipulating only that no one else should know about it.

The trust that had sprung up between us from our very first meeting now entered a dramatic new phase.

The capsule containing the microfilms was ready to be sent, but it was not a pressing matter; previous attempts had come to nothing, and there was no obvious way of achieving it. But when Khrushchev was overthrown in October 1964, things began to heat up and I believed I was in extreme danger. It was clear that the enemy would soon have his fangs at my throat, and it could happen at any moment. (Erring on the side of prudence and remembering how the regime had dealt with so many others before me, I credited it with all the dynamism of its revolutionary past. As it turned out, this energy was so depleted that it would take the authorities eleven months to steel themselves for the first search and nine years before their first decisive blow.)

The news of Khrushchev's fall found me in Ryazan, and by the following day I was already at Natalya Ivanovna's Moscow apartment wanting to know if it could be done, and if so, how soon?

Natalya Ivanovna was not only quick to reach a decision but she invariably enjoyed more than her share of luck. I had seen for myself how fortune tended to smile on her enterprises, even the apparently frivolous ones. (But perhaps it was not so much luck as the aura of invincibility that surrounded her once her mind was made up.) This occasion was no exception, for a "lucky" coincidence immediately came our way. Vadim Leonidovich Andreyev, the son of the writer Leonid Andreyev,* just happened to be visiting Moscow at that very moment. His home was in Geneva, where Natalya Ivanovna's sister happened to live; in fact, the two of them were acquainted. Natalya Ivanovna screwed up her eyes for an instant, then resolved to ask Vadim Leonidovich's help. She was quite convinced that he would not refuse!

Natalya set a date toward the end of October when I was to come back up to Moscow. By then she had already spoken to Vadim Leonidovich, and that evening in her cramped little room in a communal apartment on Malo-Demidovsky Lane she brought the two of us together. Vadim Leonidovich turned out to be a gentleman of the old school—reserved, rather dry, a man of complete integrity. And this very integrity effectively left him with no choice but to agree to our request, for the sake not only of Russian literature but of the Soviet labor camps as well, since his own brother Daniil had spent long years in captivity. (Natalya Ivanovna subsequently assured me that he had also felt honored to have been asked.) His wife Olga Viktorovna, stepdaughter of the leading Socialist Revolutionary Chernov, was also present, a most pleasant, sympathetic woman. She approved of her husband's decision and was ready to share the consequences. So there they were, officially just small fry like us in the Soviet order of things, without the protection of diplomatic immunity or even of foreign citizenship. (They traveled on Soviet passports because after the war Vadim Leonidovich, like so many other émigrés, had been carried away by patriotic fervor and had applied for Soviet citizenship, not least in order to make it easier for him to visit Russia more often.) Here they were, taking it upon themselves to ferry abroad this capsule with its explosive charge— everything I had written over the last eighteen years, from my first uncompromising camp verses right through to *The First Circle*. Of course they were not aware of precisely what they were carrying, but they had grasped enough to know that it was a bombshell. And still they took it; their minds were made up before I met them.

At the time, that evening seemed to me to be the high point of my life. Something that I had dreamed of back in the days of my exile, something I had pictured as a once-in-a-lifetime, death-defying leap, had just been quietly settled in the course of a polite conversation that was more mundane than heroic. I saw this elderly couple as nothing less than a miracle. We scarcely even discussed the practicalities. I reached in my pocket for the heavy aluminum capsule. It was not much bigger than a Ping-Pong ball, and I half-opened it to show them the rolls of film with which it was packed. Then I put it on the tea table, among the jam and cookies, and Vadim Leonidovich transferred it to his own pocket. But all the while we were discussing Russian syntax, the word order of noun and adjective, literary genres, as well as Vadim Leonidovich's book *Childhood*, which I had read in a Soviet edition. With Natalya Ivanovna egging me on, I told them about the most sensational subject matter in my repertoire—the camp uprisings. The elderly couple from Geneva sat and listened in amazement.

Could my dream have come true just like that? Would my hands at last be untied, my spirit emboldened and free? Nothing the future held in store could compare with the crises and dangers that lay behind me. It was a downhill run from here, and the rest of my life was bound to be easier. And whom did I have to thank for this amazing gift but Natalya Ivanovna, or "Eva," as I soon began to call her for conspiratorial reasons? There had been something fortuitous, even disingenuous about our first meeting at Ehrenburg's home, but it opened the way for a higher destiny: making it possible for help to reach me from the land of the zeks, from the scattered enclaves of the émigré world, from Ryazan —in short, from Russia.

On October 31, 1964, two weeks after the Collective Leadership* came to power, my little bombshell crossed the Soviet frontier at the Moscow airport, snug in Vadim Leonidovich's jacket pocket. He was not versed in the smuggler's arts, but the customs man, seeing the name on his passport, was intrigued to know whether he really was Leonid Andreyev's son. After that they spent their time talking about the great writer, and there were no serious customs checks at all. So, in a sense, the capsule went through under what seemed at the time to be the benevolent aegis of Leonid Andreyev. Eva had gone to see her friends off, and they managed to signal across from one gallery to the other that all was well.

A year later all the papers I had left with Teush were seized, the last trace of my relief at getting the capsule abroad had evaporated, and I felt as if my entire life had been crushed beneath an avalanche of black rocks. I was moping about at Kornei Chukovsky's dacha when who should turn up for dinner but Eva—an angel of light (though the glittering dress she wore was dark)! She had some business to discuss with Chukovsky and had come straight off the plane from Paris, still bearing the aura of that faraway carefree life and before she had had time to readjust to our dog-eat-dog existence. Her surprise at seeing me there was as great as my own at seeing her. To me her arrival was nothing less than a miracle: I could not have phoned her or gone round to see her for fear of being tailed, yet I desperately needed some living thread to connect me with the free world, the world *over there*. We pretended not to know each other, and Kornei Ivanovich "introduced" us. During the meal, Eva listened agog to one tale of persecution after another and could not help remarking, "Never a dull moment over here, that's for sure!" It was extraordinary: here she was, fresh from Paris (where she could have stayed for good if she had wished), yet she uttered these words without a hint of regret. Later Kornei Ivanovich took it into his head to see her to her train, while I badly needed the darkness of this evening walk to talk to her in private. It was no easy matter persuading Kornei Ivanovich and Lyusha to turn back halfway. Then Eva and I strolled the rest of the way to the station, and the pouring rain did nothing to dispel my good fortune. We talked and tried to coordinate our plans—invariably a tortuous process with Natalya Ivanovna—but her supporting presence, always so ethereal, smiling, and selfless, seemed on that evening positively heaven-sent.

Eva was soon like a second source of air to me. Thanks to her, my underground labors would be lit by a sudden glancing ray from *over there*—news of how our affairs were proceeding or how the English translation of *The First Circle* was coming along. She had only to let me know what she had in mind, and we would meet at once. And whenever I came to Moscow I would try to see her. There was hardly a corner of Moscow that did not serve as the setting for our talks. Sometimes we would arrange to meet as if by chance in the bookstore on the ground floor of the Ehrenburgs' apartment building, then wander through the courtyards, passageways, and gardens in the central part of town. (One of the places she showed me was Bakhrushinsky Court—little did I know that my future family would live there from 1970 on and that the KGB would come there to seize me and take me off to exile.) On other occasions we would talk as we strolled along an avenue or through the grounds of the Petrovsky monastery. Or again, she might come out to my dacha in Rozhdestvo, and we would sit apart from the others or go off into the woods to talk more freely. The need for so many meetings, so many agreements and arrangements—made, unmade, and made anew—was dictated less by the nature of our enterprise than by the character of this friend of ours (for by now she and Lyusha were in cahoots); in the course of our animated conversations—which, thanks to her, always went off on a tangent—she would invariably leave out something important, then phone in a panic to fix up another meeting where she would clarify the matter (more or less!). I reproached her all the time (and she me) for rushing into things without taking sufficient precautions, but however muddled she might be when dealing with incidental matters, there was a startling transformation as soon as anything serious was at stake; then she would act boldly and unerringly, and one could not imagine her putting a foot wrong.

At times of greatest danger Eva was inspired not only with great courage but with an extraordinarily convincing naturalness of manner—perhaps another legacy from her mother. (The saga of how she read *The Gulag Archipelago* was absolutely typical. She brought the three heavy volumes of the finished typescript to Ehrenburg's flat so she could read them at work. But in the middle of all this Ehrenburg died. That meant a commission to handle his papers, detailed inventories, and heaven knows what else. She had to get *Gulag* out without a moment's delay, but Ehrenburg's widow wouldn't let her go: "What's that you're taking away?" At this Eva flared up: "You mean after all these years you still don't trust me?" And she got the books away.)

The pressure of "the cause" forced such a frenetic and relentless pace on me that there was never time to have a leisurely chat with her or even have a proper look at her. Yet the impressions I gained from others and from our many encounters have merged into a single composite picture: the innate nobility of her character, which she never relaxed (never a hint of an unworthy impulse), the generosity that was second nature to her, her ability to be at once proud, unassuming, and, in her friendship, utterly simple and straightforward. The problem was that walls have ears, and indoors was no place for a conversation. (I regarded Eva's present apartment in Daev Lane as thoroughly unreliable; she knew lots of foreigners and met them quite openly, and she was forever on the telephone—in fact, this provocative openness was a deliberate tactic on her part. The fact that she was known to foreigners, including French diplomats, strengthened her position with the authorities.)

Eva and I had many a lighthearted disagreement about the West, and sometimes we fell out in earnest. In her opinion, I was far too benevolent in my statements about the West, so she would try to disabuse me, criticizing it with the same passion that had once driven her to abandon a life of well-being in Europe and face the tribulations of a voluntary return to Russia. But when I was irritated with the West for some reason and spoke too sharply against it, she was scarcely less fervent in leaping to its defense and even tended to go too far. Her main contention was always the same: that I didn't understand the West and never would. Admittedly, few would claim that Eva's political views were particularly balanced. She had left France thirty years before (and the years would grow to forty as our friendship wore on), but she did go back for occasional brief visits, and even in Moscow itself she maintained a large circle of foreign acquaintances. As a result, she was convinced that she still had her finger on the pulse of Europe. I, on the other hand, had never been there, but I did listen to several Western radio broadcasts every day, and I could not avoid the gloomy conclusion that the West's willpower, morale, and clarity of vision were dwindling in the face of bolshevism. She ridiculed my conclusions and refused to concede that Europe could have undergone so drastic a change.

Ah, the charmed touch of Natalya Ivanovna! . . . In May 1967, after I had distributed 250 copies of my "Letter to the Fourth Congress of the Writers' Union," I was keeping my head down out at Chukovsky's house in Peredelkino. It was now eleven days since the letter had gone out, the congress was drawing to a close, and there had not been a single publication or report of the letter anywhere in the West. Then, right out of the blue, Eva turned up! She was a guest at another dacha, but still she phoned me and invited me out for a walk. She hatched her plan there and then: "Do you have a spare copy? Give it to me and I'll send it off today!" (I had not been thinking along those lines at all, but the germ of this idea had been at the back of her mind when she brought the French art historian Maurice Jardot out to Peredelkino with her; he had good contacts at *Le Monde*, and she had extracted a promise of help from him.) Three days later the letter appeared in *Le Monde*, there was a great brouhaha, and before we knew it, the battle was won! No sooner had the episode of the *Grani* telegram* flared up, leaving me desperate to find out who this Victor Louis was, when—along came Eva, a regular dea ex machina, to shed some light on the matter. She had known Louis from her time in Karlag prison camp: he was a

Moscow lad who had gone in for black-market currency dealing with foreigners and whose behavior in the camps had left something to be desired.

At the very outset Eva had asked only that *no one should know* of her role—and with good reason, as it turned out. She had someone quite definite in mind—namely, my then-wife Natalya Reshetovskaya, for Eva was immeasurably quicker than I to sense danger from this quarter. At the same time, the unaffected warmth and light-heartedness of our relations could not remain hidden from my wife, especially since our endless, half-resolved schemes meant that we were always having to get away from other people to whisper together, even when Eva had simply come to visit us at home. There was no way I could have managed this or explained it to my wife without letting her know that the things we were discussing were of the utmost seriousness—things, in short, with a foreign connection. And Eva apparently understood this, too. But in autumn 1965, when the investigation into the Sinyavsky* affair was under way, she asked at one of our clandestine meetings, "Does your wife really know *nothing* about all this?" Well, she had no direct knowledge from me, but at the same time, she had eyes in her head and could see what was going on. (One thing I might have claimed with some confidence was that she knew nothing about the part played by the Andreyev family, but even that was not true for long: two years later my wife and I were among seven or eight guests at the "Princess's" apartment when Eva arrived bringing Leonid Andreyev's young granddaughter from America, Olga Carlisle, and I went out onto the balcony with her to have a word in private.)

By then a menacing shadow had already fallen over Eva, and it hangs there, dark and brooding, to this day. Her presentiment of many years' standing did not deceive her: in 1973 at Moscow's Kazan station, Reshetovskaya directly threatened Eva, singling her out by name as someone upon whom the KGB would take revenge for the publication of *The Gulag Archipelago*.* (It was this threat that prompted me to speak openly about the incident in a CBS interview in the summer of 1974.)

Yet almost two years have passed since then. Clouds that linger yield no storm . . . God willing!

———

The subsequent progress of *The First Circle*, which we had sent abroad in microfilm, continued to be directed through Eva. She arranged all my meetings with the elderly Andreyev couple on their occasional visits to the Soviet Union, as well as those with their daughter Olga Carlisle or their son Sasha.

Early in June 1968 we were out at Rozhdestvo, typing up the last pages of *Gulag*, while in Paris student revolutionaries were on the rampage. Just then Sasha (Aleksandr Vadimovich Andreyev) arrived in Moscow. He had come on a week's visit organized by UNESCO and was still exhilarated by the heroic exploits of the students. Eva received a cheery phone call from him to say that he had brought her some presents and was looking forward to telling her all about the glorious student insurrection; Muscovites, he thought, were just too philistine to appreciate it. ("What are these students ranting about? They should try living *here* for a while, that would teach them!" was the view from Moscow.) But Sasha's arrival had put an idea into Eva's head, and it gave her not a moment's peace: was this the hand of providence? Why not use Sasha to get *Gulag* to the West right away?

She made brief notes about the hazardous events of those few days as they were happening, but later burned them; then in 1974, after I had been expelled from the country, she rewrote her account, and my wife Alya brought it out when she came to join me. I am drawing on Eva's notes as I write these pages. Both before and after this episode Eva took many risks in the cause of my writing, but her words give the impression that she was not fully alive to the dangers she faced or, perhaps, that she was frivolous by nature. Far from it!

Her carefree manner was deliberately cultivated for the sake of appearances. However, the importance of the *Gulag* manuscript for her far surpassed that of our own individual fates; she came to identify it with the fate of Russia itself. The operation she devised to smuggle it abroad cost her ten days of unremitting, nerve-racking tension, an unforgettable experience to this day.

The first concern was to prevent *Gulag* from being lost. To leave it languishing in Russia unpublished was to consign it to oblivion. But for it to be confiscated from Sasha at customs would spell even greater disaster—not just for the book and its author but for all those surviving witnesses whose names figured in its pages, not to mention the consequences for Sasha himself. Indeed, was it ethical to ask one of the Andreyevs to undertake such a thing at all? And would Sasha even agree? On the other hand, these people were completely untainted: they had no mercenary motives, their love of Russia was unfeigned, and they could be relied on not to abuse the gift entrusted to them. If we let such a chance slip by, when could we hope for another? Eva was already quite carried away by the idea, and she found it hard to contemplate pulling back. She came to Rozhdestvo and took me into the woods to talk. Her notes reveal what an effort this decision cost her, indeed, she had not entirely made up her own mind—yet to me she spoke with such absolute conviction (Eva the Conqueror!) that my misgivings were soon allayed. There was no denying that it was a remarkable coincidence that this should have happened on the very day we finished typing *Gulag*, while still leaving us the time we would need to have the text microfilmed. And then to know that it would be going into unsullied hands! How much depended on our own freedom of choice and how much on God's greater design? We made up our minds—without consulting Sasha—and the decision was to go ahead! But Eva recalls that I told her, "*Don't go ahead* unless there is a 99 percent chance of success—nothing less than that." I am afraid the operation fell a long way short of that degree of certainty.

It turned out that Sasha had already anticipated our request, and he took it with fatalistic calm. "Aren't you scared?" "Of course, but I'm a Russian, too, don't forget." A day later he came up with his proposal: there was a film technician with the group who would be shipping their equipment back in a container; what about asking him to hide the capsule of microfilms inside it? "They are copies of my grandfather's manuscripts," he would be told, "and if I go through official channels, it will mean endless red tape. Will you help us out?" (For the second time my films were setting off under the aegis of Leonid Andreyev.) However, the container was not even securely sealed, much less covered by any form of diplomatic immunity. The group was due to fly back to Paris on the Saturday before Pentecost, with the technician following by train on Monday. Sasha hoped to meet him in Paris on Tuesday and retrieve the capsule with his own hands.

Everything might have gone smoothly, but then on Thursday evening it began to look as if Sasha was being tailed. We acted on the assumption that this was an indisputable fact, and the next five days became a frenzied nightmare—above all for Eva. Should she abort the operation or not? Only those who have been part of a conspiracy like this can begin to imagine that crushing, enervating state of mind when you suspect you are being spied upon, your room bugged, your phone tapped, when you feel time running out, and there is no one you can risk turning to for advice, when your energy is drained by fears of an imminent disaster and your will paralyzed by the responsibilities bearing down on you—and then you are faced with a decision that will determine the fates of so many people dear to you and of the very cause you serve. Eva made up her mind: "We shall fight for our country in the only way available to us, and we shall do it right now!" Thereupon, she telephoned one of Sasha's Moscow relatives, poured out a stream of vacuous chatter, but inserted a warning in French, gabbled as fast as she could: "Yesterday evening you were followed on your way home." (If they had really been running a serious surveillance operation, then of course that phrase would have been picked up, too.) Even though the relative was not part of the conspiracy, he understood the message and took Sasha to spend the night well out of harm's way. Then Eva and Lyusha took stock. (Eva had dropped by to pick up the capsule from her.) The more they turned things over, the more dangerous the situation appeared; they could not come to any firm conclusion, and so, in her usual forceful, intuitive way, Eva simply picked up the capsule and left with it.

Eva's meeting with Sasha on the Saturday before Pentecost went according to plan: they met up at a prearranged spot in the Kirovskaya subway station, and she handed him—not the capsule but a parcel of children's toys. Anyone who spotted what they were doing and seized the package would not have been any the wiser. They discussed the previous day's alarm and agreed that there seemed to be no one following them now. They arranged that the following Tuesday, as soon as Sasha had recovered the capsule from the container, he would phone Eva's sister Katerina in Geneva (she had been wounded in the Resistance and was now an invalid, virtually confined to her house). The sister, in her turn, would phone Eva in Moscow using a prearranged phrase to signal the outcome. As for my "bombshell," Eva would not give it to Sasha now, but someone else would pass it to him at the next subway station, Dzerzhinskaya. . . . (Eva's mother could not have hatched a better plan!) But when Sasha reached the next stop and a stranger came from behind and took his arm, he gave such a violent start that the courier decided not to hand the capsule over until Sasha had had a chance to calm down. He took him out of the station to where his car was parked on a quiet side street. (But even this did not pass without incident. There was a taxi parked right next to them with its hood up. As they drove off, it pulled out after them. But was it actually following, or were they just imagining things? The taxi dropped back and disappeared.) Now, by sheer chance, they had to pass in front of the main building of the

Lubyanka prison and make a circuit round the bottle-shaped pedestal with its statue of Feliks Dzerzhinsky, founder of the Russian secret police. As they were driving round, the driver, who had to keep both hands on the wheel, explained to Sasha how to reach over and remove the capsule from his bag. And that is how *The Gulag Archipelago* came to be handed over in the middle of Lubyanka Square!

For better or for worse, the deed was done. Now all we could do was wait. But at this point our overwrought nerves began to fail: the dangers were still lurking, but they bore down on us now in a dull, unfocused way. The microfilms were out of our hands, but they had not gone anywhere. Instead they were hovering in space somewhere, out of our control but still in danger. Lyusha dashed round to Rozhdestvo to find me, and off I went to stay in my safe house, the apartment that the "Fortune-teller" had made permanently available to me and to which I had my own key (see Chapter Ten). Eva, rather than moping about in the city, had gone out to the country for the Pentecost weekend. Unaware of this, Lyusha was trying to phone her, while the "Fortune-teller" was trying to get through to Lyusha from a public phone booth. Eva's disappearance aroused our worst fears—everything seemed to be falling apart. (Looking back, we can see what a ramshackle, amateurish affair our whole operation had been.) Meanwhile, for Eva, stretched out on the bank of a river, the blazing sun was a black and cheerless orb. Impotence and enforced inactivity are a hard combination to bear.

When she got back to Moscow, Eva managed to get through on a neutral phone line to Sasha's Moscow relative and learned from him that Sasha's departure had gone smoothly. This was a relief at first, and we managed to get through the Monday.

But then came Tuesday. Soon it was midday. The phone call from Eva's sister in Geneva should have come long ago—but there was no sign of it, and we could not call her first as that would have made nonsense of the phrasing of our prearranged message.

Tuesday dragged agonizingly on, and by the end of the day there was still no word. It looked like the beginning of the end: they must be sitting in the Lubyanka reading *The Gulag Archipelago* right now.

On Wednesday morning, at long last, came the news we had all been waiting for. (It turned out that the strikes and unrest in Paris had paralyzed communications: our *Gulag Archipelago* had crossed swords with the Parisian quasi-revolution!)

That same afternoon, not bothering too much about my cover, my friends came round to the secret apartment to release me from my suspense. They were jubilant.

But there was a painful discovery in store. For not all of the "safe hands" we had chosen turned out to be equally dependable. Ultimately, our entire effort to send the book abroad was botched, and at a critical moment we would find ourselves twisting in the wind. Sasha Andreyev, a complete novice in such matters, had been simply heroic. His father, Vadim Leonidovich, agonized over the fate of the book and even bought a set of fonts in order that he himself might be the first publisher of *The Gulag Archipelago* in Russian. But when our capsule reached the Carlisles, it got bogged down, and many years passed before the American translation would be ready. (I shall return to this on another occasion.) For all our feverish haste, for all the risks we had taken and the pride we felt, we might as well have never sent the capsule at all. It was safely in the West, but much good it did us! It had to be translated into German, but when Betta (see Chapter Twelve) asked Vadim Leonidovich to get the Russian text from his daughter, he was afraid that the affair would become public (it could cost him his Soviet passport). In the end we had to go through the whole business of sending *Gulag* out *for a second time* with all the risk and effort that involved! That was in the spring of 1971, but if we had not acted when we did, the German and Swedish translations would not have been out by the time of the 1973 fiasco, and the Russian-language edition, inaccessible to Western readers, would have seemed but a solitary, muffled shot in the dark.

In the last years before I was deported from Russia, Eva was no longer our sole link with the West (though time and again she would "pop something over the wall" for us, always in her own elegant, effortless way). But she had a sharp eye for what was needed and constantly came up with new ways of making herself useful. Eva refused to change her habits and continued, to the end, to act as audaciously as ever: she never hid herself away or concealed her friendships (she was very close to Alya despite the difference in their ages), and even in desperate times, when we were virtually under siege, she would telephone and come by to see us quite openly.

After we left Russia, Eva was the KGB's prime suspect. Denunciations and blows rained down on her. Yet far from going underground that year, she went on leading her own independent life, as fearless and self-assured as ever; she kept up her work as a freelance translator and still met with foreigners, including those we had sent her way. And in the months when our system was failing, with people being replaced, foreign correspondents expelled, channels of communication blocked, Eva was on hand. With renewed energy she restored the flow of papers from our personal archive, sending whole bags and suitcases full of them out to the West. After *From Under the Rubble* was published in the West in 1974 and all mail to or from us was systematically confiscated (not even a child's birthday card could get through), Eva handled all our more "informal" contacts with friends in Moscow.

Beginning in the autumn of 1974 there was a new face in the Cultural Attaché's office at the French embassy, a Corsican woman, Elfrida Filippi. I never saw her, but Eva describes her in her notes as:

> Beautiful, with a good figure and a smile that was enchanting to those she liked, but glacial if you were in her bad books. We were friends from the first moment; we seemed to be instantly attuned to each other without having exchanged a word. . . . She

was decisive in her actions, ready to face any terrors, anxious not to let others down, and passionately interested in Russia. . . . She was the ideal courier in a tight spot, disarming any flatfoot she met with her winning smile and graceful manner. And she was awesomely fast—it was all over before his jaw had time to drop!

Once there was a packet intended for me. The original idea was to send it out to me in three installments, but Elfrida felt the weight of it and decided, "I'll take it all at one go." This made things so much easier for me at the time. (On some occasions Elfrida had the assistance of a certain B. L.—my thanks here to any who gave a helping hand.)

The massive package that Eva sent out with Elfrida was actually delivered to us in Paris by Stepan Tatishchev (see Chapter Thirteen), and our room in the Hôtel d'Isly on the rue Jacob became the scene of a coincidence that was more than merely symbolic—the kind of coincidence that only history itself can devise. Our courier had left, and there in a heap on the couch, waiting to be sorted out, lay the contents of the package from Natasha Klimova the younger. Then, two minutes later, who should make his way up the same narrow stairs to our attic room but Arkadi Petrovich Stolypin, who as a little boy had been almost blown up on Aptekarsky Island with his father during an assassination attempt by . . . Natasha Klimova the elder! In fact, Arkadi Stolypin was coming to see me to discuss the draft of a chapter about his father that I was writing for my *August 1914*. He was a pleasant man, and we sat chatting amicably, while beside us lay bundles sent, no less amicably, by the daughter of his would-be assassin.

That was how sharply Russia had swung round in the intervening two-thirds of a century. The daughter was now risking life and liberty to work with the same flair and passion that her mother had shown before her, but for a cause diametrically opposed to hers. (That said, she did not depart radically from the Socialist Revolutionary mentality, for she not only cursed the very name of Stolypin but saw the Soviet system as a direct successor to the tsarist model.)

All the healthy forces in Russia had by now converged and were acting in concert.

1978 SUPPLEMENT

In the autumn of 1976 they actually let Eva out to visit her sister in Switzerland. While she was there, she could not even think of applying to the Soviet embassy for a visa to the United States: changing one's country of destination was forbidden, and in any case, it would have been obvious that she was coming to see us. However, we interceded, and the Americans agreed to issue her a temporary visa in the form of a loose-leaf insert in her passport. She reached Vermont without incident and stayed with us there during the spring of 1977. She took it very hard that Olga Carlisle, whom she had drawn into the conspiracy, had had a change of mind and was writing a hostile book about me, though, at the same time, Eva kept assuring me that it was all nonsense. She read *Invisible Allies* and asked if she could take it with her (one copy would be left in Paris and another would go back to Moscow with her to be read to our "invisible" friends and allies, then destroyed).

On the subject of her return to Russia in 1934, she said:

> I didn't go back actively seeking suffering. In fact I can't abide suffering. I went looking for happiness. But the suffering I was forced to endure did not take the edge off my love for Russia—quite the contrary, it heightened it still further.

And now she was faced with the tantalizing possibility of staying in the West for good. She agonized over her choice for quite some time, and the letter explaining her decision conveys this more eloquently than any paraphrase of mine. [See Appendix A.]

1986 SUPPLEMENT

Natalya Ivanovna did not abandon her conspiratorial activities, which included some very risky operations. From 1975 until 1984 she was not only the linchpin of our system for exchanging letters and books with friends in the Soviet Union but, more importantly, she helped the work of our Russian Social Fund inside the country, and we would scarcely have been able to establish such a vigorous channel of communication without her daring and ingenuity.* (I hope that one day someone may write a more complete account of the work of the fund.) The KGB was hot on her trail but could never quite catch her.

In her last years, Natalya Ivanovna suffered from inflammation of the pancreas. At the end of 1984 she suddenly experienced acute pains and was admitted to the hospital; within a week she was dead. (Before the end, she had time to send us a message: "Now it's time to lie low for a while!" She evidently felt new storm clouds gathering about her. And so she slipped out of their grasp, perhaps just in time.)

At her funeral there was a large turnout of plainclothes KGB agents, keeping a watchful eye on the proceedings. Several of them came to her apartment to draw up an inventory, purporting to be "interns" from the notary public's office. When they were interrogating Natalya's cousin, they told him, "We know everything about her. We've had her on a tight leash for a long time now, and we know exactly where she kept everything."

Braggarts! They knew things, but not everything.

Elusive as ever, she slipped away from them. And too late did they bare their fangs and lash out at her in the newspapers.

10

The Column in the Shadows

As I was writing *The Oak and the Calf*, my Invisible Allies were forever finding their way into the story. I would make a note for future reference, then pass on, pushing them into the background. And in writing the first nine chapters of the present book, I have again found my narrative bumping up against more and more of these Invisible Allies, a kind of second column of helpers. And once again I have been skirting around them—not out of fear for their safety this time, but to avoid cluttering my story line. Yet this second echelon gave me strength and succor, too, and at times their support was crucial. What holds a bridge up? Not just its piers and buttresses but every girder in its structure. And the strength of a net lies not solely in its knots but in each individual linking thread.

As I recall them now, name after name, face after face, I am uncomfortably reminded that some among them are exposed even today to suspicion or denunciations, that *they* are threatened by dangers that no longer hang over me.

The name of our Fortune-teller cropped up in the last chapter. We called her that as a joke because she loved to sit and read her future in a pack of cards. Her real name was Anastasia Ivanovna Yakovleva, and she had a Ph.D. in biology and an academic career in pharmacy, researching the harmful side effects of medicines. (If you followed her advice, you'd steer clear of medicines altogether —something I had always been inclined to do anyway.) She was getting on toward sixty, unmarried, and she always had a group of young people around her for whom she acted as benefactor, helping them finish college or get settled in life, finding them work or a place to live; she surrounded them all with an atmosphere of love, not just of freedom but also of Russia. (Love of Russia was in pretty scarce supply among the educated classes, and this made every meeting with her a rare delight.) Out of this atmosphere emerged a series of collective letters to me signed by up to twenty of these young people at a time. Even for the early 1960s, which witnessed a great surge in open letters, this was unusual and intriguing. In 1963, when I was not yet anathematized and there was no risk in associating with me, I visited their chemistry institute on Zubov Square. After that I went on corresponding with Anastasia Ivanovna. Without any real sense of how she might help, she offered to do some typing for me; I let her type up those plays that could be circulated openly, but I also gave the preliminary drafts of *R-17* to copy in case by some disaster they should be lost. She put in long hours and did a great deal for me. (In the West this is a job for photocopiers, but in our country you can't even begin to think of such a thing; you just have to type it all out, one letter at a time.) She also offered me the use of her little apartment on Thirteenth Park Street if ever I needed to work in peace and quiet. During the disastrous days of September 1965, I sometimes hid at her place to escape surveillance and snatch a brief respite from the dangers bearing down on me; it was good to know that at least for tonight there would be no "knock at the door." And again, during Pentecost of 1968, this refuge proved a godsend. (By an incredible coincidence, in a city of seven million inhabitants, containing seven hundred square kilometers of living space, my shelter for the night happened to be next door but one to the home of Sasha Andreyev's relatives: he had already put the microfilm in the container truck, and now, little more than fifty yards from where I was sleeping, he was spending his last night before flying off to Paris. If they had really had agents tailing him, I might easily have popped up right in front of them!) That night, worn out, a prisoner of my own making, I asked her, "How is it all going to end, Anastasia Ivanovna? What does the future say?" She consulted her cards in the kitchen, but perhaps because they turned out badly, all she would say to me was "A man like you doesn't need his fortune told." And she was right. (In fact, I think we are all better off without it. There's something dubious and unhealthy about it: while we do get presentiments, it is not given us to know what the future holds, and that is how it should remain.) When I was staying with her, she told me how she had stayed single, but with all the worries of those days, my mind did not take it in. In the years that followed, even after her retirement, she continued to be the heart and soul of her circle of young friends. (The contribution of people like her in nurturing new generations is simply incalculable.) But she began to fear the onset of old age and infirmity and went to Klyazma to live out her life in an old people's home.

———

Or take Ivan Dmitrievich Rozhansky. He had been a wartime comrade of Lev Kopelev, and it was through Kopelev that we became acquainted—though, as it turns out, I could have met him through Eva. He had previously had little difficulty in traveling abroad, and in 1964 another trip was in the offing. I had given him my capsule of microfilms in advance, and he was keeping it, firmly intending to take it out with him and risking his neck in the process. But on the eve of his departure, he was summoned to the Central Committee and told that his trip had been canceled (not because of anything to do with me). There would have been far grimmer repercussions if these doubts about his political reliability had surfaced as he was going through customs. (It was this same capsule that I then passed on to Eva.) Subsequently he copied tape recordings for me at a time when I couldn't risk letting anyone listen to them apart from him. During the fiasco of September 1965 I kept some important materials hidden at his home for a while. I know this because I remember calling him from a public telephone right by the Fortune-teller's apartment, without giving my name, and going round to his home for a talk at first light so that I could be sure there was no one on my tail. Rozhansky, the son of a well-known physicist, had been drawn into a token official career, from which he loved to recuperate in the company of his many books. He was a kindhearted man with a broad education, somewhat phlegmatic in conversation, as if he would rather think than do the talking. His great love was classical philosophy, and he had published a book on Anaxagoras. The code name we gave him was "Tsarevich" or "Prince." This went just as well with Ivan as with the Dmitri of his patronymic.*

It followed that his then-wife Natalya Vladimirovna Kind should come to be called "Princess." But later we found that her bearing, her quintessentially Russian manner, her high, clear brow, and a certain elusive inner quality fully justified this chance conspiratorial

nickname. She had a rich inner life and a fine mind. A talented geologist with a Ph.D. in science, she possessed great reserves of spiritual
strength and weathered life's adversities with enviable aplomb. But
what leisure did we have, in all our struggling and scrambling, to appreciate these qualities and fine feelings, to bask in their rays! What
mattered to us was that she was resolute and loyal and that her apartment was not bugged, for she lived apart from the teeming life of
Moscow. This meant that we could arrange to meet foreigners there,
Russians from overseas like the elderly Andreyev couple with whom
she had become friends while accompanying her husband on his
trips to Geneva, or the ill-starred Olga Carlisle, or Stepan Tatishchev,
whom she sent our way. The Princess was also on very friendly terms
with Eva, which closed the circle very neatly and made communications easier. I kept none of my books hidden from the Princess;
it goes without saying that she was among the first to read *August
1914* in typescript, and even before that she was one of the very few
early readers of *Gulag*, before it was even finished. She helped us
to make a map of the archipelago of prison camps, and through her
geologist connections with Pakhtusova she was able to block off the
secret that Q had leaked. After Q's death she used the same channels
to get us Pakhtusova's account of the calamitous course of events.
During the last grim and menacing months of our life in Russia,
the Princess often came by to see Alya and me, and she became more
and more part of the family; she even managed to come when
the summons from the procurator's office had already been served
on me, and she frequently called on Alya after I had been deported.
When everything seemed about to cave in on us, I would go to
her home to discuss the latest chapters of *October 1916*, though
this seemed rather academic at the time. When my friends in the
Soviet Union and I in exile were finishing our preparatory work on
the collection *From Under the Rubble*, Shafarevich* and I exchanged
manuscripts using her as a handy intermediary, since she lived so
close to him. Thus the Princess, like Eva, became an integral part of

our main channel of communications. By the time these pages are published, I expect that by no means all of our compatriots will be able to grasp just how much resolution and determination it took to commit oneself in that way.[1]

We also maintained contact with Mikhail Konstantinovich Polivanov, partly through the Princess and then through Lyusha. He was one of the contributors to *From Under the Rubble*, a mathematician, as upright and honest as the day is long and with a sharp and subtle mind. But he could rarely enjoy the pleasure of talking freely; there were few places safe enough, and few acquaintances sufficiently dependable. In this he was, like all of us over there, crippled and twisted by outside pressures and constraints. He himself was a Christian, but such was his respect for others' freedom that he did not baptize his children when they were small but let them grow up and choose for themselves (they all chose to be baptized). For many years he hid both *Gulag* and the ninety-six chapter *First Circle*, the most dangerous of my works. Sometimes they were kept in his own home—and an eventful experience that proved to be! He kept them under the bath, with the result that the pages got wet and he had to spread them out all over the apartment to dry, whereupon the slightest draft from an open window would send them flying about. Then all at once the secret police turned up to search

---

[1] The years went by and we continued to exchange brief news across the frontier. We learned of the happier moments in her life, such as her latest trip into the tundra that she so loved, or her purchase of a plot of ground for a garden just outside Moscow, or the holiday she spent in the Crimea with Eva, Danila, and Lyusha, for their shared experiences brought them closer together. She was the only one who knew of Eva's visit to our home in Vermont, and it was at her little dacha near Moscow that the last chapter, Chapter Nine of this book, was read to our friends. It seemed almost too good to be true that our news was getting through to them, fresh and untrammeled. Eva told them all about our life in Vermont, something she could never have risked doing in a Moscow apartment. But at the end of 1983 the KGB came with a search warrant (when the ring around Eva and our Social Fund was drawing tight); they took away my books and demanded that she explain where she had got them, to which she simply replied, "I've been a friend of his since the sixties." They left her in peace. (1986 note)

his mother-in-law's apartment. She was not living with them, but still everything had to be bundled into the garage and he even had to drive it all around in the car with him. Sometimes, though, he would conceal my things in his father's apartment, without his father even being aware of it. Later we relieved him of this task, but many a banned work passed through his hands, providing nourishment for him and for those readers to whom he passed it on.[2]

Anyone seeking to cast the net of conspiracy more widely naturally tends to do so on the basis of friendship or close acquaintance. Nikolai Veniaminovich Kaverin, who was the son of the writer,* and called Kolya for short, had been a friend of Lyusha's since they were youngsters at their family dachas in Peredelkino. Our code name for him was "Biker" because of his passion for cycling. On Sundays at Peredelkino it was easy for him and Lyusha to meet away from prying eyes. Kolya's generation was not feeble and enervated as its predecessors had been and he grew up understanding that the only way to win freedom was to grab it with your own two hands. He was resolute and punctilious in his behavior, as well as being reliable and efficient. As far as I know, he did not let his father know what he was up to, but he did have a group of young people around him, and it was to them that we passed on Rostropovich's whirly-printer. (It functioned splendidly, as it turned out, and they very much regretted having to destroy it in a moment of particular danger.) Kolya helped Lyusha to find new hiding places for my mi-

---

[2] By taking every precaution, he nevertheless managed to evade the suspicions of the KGB, and he continued to take advantage of official trips abroad. Once when we were in Zurich he amazed and delighted us by telephoning from Paris completely out of the blue, and then in Vermont we received a letter from him in Italy. (But such is the lot of Soviet citizens that he wrote, "There are others here with me from the Soviet Union, and it's hard to resist the suspicion that they're spying on my every move, including this letter. So don't be surprised if it has a morbid cloak-and-dagger feel to it.") In fact his letters were especially dear to us at the time, because apart from him virtually no one managed to break through the wall of silence and give us a thoughtful and substantial response from Russia to the latest "knots" of *The Red Wheel*. (1986 note)

crofilms and manuscripts.[3] He was the launching pad, so to speak, for many of my ventures into samizdat. In January 1974 he came to me at Peredelkino after dark, and I handed over a copy of my statement "Live Not by Lies"—a timely move, for on the day of my arrest this was to be one of the texts released into samizdat.* He positively exuded courage and eagerness to help, however he could and whatever the danger.

Necessity dictated that Lyusha keep an additional permanent hiding place for her own things, independent of Danila's system. I think it was in autumn 1968 that I suggested she get in touch with two individuals who worked at the Russian Language Institute in Volkhonka Street. One of them, Leonid Krysin, was already well known to Lyusha from his visits to Kornei Chukovsky. The other was a most charming woman, Lamara Andreyevna Kapanadze. I only saw her three times in my whole life, the first two in connection with their scheme to invite me to their institute, ostensibly to make sample tape recordings for phonetic study but in fact just to meet me and get hold of manuscripts that they would then duplicate. (They were also able to help me out with queries I had concerning the dialects of the Kuban and the Don regions.) The third occasion was when I asked both of them to come to Strastnoi Boulevard, a street at once so fateful yet so dear to me, to that same beloved little side street where Strastnoi widens and where the offices of *Novy Mir* stood. Once we were there, I came right out and asked them if they would look after a considerable volume of my most subversive writings. I never had the occasion to regret it, for I was not mistaken in them: they agreed without a qualm, taking and storing it like experts. Leonid picked up texts from Lyusha and brought them to her when required; this made sense, as he was still working on the literary estate of Kornei Chukovsky. As for Lamara,

[3] Only now do I learn that, unbeknownst to me, he and his friends stood guard over me at Peredelkino after I sent my "Letter to the Fourth Writers' Congress." (1990 note)

the rules of conspiracy regrettably dictated that I should never see
her again—never have a chance to chat with her, to get to know her
better. For that matter, Lyusha also saw her rarely. I understand that
Lamara had to change the location of her secret cache: initially it
was at the home of her unsuspecting elderly parents; then, for some
reason, she had to move it into her own place on Second Troitsky
Lane. By a sardonic quirk of fate, these rooms, which had been
turned into a communal apartment, had once been occupied by
Beria! Of course, concealing things there was intrinsically unreliable; Lamara lived alone, which meant that whenever she went out,
she had to leave everything unguarded in the middle of a communal
apartment! But since she was not meeting us and did not engage in
any other illicit activities, she should not have attracted attention.
However, in the summer of 1973 when were under massive assault,
we received alarming news from that quarter, too: on two occasions
someone visiting one of Lamara's neighbors had been caught peep-
ing through her keyhole. He might just have been interested in her
as an attractive young woman, but this could equally well have been
the long arm of the KGB. But with Lyusha recovering from her accident and the fiasco with *Gulag*, we were stretched too thin to be
able to deal with this problem. Finally, that autumn, we were on the
very point of extricating our hidden archive when Leonid Krysin
keeled over with a heart attack and was out of action for a long time.
Once again everything ground to a halt, and the matter was left un-
resolved. That autumn felt like one of those nightmares when you
try to lift your hand to protect yourself and find you're paralyzed.
Later on, things worked out, and we were able to get the whole
cache away from there safe and sound.

Here is another coincidence. In January 1972, on the Russian
Orthodox Christmas Eve, the efforts we were making with the aid
of Anna Samoilovna Berzer to recover a stray copy of *The Oak and
the Calf* were finally crowned with success. And where did we track
it down? At the apartment of a noted translator and literary critic,

N. N. Vilmont, who happened to live not only in the very same street as Lamara but in the house next door!

Our warm friendship with Anna Berzer continued over many years on a wonderfully steady footing; it had begun when we were first introduced at the offices of *Novy Mir*, when it was still in its old premises, and we used to meet in her apartment on Krechetinsky Lane, now renamed New Arbat, where she would tell me in confidence what progress *Ivan Denisovich* was making as it went the rounds of various Central Committee functionaries. Our friendship continued after the entire old lane was demolished and the Berzer sisters were relocated in a shoddy new apartment block on the edge of town, and it went on through the demolition of the various editorial boards and after Anna Samoilovna was forced out of the "new" *Novy Mir* and into retirement. She was the same age as I and had been a student at MIFLI* at the same time that I was taking a correspondence course there, so we shared the outlook and the memories of our generation. The way her mind worked, the way she saw things, made her a kindred spirit to me, and our reactions were invariably similar. In addition, she was an extraordinarily modest, tactful, kindhearted woman, never pushy or stuck-up—she was loved by every author who wrote for *Novy Mir*, not just by me.

Although she had not been trained for this kind of thing, whenever secret materials needed collecting, hiding, moving, or delivering, she was always ready to take on the task without flinching, and we did from time to time call on her for help. There was even a plan for Lyusha to do a complete retype of *Gulag* at Anna's flat, diving in there and vanishing without trace, as if she had gone away somewhere. But we gave up the idea: you could hear every sound in the building, and there was a lot of hostility around. Still, no scheme was so secret that you could not share it with Anna Samoilovna, confident in the knowledge that not even her sister or her best friend would get to hear of it. We would have confided in her more, but the need simply did not arise. As it was, there were lots of things she got to know about, and she would keep us informed or warn us in advance; for instance, when a copy of *The Oak and the Calf* leaked out, she was onto it at once. When I was in Ryazan and had just been expelled from the local branch of the Writers' Union, I could get no reply from Alya's phone in Moscow, so my next call was to Anna Samoilovna in her office at *Novy Mir*, and soon my news was winging on its way! The room she shared in the prose section of *Novy Mir*'s editorial offices functioned as a writers' club where one could drop in for a chat, a joke, or a grumble, and all could speak their minds. Even after the editorial board was dispersed,* Anna Berzer stayed on, together with Inna Borisova, and the two of them did what they could to keep the old traditions alive. Lyusha, too, could turn to them whenever she liked, and so even after the "Communist course correction" at *Novy Mir*, my manuscripts were still being passed on there and the statements I made for samizdat still circulated.

And Inna, who at first seemed just a pretty face, turned out to be a rock solid, self-possessed, observant, and astute individual; for years she, too, kept various of my things, including the ninety-six-chapter *First Circle*, safely hidden out at her isolated apartment in the Aeroport district. When a copy of a Russian-language edition of *The First Circle* was brought to us from the West, the name of the pirate publisher "Flegon" still meant nothing to us, so we took this for the edition organized by the Andreyevs. It had a horrendous number of mistakes, and Inna sacrificed her evenings for weeks on end comparing and correcting the texts.[4]

The writer Boris Mozhaev, one of my very closest friends, has an unrivaled knowledge of nature and village life, but he is also ex-

---

[4] The publication of *The Oak and the Calf* made life more difficult for Anna Samoilovna; there is always something we don't foresee. In my book I could not help expressing my praise and gratitude toward her, and as a result she found herself boycotted: the editorial staff of *Novy Mir* were forbidden to give her any casual or private work to supplement her income. And at the same time her eyesight started to fail. (By contrast A. D. Dementyev found himself the darling of the authorities thanks to the abuse I heaped on him in *The Oak and the Calf*.) (1978 note)

tremely cautious, just like a peasant. Consequently, he was not at all inclined to leap into conspiracies at the drop of a hat. Even when I invited him to collaborate on a samizdat journal, he turned me down. He was the very incarnation of the steady, timeless flow (or burgeoning growth) of the life of the Russian people. Our warm relations went on as if we were living in a free country where two writers could allow themselves the luxury of confining themselves to the realm of openly publishable literature. Yet even he helped me in 1965 to gather materials on the Tambov uprising, deliberately taking a journalistic assignment to provide a screen for my trip there. (In much the same way, my old prison friend, Ivan Emelyanovich Bryskin, a native of Inokovka in the Kirsanovsk district, used his relatives as a cover for my second trip to the Tambov region in 1972.) Later the Englishman Lord Bethell managed, through the Slovak journalist Ličko, to draw Mozhaev into their escapade, involving secret contacts that could even have landed him behind bars.* Boris Mozhaev behaved with firmness and dignity, never losing his nerve for a moment, as if he were quite used to this kind of thing.

Throughout the 1960s there was such unambiguous sympathy for my activities throughout Russian society and such revulsion toward the government that I could equally well turn to more remote acquaintances, friends of friends, people who just happened to come my way, and ask them for serious assistance without risk of refusal or betrayal. Even the most cautious people and those unconnected with our struggle were drawn into helping us.

This wave of sympathy embraced many anonymous well-wishers who passed on to me the contents of slanderous speeches delivered at closed-door Party meetings they had attended. I rarely knew their names and did not ask, but what weapons they put in my hands and how they helped me defend myself! From the most unexpected quarters and the most unlikely people this invaluable information flowed in.

Within this groundswell of sympathy (not just for me but for the movement as a whole) you might come across an elderly lady such as Nadezhda Vasilyevna Bukharina. At various times she offered Roy Medvedev, me, Sakharov, Shafarevich—indeed, all the prominent "dissidents"—practical help of an everyday, domestic kind, diverting her energies from her own children and grandchildren to do so. (She used to say, "Before I die I have to make up for the fact that I never saw the inside of the camps.") She was forever baking special nourishing rusks to put in food parcels for prisoners, meeting their wives and helping them out, distributing gifts and leaflets to several provincial towns. A kindhearted babushka typical of that time, she would not hesitate to accept some dangerous item from you, put it in her shopping bag, and take it wherever it needed to go. She had two selfless typists who were always available to duplicate any piece of samizdat literature, and these three old women came to constitute one of the "samizdat battalions."[5]

And what can one say of the former zeks? Show me one who did not feel compelled to help! Vilgelmina Slavutskaya, who had worked for many years for the Comintern and subsequently served a ten-year sentence, supplied me with details about Kozma Gvozdev and introduced me to the children of Aleksandr Shlyapnikov,* a unique source of information. It was Slavutskaya, too, who organized the secret meeting with Heinrich Böll at which I passed along the texts destined for the West. After my arrest and deportation, she helped Alya get my books on the Russian Revolution out of the country, even though it was forbidden to export them.

[5] Nadezhda Vasilyevna was renowned for her culinary prowess and in later years she would invite all our mutual friends to her apartment on Levshinsky Lane for a reunion on each anniversary, whether a sad or happy one. At the time of the festival of the Intercession of the Virgin in early October 1982, she was taken ill, and within twenty-four hours she had died of coronary thrombosis. She was eighty-one. The funeral service at the church of Nikola-v-Kuznetsakh was packed. During the previous night, an unseasonal blizzard had struck Moscow, the snow had come down, and it was like midwinter when she was buried at the Vagankov Cemetery, with flowers and candles in the snow. (1986 note)

Priceless testimony was provided by the Latvian Olga Zvedre. She, too, had worked for the Comintern and as a secret agent, and before that she had been a stalwart of the Cheka, on personal terms with everyone at the top.

When I was still living in Ryazan, I got to know the two elderly Garasyova sisters. Anna Mikhailovna had been imprisoned in the 1920s as an anarchist, while Tatyana Mikhailovna had been given a ten-year stretch in the thirties as a plain ordinary Soviet citizen. They collected materials for *Gulag* and hid parts of the book itself in their little ramshackle nineteenth-century provincial house, along with other manuscripts and microfilms. ("Life's cheered up a bit now that there's some point to it!") Because they had stoves in their house, they used to take away and burn all the papers and envelopes that we couldn't risk simply throwing away. After my expulsion from the Writers' Union, Anna Mikhailovna arrived at the crack of dawn, with the KGB parked outside the gates, and took away in her shopping bag a copy of my record of the proceedings so that it should not be lost in a raid on my apartment.*

Another staunch ally in Ryazan was Natalya Evgenyevna Radugina. She was connected with the Garasyova sisters and did sterling work as part of our wider network. Radugina was willing to conceal materials for us, but we did not have a chance to take her up on the offer. However, she was openly linked with us, and on the day of my arrest, the KGB descended on her with a search warrant. They ransacked the place, stole this and that, but as for incriminating evidence—not a trace!

In 1964, before I was on anyone's blacklist, I was working quite openly in the Military History Archives when Yuri Aleksandrovich Stefanov spotted my signature in the visitors' book. He came up to me to thank me for my *Ivan Denisovich* and to ask if I needed help with my archival research. He had been born in Novocherkassk and had witnessed the revolutionary events there as a small boy, but one with an unusually good memory and powers of observation. (The

Iron Broom does not sweep as clean as it thinks, thanks to inoffensive survivors like this.) Stefanov had served a ten-year sentence in his time (as had his late mother), but at seventy he was still going strong, with a massive bald head like a pumpkin, every inch the sturdy Cossack and as hardworking a man as you could hope to meet. He was a prominent engineer in the oil industry, highly regarded for his flair and indefatigable energy, but this left him only evenings and Sundays to devote to his great passion: the history of the Don region, of its Cossack inhabitants, and hence, indirectly, of the Imperial Russian Army. Needless to say, his views, as befitted a dyed-in-the-wool Cossack, were thoroughly anti-Bolshevik (though rigorously cloaked in scholarly objectivity). He knew all the ins and outs of archival research—not just what to look for but where and how to look. I cannot begin to estimate how much he helped me over the years with his extensive glossaries of various characters and units in the old Russian army, Cossacks in particular. (It is a universal feature of life in the Soviet Union that all one's helpers, all one's collaborators, have daytime jobs; the colossal work they get through all has to be done in their spare time and not a penny for their pains.) Later, when I began to receive books from abroad, the "Cossack," for such was our name for him, was quite delighted when I passed along editions dealing with the Cossacks from the White point of view. I used Lyusha as my contact with him, but he caused her no end of anxiety; on the telephone he was hopeless at disguising his meaning and getting it across succinctly, so he was forever letting things slip and putting himself in danger. But when, on top of everything else, we were inundated with the papers left by Kryukov (see Chapter Fourteen), Yuri Aleksandrovich took on the lion's share of the work, sorting through this mountain of material and finding a lot there for his own purposes as well.

In the Lenin Library, Lyusha got to know Galina Andreyevna Glavatskikh, a bibliographer who was well disposed toward me. Her prompt response to requests from Lyusha (in other words, from me) was a virtuoso performance; she provided not just reading lists but scores, if not hundreds, of real live books, with relevant passages marked. For reasons of security I never met Galina Andreyevna in person, and probably the only time I expressed my thanks was in a note I sent her. So it is only through Lyusha that I know that she was about thirty-seven at that time, a historian, "modest, refined, exhausted." And she was a Christian. Lyusha used to lug all these books out of the library and deliver them to me in the country; then she would lug them all back again.

Even in the special depository of the Lenin Library (its most restricted inner sanctum), we had a sympathizer, Vera Semyonovna Grechaninova. Sometimes she could get hold of materials that were virtually unobtainable. But whether because they traced what she was up to or because she let someone in on the secret, she was removed from the special depository. Her friend, Anna Aleksandrovna Saakyants, helped out as well; she was a specialist on Tsvetaeva, and on my behalf she sifted through an extensive volume of items from newspapers confined to the depository.

As time went by, one archive after another denied me access and information. (After the appearance of *August 1914* in 1972, the Military History Archives even launched an investigation to find out who had had the audacity to issue materials on the First World War to me back in 1964!) Yet the flow of much-needed materials, information, and answers to my various queries continued without a break. Thanks, for instance, to Aleksandr Veniaminovich Khrabrovitsky, a literary scholar and expert on Schopenhauer, son-in-law to Korolenko, and a real archive buff. Or to Vyacheslav Petrovich Nechaev. Or to the historian Professor Pyotr Andreyevich Zaionchkovsky. Or thanks to Evgenia Konstantinovna Igoshina (a retired employee of the state publishing house, Goslitizdat), who undertook to do research on the famine of 1921 for me. She was the sister of Olga Konstantinovna Kryzhanovskaya, whom Anichkova had found for me; though they both lived in Moscow, the two sisters had been entirely estranged for years until my books brought them back together. Or thanks upon occasion to people with whom we had nothing in common, who toed the official line, and to the old people who helped me (some of whom I do not even know, since Lyusha worked with them independently)—it was such a complicated time, and the intelligentsia was itself confused about whom to support, what to think, even about its own identity.

Then there was the brilliant young Gabriel Superfin, with his frail constitution but extraordinary talent for archival research. He turned up on his own initiative as a self-appointed assistant, and he did indeed help, working on Guchkov (for Chapters Thirty-nine and Sixty-six of *March 1917*) and providing general background on prerevolutionary Russia. There was not time for him to do a great deal, but at the moment of his arrest in 1973, I deliberately singled out his contribution to my work in an interview with *Le Monde*, hoping to protect him by giving his case as much international publicity as I could.[6]

I had wanted to get inside the Tauris Palace to look at the chamber where the Duma once assembled and at the locations of the tumultuous events of February 1917, but even this was categorically forbidden. And the fact that I did, nevertheless, manage to get inside during the spring of 1972—I, a Russian writer entering a Russian historic building in a land ruled by allegedly Russian leaders—was entirely due to the daring and ingenuity of two Russian Jews, Efim Etkind and David Petrovich Pritsker. Pritsker was a lecturer at the so-called Regional Party School, which had taken over the Tauris Palace and sealed it tight, turning it, in effect, into a top-secret establishment. He helped me only once and not in a matter of the first im-

---

[6] Frail as he was and dreading the prospect of arrest (because of his involvement with the samizdat journal *A Chronicle of Current Events*), he in fact coped well with the investigation and interrogation; although he did initially make some unfortunate statements, he then repudiated them completely as soon as he got his second wind. He bore up well at his trial and went on to endure prison, solitary confinement, and labor camps with the same fortitude. In 1978 he was exiled to northern Kazakhstan. (1978 note)

portance, yet it was such a comfort to me (I didn't get back to Saint Petersburg again after that, before my expulsion) that I must record my gratitude to one who helped me so selflessly. Pritsker met me at the entrance to the palace, led me past the military checkpoint, and we wandered at our leisure, savoring the delights of the Domed Hall, then the Ekaterininsky Hall, lit by the rays of the setting sun. (I even paced out its dimension, unhurriedly, noting down features of the walls, chandeliers, and columns.) Next we went into the assembly chamber of the Duma and, still taking our time, held forth about this and that. (I had done my homework and already knew where the various deputies used to sit.) I had mounted Rodzyanko's rostrum and was looking around from there when suddenly one of the military guards came running up: "David Petrovich, this part of the palace is closing now, you'll have to stop!" We hadn't got as far as the Semicircular Chamber—what a shame! Pritsker was startled, but he did not argue. I asked whether it might still be possible to see the wing where the Council of Workers' Deputies met. We had scarcely stuck our noses inside when up ran another guard, called Pritsker aside, and the embarrassed lecturer informed me that I had to leave altogether: They're onto us! I must get away! The main thing is to get past the checkpoint at the exit without being asked for my documents; then they won't be able to prove a thing. Right by the checkpoint I bowed to Pritsker and thanked him effusively, giving no sign of haste, then I slowly walked away. No challenge came. No one caught up with me in the courtyard. All the way to the corner, and still no one on my tail. Had they guessed or not? And if they hadn't, then why all the panic over ejecting me? (The following day Pritsker met with Etkind for the only time. They saw each other secretly in the Monastery Park, and Pritsker warned him, "If anyone asks, I didn't know who it was I was showing around. You'd told me he was some college professor from Siberia.")[7]

---

[7] There were very serious repercussions for Pritsker later on, and he was threatened with dismissal. He tried to object: "After all, this is the Tauris Palace, not some nu-

As for Efim Grigoryevich Etkind himself, we could never have denied our friendship; by the time of my exile it had already lasted a good ten years. (Before Etkind was dismissed from his job, Boborykin, the director of the institute where he taught, spoke to him privately in his office and warned him, "The charge against you is that you are a friend of Solzhenitsyn. Frankly, I envy you.") It began with a letter to me from Etkind's charming wife Ekaterina Fyodorovna Zvorykina. Her letters were always full of humor and were fun to read. We met in person in Leningrad. Efim Grigoryevich was erudite and witty. We went to the theater together, or out to their. *dacha, or else we would take a trip by car to Königsberg or the Baltic states. And he had an endless supply of acquaintances in Leningrad who could help me with information, advice, or practical assistance. It was always a pleasure to go and see them, and the guests they invited were interesting company. I had no reason to draw him into the conspiracy, and that was never my intention; our friendship and our involvement together was fine just as it was. But the struggle in which we were engaged generated a whirlwind so powerful that nothing in its path was left "just as it was." What could be more natural than for him to read some little thing I had just finished? But that entailed taking it and keeping it, and then perhaps, holding onto it and keeping it hidden. The openness of the Etkinds' style of living, their long-established, secure niche in the intellectual and literary milieu, did not dispose them toward taking risks or getting involved in machinations. But the whole spirit of the times was nudging them in that direction, and there was an additional factor that under other circumstances might have dimmed

---

clear submarine." To this his superiors replied, "The Tauris Palace is a classified location!" and they demanded a written explanation. In his statement David Petrovich said that he had not known the surname of the man he had shown around the palace. His bosses had no proof, and it was this that saved him.

Now that I have finished writing *March 1917*, I cannot thank Pritsker enough. How could I have managed if I hadn't seen the inside of the palace with my own eyes? (1990 note)

in their memory but that the events of these years kept bringing to mind—namely, that both his father and hers had met their deaths in prison camps. And so, when we had already been friends for some years, I let them have *Gulag* to read. Their first reaction was one of alarm; the work seemed too extreme, too destructive of the foundations of normal, everyday life. In considerable agitation the two of them came to Moscow in an attempt to dissuade me from allowing the book to circulate at all. The Etkinds did not pretend to be other than apprehensive, yet at the same time they strove to transcend and overcome their fear. For instance, when Etkind was leaving for a trip abroad early in 1967, he agreed to take a copy of my letter to the Writers' Union Congress (it was already completed, even though the congress itself was not to meet for another two months), and taking many a precaution, he did indeed deliver it. (It was this copy that eventually reached the BBC and caused a stir when it was read on the air.) I introduced the Etkinds to Lyusha, and between them they set up a kind of informal courier service from Moscow to Leningrad, through which flowed a steady stream of the latest samizdat publications and sometimes miscellaneous secret materials. At one point there was even a copy of *Gulag* buried not far from the Etkinds' dacha. And so, bit by bit, Etkind was drawn in until the day when *Gulag* erupted in international furor; caught in the blast and with no outside support, Etkind teetered on the brink of the crater —and fell. Of all who played a part in the events of this book, he was the only one so far to endure the shock of being publicly attacked and pilloried, then driven out of the country.[8]

[8] At first our friendship continued while we were abroad. Etkind came to see us in Zurich, and we met several times in Paris. (I shared with him my idea of establishing a Russian university abroad and asked for his views.) But then things changed. Two or three years later he spoke out against me in public, alleging that what I wanted for Russia was a new Byzantinism and—at a time when the wave of executions in Iran was causing worldwide revulsion—a new ayatollah, adding that the Russian ayatollahs would be even worse than their Iranian counterparts! I was completely taken aback and had to respond in autumn 1979 with a public statement, "The Persian Gambit." From that time on, Etkind became an active con-

With Lev Kopelev, things took the following course. He was the quickest of all my zek friends to establish close contact with Moscow literary circles and with foreigners. While in exile I had discussed with Zubov (who also knew Lev from their prison-camp days) what to do with the book we had made, with its hidden cache of microfilms in the binding [see Chapter One] and we agreed that Lev was the one who could most easily send it abroad. When I came to Moscow in 1956 I soon lost any illusions about entrusting it to foreign tourists or attempting to get through to one of the embassies. But I still had high hopes that Lev would help, and one after another I read him the works I had composed in the camps and in exile, waiting expectantly to see which of them he would agree to send out. But he did not praise my writing, and in that year of 1956—when the recovery of the Communist system was allegedly under way!—he was least of all inclined to harm it by giving ammunition to the forces of "worldwide reaction."

Lev promised that at least he would pass my *Republic of Labor* on to the Poles–they were supposedly making dramatic strides toward freedom during those very months, and *socialist* freedom at that! Yet he did not even give it to the Poles, and everything I, had written was left stranded. As one who was used to rubbing shoulders with the foremost Soviet and Western writers, he could not be expected to set any great store by my provincial efforts. After that, I, too, gave up trying. But by autumn 1960 I had had my first experience of being read by a non-zek audience (the Teushes and Kamenomostskys), and in May 1961, I brought the toned-down version of *Shch-854** to the Kopelevs in Moscow. Although Lev regarded it as akin to a Soviet "production novel," there clearly must have been some spice and novelty to it since he and his wife tried to get my permission for them to let a few people "have a look at it." That much they could

---

tributor to the whispering campaign about my alleged—but nonexistent—theocratism and anti-Semitism. (1986 note)

manage. At first I turned them down flat, but later I relented and let them extract a list of approved readers from me: the Rozhanskys, the Ospovats, and Koma Ivanov. That summer and autumn they started lending it out, without confining themselves to our list. Then in November 1961, after the Twenty-second Party Congress, we agreed that the Kopelevs would pass the story on to *Novy Mir*. It was Kopelev's wife Raya Orlova who took it there. (By her own account she handed it directly to Anna Berzer and conveyed its significance to her, but according to Berzer's version, Orlova said little that was to the point and laid the story on her desk as if it were just another routine manuscript. Perhaps she was ashamed of it?) Now that they had delivered it to *Novy Mir*, the Kopelevs thought they would have a pretext for circulating it widely (blaming the journal for the leak); they did not for a moment believe it would actually be published. Still I did not entirely give up hope.

Then, following the successful publication of *Ivan Denisovich*, I turned to Lev again, hoping we could "send something out" (something different). Foreigners were always dropping in on them. But no, Lev would not take it on. I had lost all hope, when in 1964, Lev suddenly told me to get ready to pass my stuff to Rozhansky. Rozhansky did not let me down: he took the consignment from me, but then his trip fell through. By now I had met Eva, and from then on I could get by without the Kopelevs. But in autumn 1965, when my personal archive fell into the KGB's hands, all I could think of was how to save *Tanks Know the Truth* and *Prussian Nights* by sending them out to the West. Eva happened to be away in France at the time, so again I turned to Lev. This time he agreed and actually did send it out via Böll. I was so delighted and so grateful to him! But what I did not know was that during the couple of weeks when it was awaiting collection, Lev lent *Prussian Nights* to his sister-in-law Lyusya to read; she passed it on to a woman she was friends with, and while it was with her, a copy was made. A few years down the line this leaked copy would put me in grave danger, for the

KGB got hold of it and used it against me, courtesy of the magazine *Stern*. At the time I could not bring myself to reproach Lev seriously, nor did he show any sense of being to blame. That is just the way he is. He does not have the steely resolve you need for a bitter, drawn-out fray. It's funny, really, but whenever I tried to send anything through him, it always went wrong. Even when he agreed to get Vittorio Strada to take out something as minor as my letter to *L'Unità*—even that fell apart at customs.* After I was deported and Alya was left worrying about how to get this potentially explosive store of manuscripts out to the West, Lev was one of those she turned to. He did not help. (And thank Heavens he didn't, or there might have been another hitch!)

In August 1973, when the dissident movement had begun to split into different factions, Lev swung back to his former Marxist sympathies ("Even fire can't clean a barrel that has once held tar" as a Russian proverb tells us) and lent his support to Roy Medvedev.* Our relations were half-severed after my article "On Peace and Violence," when he accused me of being "Moscowcentric" (I could see the oppression in the Soviet Union but not that in Chile and so on). Our final meeting took place in December 1973 at the Chukovskys' dacha in Peredelkino: I was holed up there, harassed and at the end of my strength, when he arrived bringing the American publisher Carl Proffer* and his wife to meet me, without so much as a "by your leave." He found me deep in the leafy shade of the grounds and tried to get me to meet them. I was indignant—what do I need these Americans for? I don't want to see anyone. We were both grim-faced and taciturn, and that is how Lev and I parted. After I was exiled, he got to know my "Letter to the Soviet Leaders" and then *From Under the Rubble* and became a fierce and abiding foe of the program they contained, as well as of me personally. He wrote a furious response to my "Letter," almost longer than the letter itself (a bad sign for a work of criticism). He always did tend toward verbosity. I could not get to the end of his piece, and anyway, I did not expect to find any ideas of much value in it. Then letters reached me from Moscow describing how he was going around "heaping abuse" on me. He could not restrain himself even when my friends Lyusha and Lidia Chukovskaya were present—so God only knows what he said among strangers.

But I did not lose my affection for Lev. Who could ever forget his huge, shaggy figure, his forthright, magnanimous impulses? He was generous toward all he met and, except when he lost his temper, kindly, too.[9]

Another who helped in no small measure was Volodya Gershuni, a zek since his youth and one whom I had come to know in Ekibastuz. He was indefatigable in bringing me rare old books for my work on *Gulag* and on the history of the revolution. It was he who brought me *The White Sea–Baltic Canal,** the only Soviet book with photographs of Cheka officers. And again, it was he who put me in touch with M. P. Yakubovich. Two of the expressions I use in *The Gulag Archipelago* came from Gershuni: one was the pun that turns the Russian phrase meaning "corrective-labor camp" into "destructive-labor camp"; the second was the description of true-believer Communists as having "perished comically," rather than "tragically" as in the official cliché.

Each acquaintance brings new ones in its wake, and the circles spread ever outward. It was Gershuni who introduced me to another circle of well-wishers, similar to the young acquaintances of A. I. Yakovleva who signed a collective letter to me. This circle's center was Elena Vsevolodovna Vertogradskaya, and all its members worked in a special archive housing books on the Party. It was situated—of all places—on Dzerzhinsky Square, directly opposite the Lubyanka! And what holdings they had there, too! Books that were more or less banned but that had yet to be destroyed. This meant it

[9] After he came to the West we exchanged conciliatory letters, but he was quick to associate himself with all the slanderous froth that was being whipped up against me by certain recent Russian émigrés. In 1985 came a final exchange of letters, in which we broke off relations. (1986 note)

was possible for them to "write off" books as pulped without actually destroying them, and then to pass them on to someone like me. With so much to do and so desperately little time to do it in, I took foolishly little advantage of this opportunity. (What's the point of stockpiling books when the noose could snap tight before you have read a single one?) But even so, I did accept a few things. And once they insisted that I actually come and visit them inside the archives and wander through the stacks. We did not get to know and understand one another properly, but we did consider each other friends. At our meeting we all radiated pleasure, but was it a careless move? I don't know how things turned out for them: there was an informer present, and there were unpleasant repercussions. There was no occasion for continuing contact and I never thought that this group would be useful again. But ten days before I was deported I turned to them precisely because of their distance from what was going on and asked if they would find a way of storing Kryukov's archive separately for me. They agreed!

Leonila Georgievna Snesaryova was a sad, lonely woman, half-blind and impoverished, eking out a career as an English translator after being edged out in this field by vigorous competition from rival cartels of translators. For many years she tried to assist me in any way she could, and she took pleasure in using her meager leisure time to help. (She had been born in Voronezh, the daughter of a priest shot by the Cheka in September 1919 as the Whites were closing in; this had to be concealed for the rest of her life, which is the only reason why she was able to graduate from the Department of Translation at the Literary Institute. Her mother served five years in the Solovki prison camp at the beginning of the 1930s and was sent back to the camps after the war; the pair of them were destitute all their lives and had no home to call their own.) Snesaryova undertook a detailed comparison of the two English-language translations of *The First Circle* for me (and she accumulated enough data to demonstrate their inadequacy). She also translated George Katkov's book on the February Revolution. Among ourselves we called her the "Dandelion." Thanks to the gaffes she made over the telephone, the secret police were keeping an eye on her (she had an alarming tendency to blurt things out on the phone or in rooms that might be bugged). They probably thought there were rich pickings to be had, and after I had been deported, they broke into her apartment in her absence and carried out a search. But all they found were photographs of me, and they left behind a jeering note. (By now she was so far beneath their contempt that they did not even bother to disguise the fact that they were from the KGB.) But after we had left Russia, Alik Ginzburg managed to involve her in the work of the Russian Social Fund, distributing aid to zeks and helping with communications. She was a selfless and intrepid worker, and he praised her in the letters he wrote to us in Switzerland.

In addition, there were those who lived too far away for us to be able to call upon their services or find a worthy use for their energies. Such a person was "Natanya" (Natalya Alekseyevna Kruchinina), a doctor from Leningrad. No task would have been too much to ask (but our collaboration was restricted to the matter of Kryukov's archive and *The Quiet Don*).

And stuck in far-off Rostov-on-Don, a town that warped my whole youth as well, lived Margarita Nikolaevna Sheffer, who, though older than I, had been at university with me. I went to Rostov in about 1963, and I recall her stern, dark face, as if hewn out of rock and coal. "Sanya!" she said with passionate intensity. "Give me any kind of work to do—anything for the revolution! I'm suffocating in this swamp!" All I could say was, "Move to Moscow. You won't be able to help at all from *here*." However, a few years later, she did start doing some typing for me, on a shoddy typewriter with atrocious carbon paper and, initially, with lots of mistakes. She copied out *The First Circle* and then went on to type out the whole of *Gulag*, but none of it could be put to use; it just lay there until it was burned not very long ago. (But think of the work

she put in, the risk she ran!) In the course of this episode we had another close shave: for a whole year a set of manuscripts was stuck in
Rostov in a barn owned by some casual acquaintances—it is amazing that they were not found and seized! This meant more emergencies, more trips to make. . . . In 1970 Rita finally managed to
move to the Moscow area, and we linked her into the network
through Lyusha and the NNs (this was partly a working relationship
but also partly because, in the depths of her loneliness, she needed
someone she could visit and pour out her heart to). Rita still made
slips, but in time she, too, got the hand of our conspiratorial ways.
And nearer to the present, it was she alone who was entrusted with
typing out the collection *From Under the Rubble*, thus making it
available to readers of samizdat throughout the Soviet Union, as
well as to an international public.

―――――

So far nearly forty individuals have figured in this chapter alone,
while the preceding chapters contained almost forty more, including those whose names I could not disclose. And there are more
than fifteen still to come, not forgetting a score of foreigners—in
other words, a total of more than one hundred people! And these
are just my *Invisible* Allies!

What could I have achieved without them?

Life goes by and you forget how many of them there were. Now
I look through the list in amazement.

And this does not even take into account the next line of support, an even larger group of people who made sincere offers of
help and showed themselves to be both resolute and bold but for
whose services we simply could not find a use.

And then there were those who helped us on a single occasion
without our ever knowing who they were—like those two young
men at the Radio Committee building on Novokuznetsk Street, for
instance: when a KGB man went out of the room, leaving his brief-

case unattended, they risked their necks by removing and copying the procedural instructions on how our surveillance was to be conducted. Later I was able to quote this document in an interview* (see the Third Supplement in *The Oak and the Calf*).

Or take the case of Igor Khokhlushkin. He first became involved in the struggle when he was working as a physicist at a scientific institute in Novosibirsk, and he made his voice heard even from there, until he was driven out by well-to-do academic philistines. Somehow he managed to end up in Moscow but without a proper job; at first he worked as a bookbinder, then as a joiner, but at least this gave him the freedom to think for himself. He even managed to turn this source of income to the public good, by binding many works of samizdat for no charge. When copies of *Gulag* printed in the West reached the Soviet Union—in tiny numbers, and only in Moscow and Leningrad—Aleksandr ("Alik") Ginzburg, the legendary director of our Social Fund (itself a seemingly inconceivable undertaking under Soviet conditions), managed to combine his unprecedented work of distributing aid to prisoners and their families with a scheme to have *Gulag* reproduced in Georgia, using illegal photocopies made from the Paris YMCA Press edition. The new edition was brought back to Moscow in the form of printer's sheets, which Khokhlushkin proceeded to cut, bind, and turn into proper books in the carpenters' shop at the museum where he worked. It was a quite extraordinary edition and one that exposed its publishers to terrible risk. (Apart from the faintness of its print, the striking thing about their output was its price: while foreign editions were fetching three hundred rubles a volume, ours was sold at cost for only twenty rubles.)

It was an eerie feeling to be living here, abroad, and to receive from Eva a book like that all the way from Russia! Igor wrote, "I am delighted to be able to present you with a copy of our own Russian edition of your book. (The first print run is 200 copies, with a total edition of 1,500 copies planned.) I believe that the Lord will not allow our work to be interrupted. The edition is intended less for snobbish Moscow readers than for the provinces, including the towns of Yakutsk, Khabarovsk, Novosibirsk, Krasnoyarsk, Sverdlovsk, Saratov, Krasnodar, Tver, and a number of smaller places."

So these young Russian lads put their heads on the block in order that *Gulag* could drive deep into the heartland of Russia. Whenever I think of them, I cannot hold back the tears.

And what of those unsung heroes, who had known me in the past but remained unbroken, resisting every pressure to denounce me? Should they not be numbered among the ranks of Invisible Allies? Father Viktor Shipovalnikov, for instance, rejected demands that he attack me in the pages of the *Journal of the Moscow Patriarchate*, and as a result he and all his family were subjected to a great deal of harassment, but still he did not flinch![10]

---

[10] When the KGB agent, Řezáč, was dashing around gathering scurrilous tales from people who had been close to me in the past, how are we to explain why in most cases he drew a blank? Why did he neither mention these people in his sordid book nor cite them as evidence? Surely it was because they rebuffed him and held their ground. It is inconceivable that he would not have tried to get a statement from Lidia Ezherets, who was at school with me, from my university friends, Emil Mazin and Mikhail Shlenyov, from my front-line commanders—Major General Travkin, Lieutenant Colonel Pshechenko, and Major Pashkin. This is especially true of Viktor Vasilyevich Ovsyannikov, with whom I was friends at the front—for the very good reason that he is now a lieutenant colonel in the KGB. Yet the outcome was that not one of them told him anything he could exploit in his book; not one of them would appear under this spotlight of lies. In other words, they all remained my Invisible Allies. (1978 note)

II

A New Network

In the summer of 1968 Eva kept telling me, "You're wasting your strength on things that could be done without you. What you need are some energetic young people to help you. What if I were to introduce you to some?" I agreed. Eva arranged for me to come directly to the Svetlovs' apartment on Vasilyevsky Street. But I never came to Moscow to deal with just a single matter; even when I was staying at Rozhdestvo, not far from Moscow, I always waited until a whole list of chores had accumulated. This occasion was no exception: I arranged to see the Svetlovs on the evening when Sakharov and I were due to meet for the first time. Our encounter would take place in Academician Fainberg's apartment on Zoologichesky

Street, which turned out to be conveniently close to the Svetlovs'.
(That year Sakharov's whereabouts were still being kept secret. He
could well have been under official surveillance, and so, to keep our
meeting confidential, we agreed that I would reach the apartment
before him and not leave until after he had gone.) Two hours before
my meeting with Sakharov I went to be introduced to Natasha
Svetlova.

It was a week after the Soviet occupation of Czechoslovakia and
three days after the "Group of Seven" had staged their demonstration in Red Square.* I had heard all the radio reports out at my little house in Rozhdestvo but did not have any firsthand details
about the demonstration in Moscow. And now this intense young
woman with her dark hair swept forward above her hazel eyes and
without a trace of affectation in her manner and her dress was
telling me not just how the demonstration had gone but even how
it had been planned. How could she know? It turned out that she
had close connections with the democratic movement and the
demonstrators—in fact, two of them were friends of hers. (She had
come within an inch of deciding to join them that day on Red
Square; the only thing stopping her, as it later emerged, were her
doubts as to whether she was equal to the task. There are times in
life when we find ourselves confronted with a series of crossroads,
and decisions come thick and fast. Here she was today, already facing another decision.)

I was very taken with her fervent social concern—this was my
kind of temperament. I could not wait to involve her in our work!
And indeed, either on this occasion or the next time we met, I suggested for a start that she type out the ninety-six-chapter version of
my *First Circle*. Natasha accepted with alacrity. (Even though she
was still completing a postgraduate degree in math and teaching
undergraduates classes—which meant that the only time she had
consisted of two hours each evening after her six-year-old son had
gone to bed—she managed to finish the typing in four months

without making a single mistake and with an excellent eye for presentation, something we had never bothered about before. The very next time we met she had a series of queries for me about what she had been typing, and her questions were meticulous, to the point, and ones I had not thought of myself. She even put me right on details of Communist Party history, not an area in which I had expected her to have any expertise—here, too, we were birds of a feather. It turned out that even before she left school she had begun eagerly ferreting out the true history of the Bolshevik Party just for her own satisfaction. (Her generation had had the shattering experience of seeing Stalin thrown from his pedestal while they were in their very last year at school. And one of Natasha's grandfathers, Ferdinand Svetlov, had even been a prominent Bolshevik publicist. When he was arrested in 1937, he left behind a library of Communist materials, including the banned transcripts of various Party congresses and miscellaneous Communist dross, which was strikingly at variance with the officially sacrosanct *Short Course in the History of the Party*.* All this provided the stimulus for her rummaging around. The character and momentum of Russian history in the 1950s were to a significant extent determined by this sharp about-face between generations.)

And what about keeping some of my things safe for me? Yes, of course she would take care of it.

To describe her as businesslike would be an understatement; she worked with an alacrity, meticulousness, and lack of fuss that were the equal of any man. Her grasp of tactics, of how and when to act, was instantaneous—"computerlike," as I called it—and from the outset she matched my own impetuous behavior at the time. Moreover, I had dreamed in vain of finding a male friend whose ideas would be as close to my own as were those that Natasha now came out with unprompted. As if this were not enough, she revealed a deep-rooted, innate spiritual affinity with everything quintessentially Russian, as well as an unusual concern and affection for the Russian language. This, together with her vibrant energy, made me want to see her more often.

She was thoroughly steeped in Russian poetry and knew a great many lines by heart. Indeed, she had been involved in "publishing" banned verse, typing it out and binding it herself. And I was delighted to discover as time went by that she was adroit at editing and polishing literary texts. The fourth or fifth time we met, I put my hands on her shoulders as one does when expressing gratitude and confidence to a friend. And this gesture instantly turned our lives upside down: from now on she was Alya, my second wife, and two years later our first son was born.

Though we were firmly united in 1968, our shared ability to penetrate to the essence of the individuals, events, and themes of our history did not yet link us as completely as it would later on; as Soviet society began to be torn by universal division and discord, we two remained marvelously together, and ever more so as time went on.

Our work together took its course, and it, too, went from strength to strength. At her own insistence, Alya took on and successfully completed the major task of checking and emending the quotations in the finished text of *Gulag*, especially those from Lenin: under pressure of work I had drawn them from different editions—or rather, I had plucked them secondhand from various Communist books without having time to check the sources in the library. The result was an utter mishmash. (As an underground writer I had allowed myself to be somewhat lax in my observance of the usual bibliographical niceties—a bad mistake!) Then she prepared outlines of the events falling in the interstices between the "knots" of my *Red Wheel*. (I would not draw on them directly, since they fell outside the timespan of the "knots," but I had to be aware of them, out of the corner of my eye.) She went through Shlyapnikov's memoirs, extracting the essentials, then worked on Lenin, making excerpts from individual works, then compiling and classifying them under such headings as "external features," "speech pe-culiarities," and "general bearing."

She became completely involved, contributing on various fronts at one and the same time, offering advice, helping me weigh each step I took, and by the time we had known each other for three years, she was actively contributing to the genesis of my *October 1916*. (In August 1971 we discussed it and worked at it especially intensively after a sudden severe illness forced me to abandon a trip to the south of Russia and left me bedridden for two months with what I took at the time to be some inexplicable attack of sunburn.[1]

Hitherto, I had faced all my crucial strategic decisions alone, but now I had gained an extra pair of critical eyes, someone I could argue things out with and who, at the same time, was a dependable counselor, whose spirit and manner were as unyielding as my own. It was such a joyous and harmonious development. In no time, Alya had devoted herself utterly to my work and the struggle I was waging.

———

For year after grueling year I would rack my brains over countless incidental matters: which manuscript should I work on next and whom was I to get it from? Then where should I deliver it for safe-keeping? And how should I arrange my movements to minimize the risks? Where should I telephone from in order to avoid exposing my lines of communication? Which of my caches of manuscripts must I destroy when danger threatened, and what new

[1] In April 1992 the Moscow monthly *Sovershenno sekretno* [*Top Secret*], no. 4, carried an item based on the voluntary revelations of a former KGB lieutenant colonel, B. A. Ivanov, from Rostov. (For its reverberations in the West, see *The Guardian*, April 20, 1992; *Washington Post*, April 21, 1992; and many others). Ivanov testified in writing [see Appendix B, below] that in August 1971 KGB agents had carried out an attempt to assassinate me in the town of Novocherkassk (evidently, using an injection of ricin poison—a precursor of the "Bulgarian umbrella" technique).* So that was the true cause of what we had taken for a bizarre form of "sunburn"! And indeed, not a single doctor at the time could establish what had struck me down.

hiding places would I need to set up? By overburdening my brain like this, I was consuming the very energy I needed for my writing, and a single one of these workaday chores was like a physical burden, oppressing me and ruining my mood. How much longer could I go on dragging this mounting burden after me?

It so happened that soon after we met, I lost the use of my hiding place at Professor Kobozev's (his daughter-in-law's sister had to change her apartment, as the block she lived in was being demolished, and that was where we had been storing everything for years). Now every last scrap of paper had to be cleared out. To make matters worse, this had been my *main* hiding place, the most tried and trusted of them all. I had been using it longer than any other (some eight years by now), so it contained the most complete and representative collection of my papers, including originals and master copies. And on every count the best person to take over safeguarding them was Alya—on every count, because by then I had already realized that she was the one I wanted to name as my literary executor. Now, at last, I could unburden my heart, and hand everything over to Alya, safe in the knowledge that though there was an age gap of twenty years between us, there was no gap at all in our fundamental convictions.

Without a second thought Alya undertook to arrange storage for all my papers somewhere convenient and accessible. Moreover, she would keep track of everything herself—who was storing what and how it was to be collected and returned—leaving my head clear for other things. I just had to deliver what I had finished with and order what I needed. I fixed up for her to meet Kobozev's student son, Alyosha, and the pair of them took empty knapsacks around to where my things were hidden (I had never seen the actual spot) and made the transfer. The first thing Alya did was read every single page of my writings and really get to know them, so that from then on she could recall them all in detail. Next she systematized and classified everything, at the same time getting me to add a handwritten inscription and explanatory notes to the first page of each work, in case I should die without having time to see to it. So everything was gathered together—finished manuscripts, works in progress, and discontinued projects.

However, now that she had taken over this store of papers, she could not keep it at her apartment much longer, since reasons of the heart often brought me to her door and I needed to be free to visit. It would all have to be deposited at some remove from me, in places I never visited, in the care of people whose names I deliberately chose not to know or ever inquire about. (It is best when each individual knows only as much as he needs to; then nothing—either delirium or depression, hypnosis or drugs—can loosen his tongue.)

Alya wasted no time, even though as yet she had no idea where she could house everything. She still had to devise a network and then seek the agreement of those who would be involved. Moreover, she had the wit to realize that her system must fit in with the normal pattern of their lives so that any changes in their movements and their circle of acquaintances were kept to a minimum. In other words, those who handled the "pickup" had to be people who had previously called regularly and would continue to do so in the future, so that their visits could be explained away convincingly. One such close acquaintance and high-profile visitor was her exhusband, Andrei Nikolaevich Tyurin, who for years had been coming to the apartment to see his son by their former marriage. (Later she would use other similar connections. Once she hid a copy of *Gulag* all winter at the home of her relative, the artist Leonora Ostrovskaya—the same Ostrovskaya who designed the mock-up for the front cover of *August 1914* in her own apartment; later it was actually used for the Paris edition.* On another occasion, when things were looking bleak and Alya was virtually under siege, she came up with the idea of smuggling sensitive papers out with Nadezhda Vasilyevna Bukharina, who was always dropping in to lend a hand or baby-sit and who invariably carried some kind of shopping bag.)

Andrei Tyurin did not hesitate in agreeing to Alya's request for help. At the time he was not yet thirty, a gifted and successful mathematician who had already finished his doctorate in physical and mathematical sciences. He was resolutely embarked on the road to spiritual and religious emancipation (it is through our hearts that God transforms our miserable and foolhardy societies). He had a forthright, courageous temperament, and by good fortune, his personal relationship with Alya had survived unscathed—indeed, it was marked by mutual high regard. He agreed to help and for the next five or six years acted, in effect, as "manager" of our safekeeping arrangements. He was unfailingly responsive to our needs and never complained, but acted swiftly and with the precision of a trained mathematician. His storage operation was not only the biggest but it was also the only one that functioned without any interruption. (The system I had using Danila's "moles" had almost ground to a halt; items could only be picked up and deposited intermittently, and there were times when it was unavailable altogether.)

But since Andrei was a frequent visitor to Alya's apartment, not even he could keep anything of mine in his own home; he had to hide it further afield. (If the number of direct contacts is n, then the number of secondary, indirect contacts is n^2, and you could never ransack every one.) Andrei also came up with the simplest of solutions—he would keep it all at the apartment of his sister, Galina Tyurina. Like her brother, she was a brilliant algebraist, a university teacher with an advanced degree in science. She had no contact whatsoever with dissident circles and was interested only in mathematics, canoeing trips, and mountain skiing. At the same time she was a straightforward person, reserved and reliable, just like her brother. And she, too, agreed to help! It was a sign of the times. (She would probably have refused to become involved in any explicitly underground revolutionary activity. Under Khrushchev I had been hammered into Soviet society like a wedge, but the extraordinary thing was that every educated person felt duty-bound to lend me support—for the time being! Khrushchev himself was so scatter-brained that he died without realizing what mischief his hammering had done, and it was left to his heirs to try to undo the damage.) Galina started storing my things in the loft where she kept her canoe and skis. The whole system worked smoothly without Alya ever needing to meet her, thanks to the method Aleksandr Aleksandrovich Ugrimov had proposed for facilitating the identification and retrieval of bundles of papers. Duplicate sets of postage stamps were bought, as gaudy and distinctive as possible, and one of them was stuck onto each of the packets intended for storage, while Alya kept its counterpart in what looked like a stamp-collector's album. Every stamp was numbered, and elsewhere she kept a separate coded list of my manuscripts. When I needed one of them, Alya would look up the appropriate stamp, give it to Andrei, who would pass it on to Galina. She then had no trouble identifying and retrieving the right packet. (Alya operated an identical system with Ugrimov himself for items kept in deep storage.) Doing things out in the open like this was entirely safe and reliable. When a packet was picked up, the stamp was left behind to confirm that it had been collected. The same procedure could be used for adding papers to a packet already in storage; you just sent the appropriate stamp along with them. I could ask for any manuscript I liked, and it would take between three and five days for our system to deliver it to me.

In November 1969 I was expelled from the Writers' Union in Ryazan, and still smarting from this setback, I rushed to telephone Moscow. The first number I dialed was Alya's, but she was not at home. (For one last time she was indulging her youthful habits and had flown off to the Caucasus with a group of friends on a skiing trip.) A few days later I arrived in Moscow after leaving Ryazan for good. As soon as I was finished at *Novy Mir*, I went straight round to see her, ignoring the three KGB sleuths I had in tow. She was already back by then. "Did you read about it?" I was referring to the newspaper reports of my expulsion.

"Yes."

"And what do you think?" I was testing myself as much as her.

"We've got to hit back!" she replied without a moment's hesitation.

"How about this, then!" I said, taking out the reply I had already composed.

When one of us was itching for the fray, the other invariably felt the same.

I had brought the Lenin chapters* from various "knots" of *The Red Wheel* with me to Alya's expecting to have them passed on for storage in the normal way, yet for some reason I did not take the chapters away with me to Zhukovka but left them with Alya, even though, looking down from the seventh floor, we could clearly see the KGB agents standing around outside (indeed, Eva dropped in at that moment and confirmed it). The morning of my second day at Zhukovka, Lyusha's cousin drove out to see me with an urgent message from her begging me to come round at once. What could it be now? Then suddenly it hit me: disaster had struck! After I had left, they must have come to Alya's with a search warrant! How could I have done it again—ruined everything through my own carelessness? Apart from *Gulag* it was hard to imagine anything more incriminating than those Lenin chapters, and I'd left a chapter set in the Soviet period there as well—the one where Dzerzhinsky appears, from the fourteenth "knot"* of *The Red Wheel*. The young man who had come for me was completely in the dark, but still I asked him as we drove back, "Any idea what's going on?"

"I don't know any details, just that something really bad has happened," he replied.

Just what I feared! Now there could be no doubt about it! I sat squirming in the car, consumed with apprehension, as we crawled along the Rublyov Highway and through the hideous densely packed buildings of the Minsk district. By the time we arrived, I was more dead than alive! During the half hour's journey I had relived all the torments of 1965 and the loss of my archive, and with them the agonizing awareness of my own mistakes and the shambles they had made of my defenses.

And what was it all about? *Literaturnaya gazeta* had published some piece about me, and Lyusha and the people at *Novy Mir* felt I ought to reply at once. . . . Big deal!

But the full force of that crushing blow had been brought home to me once again, and what bliss it was, after such a reminder, to know that everything would be hidden deep and safe from harm.

It was less than a year, however, before our storage arrangements were again disrupted. In July 1970 Galina Tyurina took a group of friends on a canoeing trip in the north of Russia. As she was negotiating a stretch of rapids on her own, she—the most skilled and experienced of them all—was drowned, leaving the helpless group of city dwellers to return to Moscow without having found her body. She was thirty-two years old, and her death was a shattering blow to her friends and relatives; her husband was almost out of his mind for a time, while Andrei flew off to try and find the body. Alya, who was pregnant and could not get around, spent days on end telephoning all over Moscow trying to organize a search party and the equipment it would need. A number of selfless volunteers were found. (At the scene of the tragedy, Andrei found the local authorities consistently apathetic and uncooperative. He did manage to discover the body, lying further downstream, but only thanks to a pilot who ignored an official ban in order to help him. The remains were brought back to Moscow for burial.) And all the time that Alya was trying to get the search party together, through all the pain and commiseration, we felt a nagging fear: the dead woman's relatives knew nothing about the cache of manuscripts, but with Andrei away they might stumble across them in her apartment. Someone would have to go and save them. With people so unsuspecting and dazed with grief, who knew what might happen! So Aleksandr Ugrimov and Dima Borisov drove Andrei's wife, Sonya

Tyurina, over to the dead woman's home and hauled out knapsacks full of manuscripts, weighing some sixty pounds, without arousing the suspicions of a succession of visitors arriving to pay their respects. (When Galina's husband learned that she had been storing things for me, he was upset at the thought that she would have kept anything from him.)

For several weeks these knapsacks lay in Andrei's apartment, and even in the midst of so much grief we still had to work out what to do with them next.

The kind of people who made up our immediate circle of acquaintances gave us a clue. They tended to be mathematicians and to go off on trips to the mountains together (losing toes and suffering frostbite together); on Sundays they went walking in the countryside near Moscow, treating their overworked mathematicians' brains to some welcome fresh air and debating social issues without fear of microphones. (Alya had once been a regular participant, but the burden of working for me had long since forced her to give it up; Andrei, however, still went hiking and used to take that opportunity to incinerate things for her—all kinds of scraps and leftovers from our clandestine copying. The impracticability of burning paper in a city apartment was one of the perilous complications facing the modern conspirator.) Now it fell to Sergei Petrovich Dyomushkin to take over the custody of my papers, a man who, though only thirty-five years old, was scrupulously circumspect in all he did. He agreed to help on condition that nobody, however close or irreproachable, should be let in on the secret or become involved in any way.

Because he was so cautious and studiously reticent, Alya and I between ourselves referred to our new custodian as "the Badger." Sergei Petrovich was also a mathematician, and he worked at the Steklov Institute. He was very serious, placid, reserved by nature, but though calm and soft-spoken, he was a man of firm convictions. Born in a village, he had acquired his entire education through his own efforts. He lived inconspicuously, never thrusting himself forward, yet he was one of the first in Moscow to start contributing, quietly and unobtrusively, to the welfare of needy zeks and their families, and these donations never stopped. At a mature age he took up the piano. An illness left him with a limp, but he still went skiing or hiking in the mountains with his friends.

Even with Sergei Petrovich looking after my manuscripts, we still had quite a scare. He was storing them not in his own apartment but at his brother's and without the knowledge of his brother's wife. When their marriage suddenly began to deteriorate, Sergei Petrovich decided to play it safe and move everything out. But where to? He found yet another hiding place (to this day I do not know where), and there he looked after everything until I was deported from the Soviet Union; then he delivered it all, one batch at a time, ready to be sent abroad. (Later he was expelled from his institute but not because of his links with me.)

Andrei Tyurin, on the other hand, made little effort to disguise his political antipathies; moreover, it was perfectly obvious how close he was to our family. After my expulsion he not only used his rights as a relative to come and guard the apartment every day against uninvited visitors but during the weeks when surveillance was at its most intense and everything hung by a thread, he delivered one bulky consignment of confidential materials after another. In so doing, he had the added constraint of a very strict timetable: since Alya could not have anything incriminating lying about the apartment for a moment longer than necessary, she could only take delivery on days when foreign correspondents were due to call and could ferry the bundle on its way.[2]

---

[2] They tried intimidating Andrei's mother as well, summoning her to the KGB and giving her "friendly" warnings (she had worked for them for many years as a radio engineer): "You must save Andrei from himself; he's always going to Kozitsky Lane." They got their revenge on Andrei after we had left by subjecting him to annual academic reappraisals. There was no legal or procedural justification for this, and he had defended his doctorate with distinction, yet they nagged and niggled

The following year they were still sending the remnants out to the West, making good any omissions and burning what was left over.

As I write these lines in the summer of 1975, their custodianship has finally been completed with flying colors.

———

Another of the duties that Alya lifted from my shoulders was the business of photographing my finished manuscripts and transferring them to microfilm for smuggling abroad. For many years this skill had been an incomparable blessing to me, an insurance policy for my whole clandestine operation. Yet even then, the volume of work was proving burdensome and time-consuming, so I passed the technique on to my first wife (who, it must be said, did an excellent job of copying the whole of *Gulag* in 1968). Now the volume of copying was growing steadily, but that was not the main thing: in the spring of 1971 we had decided to make another copy of my entire output and send it to my lawyer in Zurich;* this meant that everything I had written, all the most important of my private archives, would be concentrated in one place and at our disposal. This set would serve as our "safety deposit." (We even had to make a duplicate copy of *Gulag*, since we no longer had access to the one we had sent out first and could not use it for translations into European languages.) An immense amount of work was involved.

And Alya suggested that it should be done by our mutual friend Valeri, a physicist from Moscow State University.

I had seen Valeri Nikolaevich Kurdyumov once before in Andrei's company and had been struck by the air of gentle melancholy that hovered perpetually about his eyes and lips and by the oppressive pessimism of his outlook. Though he was barely into his thir-

———

away at him in one committee after another, denying him a professorship and interrogating him on his "sociopolitical" views.

But the Lord spared them the most serious of repercussions. (1978 note)

ties, his morose and despondent manner seemed more appropriate to the world-weary hopelessness of old age.

His father had been a zek, working on the White Sea Canal project, then on the Moscow-Volga Canal. His parents kept nothing from their children, and the young Valeri, a child of the notorious year 1937,* grew up to be a worldly wise skeptic, bereft of all illusions. He was skillful at fixing radios, and even when jamming was particularly intense, he could still pick up the gist of Western broadcasts. Valeri kept abreast of politics—both the broader developments and their specific ramifications—and his opinions were considered and to the point. He was convinced that "our" leaders would never relent or give an inch, let alone change for the better (a sober and sensible outlook), and that they would end up by devouring the gullible West. Moreover, Valeri dismissed as utterly hopeless even the slightest resistance to Communism, let alone any full-blown struggle, within the country or without. By the same token, he regarded the struggle I was waging as a one-shot event, miraculous in its way yet doomed to achieve nothing, while I myself would either be locked up or murdered, and even the publication of my books in the West, in his view, would merely hasten my downfall.

On the other hand, there was one thing of which he was energetically, even zealously, convinced, and that was the need to *save* all that had been written, every document, every *word*. On his own initiative and with his own two hands he created a complete collection of samizdat in photographic form with homemade bindings— an entire library, almost unique in Moscow, which he lent out to all and sundry, even the most inflammatory items such as works by Avtorkhanov. He readily agreed to make copies for me as well. Alya was afraid of letting him take the volumes of my works back to his apartment, so he carted all his equipment around and for three days and nights he did his photographing, developing, and drying at her place. The result of his labors was a new film of the text of *Gulag*, which would eventually serve as the basis for every foreign translation except the English-language one, and in addition he copied half of the entire "safety-deposit" set of my writings. Later on, as a precaution lest the only extant manuscript should be lost, Alya got him to photograph interim versions as well, and even raw drafts of novels, just as they looked when I stopped work on them or was forced to discontinue. (This need to make duplicates at successive stages put a massive additional burden on our conspiracy.)

In August 1973, when I was steeling myself for the final battle, I was anxious to send a filmed copy of what was then the latest version of *October 1916* out to the West, to be on the safe side. I took the manuscript around to Valeri in person; we had arranged to meet in a dairy store on the block where he lived on one of the various Peschany Streets. I followed him out of the shop, keeping my distance, and not until we came to a little public garden surrounded by apartment blocks did we greet each other. It was broad daylight, there were no benches to sit on, so we kept walking around. I already had a mental picture of how the successive stages of my attack would unfold day by day, and knowing Valeri's passionate loathing of *them*, I thought I would cheer him up by telling him a little about what was in store. He smiled as I spoke, but it was a joyless look, lost and regretful like the smile with which he had first greeted me in the dairy store. He was pleased at the ferocity of my impending onslaught, but felt only sadness at the thought that *they* would win the day once more, while we would once again go under.

In autumn 1973 we were under such intensive surveillance that it became decidedly difficult to get in touch with any of those whom we were anxious to protect. Yet we often needed to have manuscripts made into film right there and then. So I fell back on my own resources, buying equipment to replace what had been lost over the years and setting about making my own copies behind the perpetually lowered blinds of our Moscow apartment in Kozitsky Lane. (Sasha Gorlov put his awesome dexterity to work in adapting an unwieldy Soviet-made photo-reproduction stand specially for our purposes.) These were menacing weeks for us, and then in the midst of it all Valeri suddenly dropped by to see Alya, unannounced and uninvited, blithely ignoring the fact that the KGB was almost certainly photographing callers from the building opposite our front door. There was some filming waiting to be done, so he took it and returned it through an intermediary a couple of days later. However, a few days after that I discovered that an important section was missing. Could it have been dropped somewhere? Or mislaid? Or even seized? It was around midnight when we discovered the loss, and I seem to remember that it was due to be sent off the very next day. Alya and I went out "for a walk," and by the time we called Valeri from a telephone booth, it was almost one o'clock in the morning. (An added difficulty, as I recall, was that Valeri's wife could not abide hearing unidentified female voices on the phone, so Alya had to say who she was.) Valeri was embarrassed to hear of the loss. There was a pause while he searched for the missing section, then he announced with a jovial laugh, "Yes, it was tucked away in the back of the drawer." Thank Heavens for that! The next day he brought it around in person. And bear in mind that this was at the time of our greatest danger, the final days before my deportation.

Being such a frequent visitor, Valeri did not get away scot-free. You have to take care when passing a working X-ray machine or the repeated exposure will give you radiation sickness before you can feel a thing; it was the same with being around us. After we had been expelled from the country, letters from friends reached us by devious means, and we learned that they had started badgering Valeri. The institute of physics where he worked was a classified establishment and boasted a "director of discipline"; Valeri was summoned to see him and threatened with dismissal. Then in September 1974 they hauled him in to the Lubyanka and grilled him about the nature of his contact with us; they knew all about our meeting in the dairy store and even offered to show it to him on film. Valeri admitted to having helped us but refused to identify what exactly he had photographed. They tried intimidation: "Seems very quiet in here, doesn't it? But that doesn't mean people don't get shot." Still, that seemed to be as far as it went, for the time being.

I can still see the sad desperation of that smile, still recall his constant foreboding that any resistance we offered *them* was futile—a presentiment that Q shared to some extent.

And I can only thank the Lord that in the year and a half since my deportation our friends have as yet experienced so little in the way of harassment and victimization, that we have managed to destroy so much potentially incriminating evidence, and that many individuals have been able to establish a more secure position. I don't know what it was that kept our whole circle of friends and helpers going throughout those perilous months. We had nothing but our prayers to sustain us. But as time goes by, the past recedes ever further and becomes less and less relevant to the immediate practicalities of the struggle. New irritants come along, such as the speeches I gave in Europe and America; new fields of battle open up, and enthusiasm for digging up the old ones starts to wane.

––––––––

My working partnership with Alya had barely begun before it was brought home to us how much we needed to establish a new and permanent "channel" of our own to the West. Eva's route worked intermittently and essentially by improvisation. And in 1968, after we had sent out *Gulag*, she refused to pass on the microfilm of a book by Dmitri Panin,* which he had intended for the pope (at one fell swoop, it was supposed to "change the thinking and direction" of the whole of the West and the world at large). Eva sensed that this was something alien to us, and I, too, had no confidence in it, but still I felt duty-bound to help out an old friend and fellow zek. Just in time I made the acquaintance of the charming Father Aleksandr Men. Knowing that he had connections with the

West, I asked him whether he would help. He agreed readily and with great assurance: "Yes, of course, *my channel* is still working smoothly." (How I envied him! Here was a man with his own channel to the West. If only we had one, too!) He took the film from me—and was as good as his word.

Only when we got to know him more closely did we discover how the mechanics of this transmission had operated. Father Aleksandr was the spiritual leader of a faction that, though still small, was seeking its path within the Soviet-dominated Russian Orthodox church. He conducted unofficial seminars and was mentor to a group of young people. (This initiative gave rise to a collection of essays that appeared in the émigré journal *Vestnik*, number 97, as well as to subsequent publications.) On the organizational side his right-hand man was Evgeni Barabanov, a man with an endless flow of schemes and projects (the most successful was the channeling of samizdat into the Paris-based *Vestnik*).* We met—and formed our own direct link in the network—at Father Aleksandr's home, where we arranged for consignments to be sent out using their route. After that, to minimize the risk to their channel to the West and to the group as a whole, I not only met them extremely rarely—no more than three times in four years—but Alya saw little of them as well. Once again we had to protect the link by putting another factor into the equation, and that meant finding another intermediary who could meet Alya and Barabanov without drawing attention.

The person Alya chose to fulfill this role was one of her friends and the godfather of her eldest son, Dima Borisov. He was a pleasant, shy young man with curly black hair and glasses, a discerning poetry lover, expert on Russian songs, and no mean singer himself. He seemed to have trouble applying himself consistently to his work and was somewhat disorganized. When we got to know him, Dima was a graduate student at the history institute, writing a dissertation (suitably camouflaged with sociological terminology, of course) on the history of the Russian church in the eighteenth century. It was a miracle that he had been accepted to do research, a miracle that a topic such as his had been approved, and a miracle if he should ever be allowed to defend his dissertation (ultimately, the miracle would fall apart). He had been born into the family of a prominent Soviet official but had rejected his father's convictions and chosen his own path, to his father's alarm and consternation. Dima Borisov was a man of considerable and steadily developing erudition: his essays in *From Under the Rubble* (as well as his "Rumor and Controversy" in the samizdat collection *Russian Responses to "August 1914"*)* were just a foretaste of what might lie ahead. It goes without saying that he should not have been spending his time ferrying illicit packages around (or coping with the pressures of poverty and unemployment, for that matter), but Russia's vitality had been so sapped over the last sixty years and our casualties had been so heavy that we did not even have the manpower for such basic cloak-and-dagger work. Dima Borisov was in general a mild, pensive, contemplative person, but he had his trials of strength with the KGB (first in the spring of 1973 when they pulled him in for interrogation, then came the last days of the campaign against me, the shattering moment of arrest, Alya's six weeks of getting everything together, the operation to smuggle my archives out to safety after me, and the threats he faced in 1974 after we had gone). And from the outset, he displayed such firmness, indeed such unexpectedly vigorous retaliation, that to this very day they cannot bring themselves to seize him or go on pushing him around.

Dima Borisov became an intimate family friend; he was best man at my wedding and godfather to my son Stephan, while Alya is godmother to one of his daughters and I am godfather to the other.

The chain led from Dima through Evgeni Barabanov to an unknown contact in the French embassy, to whom we provisionally gave the male name Vasya (only to discover belatedly from Barabanov's hints that "Vasya" was a she—and a nun to boot!), and for three years it worked without a hitch, starting in 1971 when we sent the typescript of *August 1914* out to the YMCA Press in Paris. This was our main, permanently open channel to the West. The KGB never got wind of it, and nobody else in the embassy knew of its existence. (In September 1973, when Barabanov was under surveillance and had put himself in danger, he promptly made an outspoken statement to a foreign correspondent in our apartment, openly admitting that he had sent things to the West. In the process he was all set to mention that works of mine had been involved— what was there to lose? But I restrained him: let's bide our time and keep that under our hat for now. And I think it was pretty sound advice. After I was deported, they were hardly likely to forgive and forget. As it was, he survived unscathed.

———

It was only when we were in the West that we began to piece together the details about this legendary "Vasya," and in the spring of 1975 we finally met her in Paris. She was a Catholic nun, that much was true, but not the delicate angel I had envisaged. The woman who walked into our hotel room could have come straight from a Russian village; she was plump and kindly and would clearly have made a splendid housewife (one could just picture her dishing up pies and pickles to a houseful of guests). And her Russian pronunciation was not only perfectly preserved, which is rare enough among émigrés, but marvelously rich and fruity. Speech like that has been obliterated in the Soviet Union. There, too, it is a lost art.

It had been her constant dream to live in Russia.

Asya, whose full name was Anastasia Borisovna Durova, was born in 1908. Her family had been scattered by the civil war. Asya and her mother were living near Dzhugba on the Black Sea, but her father was missing. Then one day when the Whites were occupying Dzhugba, they happened to look in a newspaper, and there was his name: he held a prominent post in the government of Arkhangelsk.

When Arkhangelsk fell to the Bolsheviks, her father emigrated to Paris and from there managed to rustle up visas for his family to join him. This was at the end of 1919, shortly before the nightmarish evacuation of Novorossiisk. Her father had founded the Russian Lycée in Paris, together with a number of fellow officers. (After all—the perpetual delusion of the émigré!—we'll be going back any moment now, so we must make sure the children are brought up as Russians. The school survived until 1962.) That was how Asya was brought up, raring to get back to Russia, though her grandmother in Leningrad sent warnings by roundabout routes: "Stop dreaming about Russia—it's ravaged by man and forsaken by God." When she left school, Asya entered a religious college and converted to Catholicism. Her former aspirations stayed with her but in modified form; now Catholicism was to be the means of saving Russia. After graduating, she was also certified to teach Russian. The second, postwar wave of émigrés came flooding in, bringing a vivid taste of the real Russia; this, followed by the voluntary repatriation to the Soviet Union of sections of the first emigration, made her even more impatient to return.

In 1959 she visited the Soviet Union as a tourist and set foot on the soil of the Luga district, the place of her birth. In 1962 she traveled to Moscow to work as a translator at the French exhibition in Sokolniki Park. Then, in spring 1964 the new ambassador, Baudet, left for the Soviet Union. He had lost his wife not long before, and now he would need a housekeeper to run his Moscow residence, ideally someone who was unmarried, with no relatives in the Soviet Union (an ambassador must not be exposed to inducement or reproach), yet someone with an impeccable command of both French and Russian and excellent domestic skills. It was an improbable combination of specifications, but Asya Durova fitted them to a T. She was vigorous, spirited, quick-witted, and at the same time she had that warmheartedness and breadth of vision so often found in Russian and Ukrainian women. She quickly got the hang of Soviet conditions, dealing firmly with bureaucrats and tradespeople while managing to stay on good terms with them and coping with the erratic supply of household provisions. So indispensable did she become that subsequent ambassadors were glad to keep her on. She merged so effortlessly into the Soviet way of life that she could evade the clutches of the KGB without turning a hair ("We could meet in the Hotel Evropeiskaya, if you like?" "Do you fancy coming out to my dacha on the Gulf of Finland?"). So effortlessly, indeed, that she soon fell in with some of the incipient "dissidents" of the day (the term was not yet in use, and they were not singled out as such). Soon she was going to some of their homes, and in 1966, she visited Barabanov after they had been introduced by a French student, Jacqueline Grünewald; later she attended his wedding and was godmother to his children. Gradually she became more and more involved — Russian dissidents always have something that needs "passing on," so she passed things on (including works by Sinyavksy and Daniel, in which Hélène Zamoïska was also implicated); then that same Jacqueline Grünewald and another student from Paris, called Anya Kishilova, put her in touch with Nikita Struve at the YMCA Press (see Chapter Twelve). Over the years, that special combination of practical efficiency, resourcefulness, common sense, audacity, and disarming, good-natured simplicity that Asya Durova embodied allowed her to keep open a channel to the West that was used intensively and may well have been the principal illicit outlet from the Soviet Union at the time. Without so much as the benefit of diplomatic immunity, she achieved things that well-protected (but career-minded) diplomats would never have risked. Her usual method was not to use diplomats but to send things with various casual acquaintances—people she had known in Paris in the old days, fellow students, and the like—usually without telling them that they would be carrying anything incriminating: "It's always easier to get people to take something innocuous." She had a "kind of hunch" about who could be trusted and who could not, and this intuition never let her down. And so, from autumn 1968, when Dmitri Panin's microfilm was first sent out, we, too, became hooked up with her via several other links in the chain. In February 1971 she agreed to take a manuscript of *August 1914* from us, even though nothing had been planned or decided. But she happened to know a French policeman who was going back to Paris, so Asya, the efficient housekeeper, who (as everyone knew) was forever preoccupied with flowers and pies and cakes, asked him if he would mind taking out *a big box of candy for a sick nun*. No doubts troubled the gallant policeman's mind as he took the gift, and no inhibitions prevented him from bringing it through successfully. That was how *August 1914* reached the West.

In May 1971 Asya used another chance traveler (but this time one who knew what she was carrying) to bring out the crucial consignment: my "safety deposit," the set of microfilms that would at last leave my hands free. The courier was met at Orly Airport by Nikita Struve and his family, who took her off to a café for a cup of tea and a family reunion, leaving their various bags on the floor beside them so that he could "accidentally" pick up the wrong bag when he left. (His children were nervous: a lady at a nearby table was watching them all with more-than-usual attentiveness.)

But that was nothing compared with another completely improbable scheme that Asya came up with and actually carried through. This was the September 1970 meeting in Warsaw between Evgeni Barabanov (a member of a "delegation of Soviet decorative artists") and Nikita Struve (a tourist from Paris). The Warsaw encounter transformed Struve's *Vestnik RKhD* (*Herald of the Russian Student Christian Movement*) into a thicker, more ambitious journal, with contributions from authors living in the Soviet Union. (In fact, their involvement was already under way, and the meeting was not sufficiently necessary to warrant the risk, but what a plan to think up! It entailed intricate prearranged phone calls to Paris and Warsaw, all of which were child's play to Asya.)

She recalls these events nowadays without a hint of pride, as unaffectedly as if she were discussing a particularly successful cake that we finished off last week.

Not for the first time do we see how the spurned children of Russia are drawn back to her bosom. When Asya Durova finished working at the French embassy in Moscow, she could no longer settle down in the West, but kept coming back for long stays at the embassy, since her younger sister and her nieces were employed there. Asya came not to work but simply to live there again.

12

Three Pillars of Support

Yet for all the thunder and daring of my overt attacks on the authorities, in reality my opposition lacked any effective underpinning. Any night they chose—or any day, for that matter—the KGB could have simultaneously raided my home and those of a few people close to me, sweeping away much, if not all, that I had written, collected, and constructed over the years and dragging it off to their lair. Time and time again, from the 1920s through to the 1970s, my predecessors, my elder brothers-in-arms, many of them nameless, had seen everything vanish into oblivion, swept away once and for all into those gaping jaws. I have already written elsewhere that an entire national literature perished in the Gulag, and not just in the hearts and minds of convicted writers but earlier still, during the searches that accompanied their arrest. But I, who bore the accumulated experience of the labor camps within me, did not dare to leave myself exposed in this way. And the various hiding places I set up in Moscow with the aid of my Invisible Allies did not amount to real security either. I needed to have all my manuscripts in safekeeping in the West and someone there to back me up, someone capable of ensuring that, come what may, my books would see the light of day in the event that Alya and I should perish.

In order to achieve this, I would clearly need first of all to have a permanent Russian publisher in the West (as well as a permanent line of communications with him). Next, I had to have an official representative (a lawyer, perhaps?) who could take legal steps to ward off the KGB's various dirty tricks, such as the practice—demonstrated more than once by our old friend Victor Louis—by which the Soviet authorities would tout in the West the confiscated manuscripts of authors whom they had actually banned at home.* (Again, I would need to have a permanent channel to such a lawyer.) But even more important was to have someone who was utterly trustworthy and had an inside knowledge of our affairs, someone with a good understanding both of me and of Soviet conditions yet who lived beyond the reach of the secret police—someone, in short, who could skillfully manage everything that we smuggled out to the West. That meant three points of support. And they would need to be interconnected—a rigid triangular structure.

The choice of a publisher was obvious enough—Nikita Alekseyevich Struve. (On the other hand, we had only a hazy picture of the nature and organization of the publishing house he represented, the Paris-based YMCA Press.) In fact, even Struve himself was still a complete stranger to me. Barabanov and Durova put us in touch with one another, and it was from Barabanov that I gleaned my first impressions of Struve. He was the grandson of that historic figure, Pyotr Berngardovich Struve, and the nephew of the well-known literary scholar Gleb Petrovich Struve, from whose book I had once pieced together my first impressions of the scale and substance of Russian émigré literature.* Barabanov's connection with Nikita Struve was of long standing, dating back to about 1966. In letters from Struve that reached Barabanov by surreptitious means, there were confessions such as the following: "We [that is, émigrés, and especially those descended from émigrés] are disembodied Russians." "Russia [for us] is scarcely a fact at all, but an idea . . . and that is why it is even more important for us to believe in Russia, against the evidence of facts and outward appearances, than it was at the time of Tyutchev.* We believe that Russia is marked out as God's elect: it is the only great country in which the Orthodox religion survives, and Orthodoxy embodies truth and life in all their fullness. . . . The link between Russia and Orthodoxy is for us one of the supreme values of God incarnate." (Ever since my youth I had been extremely interested in imaginatively recreating the whole émigré worldview. But here were everyday concerns that had not occurred to me in those days: "We make superhuman efforts to keep our children Russian, illogical and disadvantageous as this may be, and, in so doing, condemn them to the agonies of moral uncertainty, as this monstrous form of upbringing tears them away from the very environment in which they live." I would come to grasp the truth of these words a dozen or so years later, when I myself was living abroad with my sons.) Subsequently, Nikita wrote to me in Moscow, saying, "Being an émigré is the most difficult skill to master."

And in the years that lay ahead, this man, with his cherished hopes and spiritual reliance upon a Russia that might not even exist ("Nowadays it is hard to imagine how cut off we were up to the 1960s"), was destined to achieve no mean spiritual feat, to create for that same Russia something that certainly did not exist there: a religious and literary journal that would be eagerly awaited and widely read in Moscow and that would help Russia's scattered intellectual forces to regroup. Publishing such a journal without living in the country for which it was intended and without being able to rely on the open mail for receiving manuscripts and readers' responses or sending out subscribers' copies was an unusual and daring enterprise, fraught with difficulties. But Nikita Struve managed it; beginning in 1969 he succeeded in transforming the hitherto slim émigré journal, *Vestnik RSKhD,** into a spiritual bridge that linked the worlds of émigré and metropolitan Russia and grew in strength with each successive issue.

It was even earlier than this, probably in autumn 1967, that the Kopelevs first introduced me to Liza Markstein. The meeting took place in the Chukovskys' town apartment, whose ceilings we had not yet come to suspect of being bugged. Liza's name had long been familiar to me; her father had been the head of the Austrian Communist Party, no less, and though Austrian by birth, she had spent the whole of her youth living in the Soviet Union. When she left to go back to Austria, she continued to make frequent trips to Russia (visas were no problem for her), and as a result she combined an intimate knowledge of both languages, both cultures (a great asset when she later came to translate *Gulag!*), and she had ample firsthand experience of both the Western and the Soviet ways of life. Furthermore, she was quick on the uptake and thoroughly straightforward, with a fervent, eager heart. Liza was predestined to play a special role as an intermediary between these two worlds. We liked each other from the moment we were introduced; she is businesslike, takes a forthright, precise view of things, and gives clear judgments without beating around the bush. However, on that occasion no practical proposals were put forth.

A few months later Lyusha passed on to Liza my corrections to *Cancer Ward*, which were not very extensive, and Liza took them out to the West by interspersing in her own handwriting fragments of lines from my book with the notes on Russian syntax she was making. (These corrections were delivered to the publishers, and later they would have an unexpected role to play as evidence in the litigation surrounding *Cancer Ward*. Which publishing house had the authentic text? The one that had received the author's corrections. It is so difficult, when you make a move in one world, to anticipate all its possible consequences in the other. Later Liza was even subpoenaed as a witness in a case between two publishers, but she appeared anonymously for fear that her links with us might come to light.)

In May 1968, while we were hard at work typing out *Gulag Archipelago* at Rozhdestvo, I was given a letter that Liza had sent from Paris by circuitous means to her friend in Moscow, Naya Mirovaya (Lazareva). In it she spoke of how much it hurt her to see my books helplessly exposed to the machinations of scoundrels or impostors in the West and of her readiness to protect my interests unstintingly if I would give her power of attorney.

Slowly but surely the idea began to take shape. That autumn Liza took the bold step of turning up at my little dacha at Rozhdestvo, where I was in the process of burning the autumn leaves. We sat down by the bonfire—it was hard to believe; we had only just been finishing off *Gulag*, and now here was a visitor from abroad, a sincere and intelligent well-wisher who was prepared to set the wheels in motion! Another year passed and I started telling Alya about a certain splendid woman called Liza, but it turned out that Alya had already known her for some years. I do not know whether the world was becoming so small a place or Moscow society so narrow, but Alya had been introduced to Liza, newly arrived from Austria in order to find out about the dissident movement in Moscow and how she might help. (Since the Bolshevik coup, the world has seen a 180-degree turn in the way people think and feel, but how much longer will it take for this change to find a more tangible realization?)

So we were already preparing to forge a link. During one of Liza's next uneventful visits to Moscow, Alya negotiated with her on my behalf about having her act for us in Western Europe; they were just two women strolling innocuously down Prechistensky

Boulevard, a street they knew well, two women trained to keep their eyes peeled and not miss a thing, speaking only Russian so that nothing should jar on the ears of passersby—what could be more natural?

In September 1969 I met Liza at Alya's apartment on Vasilyevsky Street. She had brought with her the printed text of a German legal agreement granting power of attorney, and she advised me to engage a lawyer in the West. In fact, she could recommend a good Swiss lawyer, Dr. Fritz Heeb, in whose name I might wish to make out a basic authorization, empowering him to handle my affairs. We were not aware of a single rival candidate in any other country, so we welcomed Liza's recommendation as a godsend. I reasoned that having my own lawyer in the West was a forceful move and one that would take the authorities completely by surprise. Nor was it actually illegal as far as we knew. Alya and I agreed at once, and it seemed embarrassing even to inquire any further about this Dr. Heeb.

At the beginning of 1970 Liza returned, bringing a final, comprehensive version of Dr. Heeb's power of attorney; once again I signed—eagerly, in fact, as I thought I had found the ideal way of directing and resolving the fate of my books abroad. At that stage they were not searching Liza at customs, but just to be on the safe side, Katya Svetlova, Alya's mother, made a fine job of sealing the document inside the lid of a cardboard candy box.

Liza ("Betta" was our nickname for her, from her German name Elisabeth), Fritz Heeb ("Yura," a Russian name sounding like the word for "jurist"), and Nikita Struve (we turned Nikita into Nikolai, then into its short form "Kolya")—together they formed the Western triangle we had longed for. Now all my illicit correspondence was passed to or from these three points (Betta in Vienna would receive from Heeb in Zurich a photocopy of my letter to him, or else she would get directly from me a smuggled letter intended for Heeb, which she would then translate for him, sometimes in writing but as far as possible over the phone.)

As a diversionary tactic, I also exchanged letters with Heeb through the regular mail—a superficial, fairly vacuous correspondence, with him writing in German and me replying in Russian. (The letters were generally sent by registered mail, and they did get through; the KGB did not stop them—perhaps in order to keep tabs on me?) Sometimes I would use this open correspondence to divert the secret police's attention from my true intentions or to warn them about something I would fight tooth and nail for, and I would allow myself the occasional joke at their expense. When they failed to deliver a package of Western newspaper reviews of *August 1914* that Heeb had sent me, I wrote telling him that I had not been angry, for it had been done with my best interests at heart. Abusive reviews would have left me feeling dejected, while rave reviews would have turned my head; either would have slowed down the pace of my work, and I would not have managed to get my new book into print before the Soviet Union acceded to the Copyright Convention, a development that would have meant long delays.* But when the Soviet authorities committed flagrant violations affecting the course of my divorce proceedings, I told Heeb about them, too, as an example of the paradoxical Soviet way of things, and these letters *were* seized, for fear of adverse publicity.

Eventually they became suspicious of Betta and started refusing her an entrance visa. The last time I saw her was in autumn 1970, while Alya met her again a year after that (through the agency of Dima Borisov). That marked the end of Liza's trips to the Soviet Union and of our open discussions with her. All our advice, requests, plans, proposals, and decisions vanished below the surface into our underground correspondence. In emergencies Betta would contrive to pass information and inquiries to us disguised as innocuous messages in ordinary letters or phone calls to the Lazarevs.

It goes without saying that we burned our end of the correspondence, but Liza and Nikita preserved it intact, and now I have those letters in front of me. They vividly recall a situation that was already beginning to fade from my mind.

From autumn 1970, as soon as I had completed *August 1914*, my mind was made up: I would send it to Struve at the YMCA Press and have it published openly, under my own name, but keeping everything under wraps until the very moment it came out. In early spring of 1971 back came the reply, saying that the typesetting was already under way in secret and that he and his wife were correcting the proofs. (It was a new experience for them, too, to be working directly with a writer from Russia like this. On a previous occasion, when they had managed to get hold of a text of Bulgakov's *Heart of a Dog*, they were delighted with it and wanted to publish it come what may, but then the publishing house heard that Bulgakov's widow was threatening to sue them and they had to think long and hard before going ahead.) We were able to get some additional items to them—a map, then a sketch for the cover design, and eventually the afterword, in which I appealed to émigrés to send me historical materials. Our limited ability to consult and coordinate led to a major blunder over the use of italics in the text: unfamiliar as we were with publishing practice, we had used block capitals to indicate italicized words; the YMCA Press went ahead and printed them in capitals, which looked pretentious and affected, and this annoying gaffe would go on to be repeated in the foreign translations as well. When the book reached us in Moscow we started checking the text and found that there were still a fair number of typographical errors, and even by the time of the second edition they still had not been corrected. In writing to Nikita about this, my tone is decidedly constrained: "The edition seems to fall rather short of the ideal."

Durova's channel to the West was working splendidly at this stage, and by spring 1971 I was already sending important consignments to Heeb, via Nikita (*Gulag* was going out for the second time): "This means more than the fate of any individual; treat it with the utmost caution and circumspection." In my letters I try to teach him the tricks of the conspirator's trade, Soviet style; go to Heeb's in person but be sure to have someone with you so that the bags are never left unsupervised for so much as a moment, and you must go *before* the publication of *August 1914*, in case they start tailing you then. And another warning: if any new staff are taken on at YMCA Press after the appearance of *August 1914*, don't trust them, however naturally they may behave. In the West, of course, such admonitions sound ludicrous, for who there has experienced what it is like when the KGB gets its claws into you?

After his meeting with Heeb, Nikita shared his reactions with me: "He made a favorable impression on me, although he is rather stunned by how complicated everything is." Being unfamiliar at the time with Nikita's exceedingly tactful manner of speech, I attached no significance to the latter part of the sentence and took it by and large as an endorsement of Heeb. (In fact, Nikita intended to suggest that Heeb might not be up to the task.)

The channel to the West was working splendidly—and my appetite grew. I asked them to send me various émigré memoirs of the revolution, if they would get through. (And Nikita sent me the invaluable memoirs of V. F. Klementyev.)[1] I ordered a copy of Gurko's memoirs in German, and it arrived, too, as did books by Melgunov* and others. (Here they were, the books I wanted, crying out to be read, but how could I squeeze them into a life already filled to the bursting point?) In March 1972 Nikita acted as the intermediary when I sent abroad a microfilm of Teush's study of the destinies of the Jewish people, intended for Zilberberg.* (But there was a long silence before Zilberberg acknowledged its receipt; meanwhile, Teush was growing anxious, so we sent a second roll of film out by the same route.) The collection *Russian Responses to "August 1914"* was smuggled out for publication by YMCA Press, as well as my "Lenten Letter to Patriarch Pimen." (The furor it

---

[1] Captain Klementyev duly figures in *March 1917*, under his own name and with his own biography. (1986 note)

aroused in émigré religious circles is reflected in the pages of *Vestnik*.) I sent Nikita my "safety deposit," the cherished set of microfilmed manuscripts, for his next meeting with Heeb. I sent the authentic text of *Cancer Ward* (not realizing at the time that this same YMCA Press—that is, Nikita and a group of French translators—had three years earlier published a French version of *Cancer Ward* on their own initiative, using a stray samizdat copy in which my characteristic lexical innovations had been "emended" and rendered "more literate"). Another letter warned him in advance: we are planning a series of pamphlets under the title "Contemporary Russian Thought" (the germ that would eventually yield the collection *From Under the Rubble*)—let's print that, too! (I mentioned it more than once, but the series failed to get off the ground; there was no time to organize it.) Elsewhere I insisted on preserving the peculiarities of my own grammatical rules. I even went so far as to think that the non-Russian editions of *The Red Wheel* ought to be abridged. (It was a sound idea but one that was never put into practice.)

The correspondence shows me arguing with Struve, too. The collection of essays published in number 97 of *Vestnik* aroused my indignation, as did the subsequent essay by "Telegin" in issue number 103: they were an insult to Russia but were not accompanied by any editorial comment or disclaimer. The distorted view from Paris was to blame; they could not see the unrestrained outbreak of irresponsible anti-Russian feeling that had flared up in samizdat, and they failed to appreciate the danger of the movement splitting in two. In a heated letter I tried to explain this to Nikita, and I sent him the draft of an essay I was writing in response—not for publication but for his eyes only. But he replied, quite unruffled, "There was a good deal in these essays that was not to my liking, but I saw them as a reasonably literate first attempt to make sense of the recent past. Their infatuation with the West is due to their youth and inexperience. I do not regret letting them have their say."

In our surreptitious correspondence, spurred on by the forces of oppression, we did, nevertheless, find time for an occasional exchange of views on other topics. In one letter, for instance, I react bitterly to Bunin's *Dark Avenues*,* and Nikita heartily concurs. In another, he tells me about a ludicrous essay by the émigré writer Nikolai Ulyanov,* printed in the newspaper *Novoe russkoe slovo*: Ulyanov argues that there is no such person as Solzhenitsyn and never has been; he was dreamed up by the KGB and composed through a team effort, for no single author could have such a thorough grasp of science, medicine, military affairs, as well as politics and history. Struve sent the paper a blistering reply. In one passage, I shared with him my admiration for the sermons broadcast over Radio Liberty by a certain "Father Aleksandr." This turned out to be Father Aleksandr Shmeman, and Struve sent him a copy of my enthusiastic letter. (Somehow it later found its way to that same *Novoe russkoe slovo*, which was tactless enough to print it.)

But while my correspondence with Nikita was still perfectly calm, my frenetic exchanges with Betta were a whirlwind of a very different order. Here I am, driving, pushing, spurring her on with messages written on cigarette paper in minute handwriting. Much as I longed to sit and work quietly at the "knots" of my *Red Wheel*, I had built up too great a head of steam in the recent struggle. Take the film of my *Tanks Know the Truth*. To my mind it would deal a crippling blow to communism, and I could picture the prison-camp uprising being enacted on cinema screens the whole world over! From the beginning of 1971 I asked our people to start negotiating with film directors and preparing for shooting — this was bound to be a drawn-out procedure. We needed to find a director who would not be afraid to bring out the full political impact of the film—who had an understanding of Russian themes and a feeling for Russian character types—someone who would not turn the film into a tawdry Hollywood epic. . . . (But how were we to find someone who fit the bill? Negotiations did get under way, but for three whole years little progress was made. Of course, Betta already had too much on her plate without getting involved in yet another sideline, while Heeb did not understand the first thing about such matters; directors were proving hard to find, or else their leftist sympathies made them afraid of being associated with an anti-Communist film, afraid of boos and catcalls from the left.) Counterproposals arrived from Betta: they wanted to dramatize *Cancer Ward* for German television, and she asked whether she should give approval. Yes! And she herself suggested preparing a television production based on *August 1914*. All right, why not? Let's hit them from all sides!

Then I began to cool toward the production of *Tanks*, and I asked Betta to take her time over the negotiations: "Let's leave 1972 nice and quiet. I want to write *October 1916* and make a start on *March 1917*." And in 1972: "A feeling of lightness and freedom that I haven't known for a long time. To spend both 1972 and 1973 working, never stirring from my desk. . . . Just to work on the novel, nothing but the novel, without troubling my head about the public arena"—the writer in me was asserting himself, and that was a healthy sign. And anyway, over in America the Carlisles had had the translation of *Gulag* well in hand ever since 1968 (or so we thought), and by summer 1971 my duplicate microfilms of *Gulag* were with Heeb, while by February 1972 Betta had started translating the German version, too. So let the translations do their work, silently undermining the Ogre's magic mountain! Meanwhile, I shall feel free to get on with my writing.

And here was something new: during my sleepless nights I picked up a series of programs on the history of the revolution, broadcast over Radio Liberty at 2:30 in the morning. I listened avidly, as best I could through the interference. It seemed as if a huge amount of my work had been done for me quite unexpectedly—a whole team of assistants beavering away, collecting materials, conducting interviews! But what would be the most reliable way of utilizing all this? I wrote to Betta: Let's call it "Operation

Two-thirty" and start looking for a go-between who can get hold of these materials and send them on to me. In addition, I asked, What are the chances of having the contemporary European press responses to the February Revolution copied out for me? The idea of having chapters consisting entirely of newspaper cuttings was taking shape even then. And Betta agreed to take it on (her husband would do the research).

Now, with my supporting triangle in place and all my microfilms safely in Zurich (it was a long time before I stopped worrying—don't keep them in your office, they'll raid it, put them in a safe in the bank, put them in the vault!—and at long last we received confirmation: Yes, that's exactly where they are!), all that remained was to work out an effective defensive strategy based on my will. In February 1972 in our Moscow apartment Heinrich Böll had earned my undying gratitude by signing and witnessing every page of my will and taking it away with him in his pocket—hence the feeling of lightness I experienced at that time. Böll was on excellent terms with Liza, and by now my will was safely in the hands of friends! (And who is Böll, if not another of my Invisible Allies? As early as 1965, the most precarious of times for me, he had brought my film scenario and long poem home from Moscow and looked after them for years before handing them over to Liza. Yet who can foresee the twists and turns of fate? Böll's standing in West Germany would subsequently deteriorate—he had, after all, described the young terrorists, the future Baader-Meinhof gang, as "youthful idealists, driven to the point of despair." It would reach the point where he, living in the free West, now needed me, from the captive world of the Soviet Union, to defend him! I duly sent him a letter of thanks via Liza, with no intention that it should remain private.)

This was no mere will and testament but a vital move in the struggle that lay ahead, an invaluable reinforcement of my defenses, and that is why the spring of 1972 brought such a sensation of lightness. Just try and touch me now! From now I know that, even when

Alya and I are no longer here, all *this* will still be published, and book after book will rain down on your heads after I am gone! Now all we had to do was agree in our secret correspondence what pre-determined phrases we should use in the letters I sent openly to Heeb through the regular mail or in an unannounced phone call to Zurich in order to trigger the explosion and set some or all of the plan in motion. (In the same way, we worked out similar phrases and code names for a range of other situations as well; as with everything, their number kept growing.) In the meantime I had not yet sorted out all the details of the will in my own mind; the plan to build a huge Church of the Trinity out in the open fields at Zvenigorod now seemed overambitious. Perhaps it would be better to aim for something more modest, such as restoring the Church of Saint Panteleimon in Kislovodsk where I was baptized, or the church at the cemetery in Georgievsk where my father's grave lies under the foundations of a sports stadium? Or perhaps there might still be enough space to build a little chapel right next to where the Rostov Church of the Kazan Virgin stood until it was torn down? I could thus atone for my unthinking behavior when, as a boy, I used to run wild in its churchyard, playing soccer. And then there were various amendments to the will, and new works to be added to the list for publication—*Victory Celebrations*, now that it has unexpectedly been rescued, and an abridged collection of prison-camp verse, and, of course, *The Oak and the Calf* itself, as far as the "Nobeliana" section, as well as my *R-17 Diary*,* which by now had grown to substantial proportions—let's publish it all, every last thing, and set the Dragon reeling! I drew up the sequence in detail for Betta.

At this point the Soviet Union's imminent accession to the International Copyright Convention cast its shadow over our correspondence. (Not so long before I myself had been urging them to join, but we had all realized belatedly that this was just another device to dupe us with. Alya wrote an article—"A Knife in the Back for Russian Literature"—and sent it anonymously to *Le Monde*,

where it was published in March 1973—the topic was in fashion!)
But all this time Nikita still had not managed to publish the authentic texts of *Ivan Denisovich* and "Matryona's Home" and I kept pushing and pressing him: they had to be out by the day the convention was signed (June 1, 1973), because if I had to fight a copyright battle, it was not worth doing so over these particular texts.

But there was more to it than that: we were already secretly working on *The Quiet Don*, and I anticipated that it would cause a sensation, but how could I best secure in advance the rights of the anonymous author "D★"? Should I leave Heeb out of it? Or should I work through him? (I say first one thing in the letters, then I contradict myself.)

Although I had been around long enough to know perfectly well that in Rome one must do as the Romans do, I still kept on at them in letter after letter, getting more and more worked up about my brainchild: how to make drastic cuts in the retail price of the forthcoming edition of *Gulag*. It is simply appalling! In the West the book will cost ten dollars; that comes to between forty and fifty rubles per volume in real terms! How can I possibly allow such a thing? A volume of *Gulag* should cost a third of that price! No, a fifth! I want *everyone* to read it! Just so long as it makes its impact, just so long as it smashes into the Soviet monster! Let tens of millions read it in the West—and there is nothing more I want from it! "For me it is a profoundly moral issue: *this* is not merchandise for haggling over, but blood shed on a sacrificial altar, blood that must ascend to Heaven. I want to introduce this high-minded view into the world of books and publishing and appeal to the conscience of the publishers themselves." Let the translators, typesetters, and publishing-house staff be paid the normal rate for the job—and let any losses be split between the publisher and the author in proportion to what their share of the profits would have been. "Many publishers will not touch a deal like this, and good riddance to them! But for every language there must be at least one publishing house prin-

cipled enough to agree, and we can make it up to them later by giving them the rights to other books." Betta knew the Soviet Union
and had no trouble understanding this fighting spirit of ours. She
did not object in the slightest. Heeb, on the other hand, did have
objections, albeit rather confused ones, and he subsequently sent
me a vaguely worded report he had composed on the subject.

While this was going on, copies of foreign editions found their
way to us and left us far from elated. What has Luchterhand done to
the German edition of *August 1914*?* Even the title page omits the
words "First Knot" and the dates covered by the action. The film-
scenario sections have been garbled, without the slightest understanding of the principle on which they were supposed to be set
out. They have blurred the arrangement of the proverbs. And even
the map of East Prussia is wrong—in the *German* edition!—with
several locations misplaced by up to fifty miles! How can they be so
lazy, slovenly, negligent? All the work we have done seems to disappear into some callous mincing machine. How are we to prevent
this kind of thing from happening with other editions, and *who* will
find the time to keep an eye on them? Betta can't do everything
single-handed. We are woefully short of helpers!

And the trouble we had with foreign translations! In the Soviet
Union outstanding writers have poured their skill and energy into
translating. In the West, by contrast, literary translation is underpaid,
and good translators tend to work for love, not money. I wrote to
Betta, "It's better to have no translation at all than a botched, lop-
sided, mechanical one!" The English translation of *August 1914* had
taught us a lesson we would not soon forget. Glenny had done a
thoroughly bad translation* for The Bodley Head,[2] and *August* had
been damned with faint praise in England, if not actually panned.
Glenny stooped to justifying himself on the grounds that *August* was

[2] As I learned later in England from a member of Glenny's "team" of translators, he
had divided the text of *August* up into chunks and distributed them to his graduate
students to translate, all working at sixes and sevens. (1978 note)

"so badly" written that in places he had had to "correct phrases," while a representative of the publishers said, "If we translated *August 1914* literally, we would be a laughingstock." Then suddenly—a ray of light! I came across a translation of my "Lake Segden"* in the *Intellectual Digest* of April 1971. I read it and trembled with excitement: this went far beyond any mere translation! It was as if I had written every phrase of it in English myself. How well it captured the rhythm of the whole, its tone and modulations, the sweep and dynamism of every phrase. This was what I needed—not just a translator, but a close and trusted coauthor! I could not find the translator's name on my copy. Off went an urgent letter to Heeb: look for him, find me this translator in a million! (And look he did—for a little less than three years! In 1973 he was still trying to track the translator down in New York. And the answer I got was—no luck, he's moved to Australia and can't be contacted. And this was Harry Willetts, who lived in Oxford and had not the slightest intention of going anywhere! Meanwhile we had wasted three precious years in which he might have been helping us! When I came to the West, I found him.)

All the more crucial would be the translation of *Gulag*. (I did not yet suspect how casually the matter was being treated by the Carlisles and company.) The German version was being translated by Betta herself, and she wrote that she was "devoted to it, heart and soul." Her good understanding of Soviet life was a considerable asset, too. (It was she who suggested using two different ways of highlighting words—italics for specialized terminology and bold print for emphatic expression. I was very taken with this idea, and all through 1973 Alya and I put in many hours of work sorting the relevant words into categories and sending off lists of corrections; this was in addition to the unremitting flow of substantive corrections. And after all that, the other Western editions did not follow suit.) Meanwhile, the search for a French translator was not going smoothly; with such a high degree of secrecy involved, it was hard to know to whom to entrust it. Stepan Tatishchev was lent the first

chapters on trust by the Andreyevs, but the translation did not get
under way. Nikita also tried in vain to find a translator; then, with
his approval, Betta contacted Éditions du Seuil directly. Later still
we would need to get a group of translators together, in order to
speed up the translation of the first volume. I was straining at the
leash: we must start looking for a Spanish translator as well—after
all, there is the whole of Latin America to think of! We decided
that, given the secrecy of *Gulag*, we would adopt the following procedure: first we would find translators for the different editions,
paying them for their finished work out of our own pocket; only
then would we look for a publisher, with the assistance and approval of our translators.

Unforeseen calamities were raining down on us from all sides; no
sooner had we warded off one than the next would be upon us.
First an excerpt from *Prussian Nights* suddenly turned up in *Die
Zeit*,* a paper we had thought of as sympathetic—must get Heeb to
suppress it! Then a piece by Patricia Blake in *Time* magazine, so
dangerous that it threw us into a panic:* it reported that a certain
group of people were working on a translation of *Gulag*. But who
were they? And which copy were they using? There was no way of
finding out and no point in putting pressure on them—the title of
the book was a secret no longer! All this threatened my grand plan
of attack and exposed my flank prematurely. Next came a warning
from Betta herself that Scammell was rumored to be publishing excerpts from my long poem, *The Road*, in the magazine *Index*;* apparently they had been passed on to him by Zilberberg. Now I was
on tenterhooks: someone must have stolen them! And how long are
the excerpts? Nobody had ever had a copy of the poem except for
Teush. Sound the alarm! Get it stopped! And the nervous energy
expended as the letters raced to and fro! The explanation came at
last—these were the same excerpts that Teush had already published
anyway in his "Blagov" essay.* Nothing to be done! Hard on its
heels came another shock in the shape of Feifer's biography.* Now,

a biographer can be a kind of amateur detective; he may have sniffed something out and be on the point of publishing things I have painstakingly hidden from the KGB. What can I do? Try to get an injunction? We don't have any grounds. But perhaps a statement from Heeb would cool their ardor? I wrote to him formally as my lawyer: "I request that you issue a statement directed against unauthorized biographies. I consider it shameless and immoral to reconstruct the biography of a living author without his permission. Such activities are indistinguishable from investigations by the police or private detectives." (Heeb writes back by unofficial channels to tell me that there are no legal grounds for restraining Burg and Feifer, provided they do not defame me; even if the pair of them tells lies about me, without themselves being aware that they are lies, they cannot be held accountable.) Next in line is my "ally" Zhores Medvedev, who shows off to all and sundry by including in his book a copy of a written invitation describing how guests can find their way to our apartment through the back alleys of Bakhrushinsky Street*. I sent an urgent demand that he remove the offending map from his book. And then a rumor went the rounds in Moscow about Natalya Reshetovskaya and how she was collaborating with agents of the Novosti Press Agency: she was writing either her memoirs or a biography about me, generously spiced with quotations from my letters.* She couldn't even wait till I was dead! (She did, in fact, hand over my letters to her for Novosti to publish or sell, beginning with those from my years at the front. In June 1974, immediately after my deportation, the Italian magazine *Tempo* was already printing "The Love Letters of Solzhenitsyn," and they were offered to the *New York Times* as well; after that, an agent, Alain Daveau, offered them for sale in Geneva.)

To add to all this, there was a new scheme afoot. The Nobel Prize meant that we now had money abroad, so how could we fail to help all those who had assisted us so selflessly? They were all short of money and scraping to make ends meet, while hard currency was far

and away the most valuable item in the Soviet order of things. There
was nothing to stop us from making a list, numbering them one,
two, three, and so on—twenty "ciphers" in all (we borrowed the
term from Zamyatin for use in future letters*)—and so, throughout
this period, they figure in a series of tense individual paragraphs in
our secret letters. Betta was sent a copy of the key to the list, giving
names and addresses. For some of them this involved little risk, but
our links with others were so secret that there could be no question
of including their name and address in the same letter. So we sent
those in fragments spread over two or three letters: first the street
name, but omitting the house number, which came separately in another letter; then we would break up the surname and first names
and tack them on somewhere else, with no apparent rhyme or reason. Another chore was to decide which country the money should
be transferred from and above all from *whom*. One of the recipients
had a well-known foreigner for a friend, another had a genuine relative living abroad, and in those cases we could transfer money in
their names. For the rest of them, however, we had to fabricate
senders, and here the KGB might well grow suspicious (as indeed
it sometimes did, with dangerous consequences). Or what if the
money for number eleven should be transferred so promptly that
they ask him from whom he is expecting to receive it before he has
had time to prepare a plausible reply? This was a very ugly situation
indeed, and one such experience was enough to make us send out an
urgent written inquiry (which in turn entailed handing over each
individual note at a secret rendezvous). It was all very fraught: in
every letter a lot of space was taken up by our "ciphers," and there
was no shortage of mix-ups; all the misunderstandings left us utterly
drained, but think what it was like for Betta, who had to disentangle
the whole mess and send Heeb full, unambiguous instructions before he could proceed.

Lidia Chukovskaya was losing her sight, and we had to get hold of
a certain optical appliance. We did not quite know what we were

looking for, and neither did anyone else, except that the lens had to be large enough in diameter to take in a whole page and strong enough to magnify by a factor of between five and seven. (Normal magnifying lenses combine powerful magnification with a tiny diameter, or the other way around.) This one also had to illuminate the page from below. But how were we to find out what type we needed, and where did we order one from? Perhaps from Holland? They are supposed to have experts in this kind of thing there. As for sending it over, we would ask Heinrich Böll, even though it was an imposition. But the correspondence between Moscow, Vienna, Zurich, Cologne, and other unknown locations dragged on interminably, and when at last the appliance came, it was the wrong kind! This meant starting all over again! But in the meantime Lidia's sight was deteriorating catastrophically, and it is hard to imagine eyes more precious than hers. So we sent new, urgent requests and kept piling on the pressure. And at last the right appliance arrived and we were saved! But it took nonstandard lightbulbs, and it arrived without a single spare, so now we had to put in a separate order for bulbs.

Grueling as it was, the various orders were gradually fulfilled until the money for the twentieth and last name on our list finally arrived. Now Alya and I could think of expanding the scheme in a new direction: what if we were to extend the same kind of help to former zeks (an embryonic version of our future Russian Social Fund)? This meant going through the same procedure, extending the list from number twenty-one to number forty, then deciding who would be the nominal sender. New inquiries flew thick and fast.

While all this was going on, the Soviet authorities, stung by one of the articles Betta had published in Austria, finally decided to bar her from entering the Soviet Union. At the beginning of 1973 the Soviet consul in Vienna said, to her face, "Why go to a country you dislike so much? We're not issuing you a visa, and it will be a long time before we do." How much simpler it would have been if we could have met for a talk. We could have cleared up so many loose ends in next to no time! There were a few small consolations, as when Betta's elder daughter came to Moscow instead and met with Alya, or when Eva traveled to Switzerland and met Betta there— but Eva's meetings led to a good deal of confusion.

And so a whole torrent of questions, proposals, and decisions had to be channeled exclusively through our smuggled letters, which then had to wait for a suitable courier to happen by. Sometimes a letter, written and ready to go, would languish in our hands for a couple of months before anyone could take it out, and in the meanwhile things began to look different and we had changed our minds —so scrap it and write a new one!

By now it was hard to remember whether we had already written something or not, and I sometimes repeated myself—after all, we dared not keep copies of our letters, so I would write about the same thing a second time—or, buffeted about by changing circumstances and more up-to-date news, I sometimes changed my mind in the course of a single letter. And Betta, meticulous as ever, extracted our instructions, requests, and corrections from this flurry of letters and entered them by subject into a card index she had set up for the sake of clarity. Then, too, a lot of what we sent came on film, the quality of the exposure varied, and occasionally they were out of focus—don't forget that we were working in secrecy, under constant pressure; sometimes we had to dismantle our equipment in a hurry. We would be sending corrections out on film, while back in Zurich the films with the original text had yet to be transferred to paper. And Betta, inundated with this mass of communications, had to work through it all systematically, making contact with various parts of Europe, spending whole weeks writing letters and making phone calls. ("How I loathe the telephone!" she wrote, and how I share her sentiment!) And this does not take into account what had been her main task ever since February 1972: that of translating the entire first volume of *Gulag* and of doing so in strict secrecy, consulting no one except me and then only through the furtive correspondence I have described. "The hard thing isn't the work itself," she wrote, "so much as the sense of responsibility." She had given herself up heart and soul to *Gulag* and to our clandestine work in general, abandoning herself to it in a way that is quite alien to the Western work ethic: "I am leading a double life. My heart and head are over there with you. Sometimes when I walk down the street, I suddenly wonder where I am." The boundaries between free Vienna and the oppressive world of Moscow became blurred. Her letters on practical matters nevertheless exuded an unfailing warmth and faith in the task I was facing. I wrote back, "Reading your letters, we were struck by the way neither time nor distance seems able to come between us: it is as though we are together, constantly sharing the same thoughts and feelings, and what you decide to do coincides almost 100 percent with the decisions we would have made together. . . . Your spirit is cast in a mold so similar to Alya's and mine." Once when a misunderstanding of a personal nature arose, she telephoned the Lazarevs and left a cryptic message, to which I replied, "I think our love for you and yours for us is something higher than any differences of opinion that might arise between us. Over the years we have drawn such comfort and reassurance from simply knowing that you are there. I will always believe in you, and this gives me peace of mind."

It is inevitable, of course, that people from different worlds will not see eye to eye the whole time; sooner or later the cracks will show. I heard from someone that Betta was "upset" by my August interview with *Le Monde*: there were many points I "had not got right," and the same was true of my essay "On Peace and Violence." With the heated objections of Moscow acquaintances on this very subject still ringing in my ears and with my thoughts on *From Under the Rubble*, which by now was taking shape, I told Betta in one of my letters, "In the very near future, I believe . . . public opinion in the West, both democratic and socialist, will have to face up to some devastating home truths, when voices from Russia declare the most sacred, centuries-old deities to be false idols. . . . And it is my most ardent hope that you will be among the first Europeans capable of receiving this message with sympathy and understanding." A month later we hear from Betta that she is distraught: "It grieves me deeply that people have misinformed you about me. I not only approve of everything you are doing but regard it as a great undertaking; we differ only over trivial points of detail."

By now we were but days away from the catastrophic seizure of *Gulag*. And how could I have had such a clear premonition of it? On August 22, 1973, I wrote to Betta, "This autumn will be especially hard. We may no longer have the leisure to discuss what to do. You may have noticed how for many of us events seem to be raining down thicker and faster than ever before. This is due to some movement of the stars, or as we prefer to think, to God's will. I shall be going into battle much sooner than I thought, many factors are pushing me in that direction, and there's no doubt it will come. We cannot foretell any of what will happen, but it is clear that the day [we shall need *Gulag* to be ready] is closer than we supposed. If it turns out badly, you will have to decide matters without the two of us."

Two weeks later Betta heard about the loss of *Gulag* from news agency reports. Her letter reads, "Life has speeded up in our household, and it's a case of 'Everything for the Front! Everything for Victory!' I just hope I can keep it up without spoiling the quality" (of the translation, that is).

And I collected my wits: "We've been putting this confrontation off for Heaven knows how many years! I should have known things couldn't go on like this any longer." But with this came a feeling of relief. Now we could keep the whole text of *Gulag* at home, we did not have anything to lose, and that made it so much easier to refer to it. On the other hand, I was afraid that Betta's apartment would be targeted for a raid, and I sent her a warning.

During those autumn months of 1973 (though we did not know it, Betta, Nikita, and Heeb met to confer in Zurich that October), our underground connection throbbed more convulsively than ever. I send Betta a parting epigraph to add to *Gulag*: "For years I have with reluctant heart refrained from publishing this already completed book: my obligation to those still living outweighed my obligation to the dead." But now how could we speed up publication? Perhaps we should photocopy the text straight from the typescript? Never mind what the edition looks like, it's speed that counts now! And I told Nikita: It doesn't matter if *Gulag* looks amateurish so long as it sells a bit more cheaply; it is not the kind of book people should have to save up for. (But Nikita, worn out with trying to make ends meet in his impecunious publishing house, implored me to relent; the Russian-language edition could not possibly be priced more cheaply. I accepted this.) He promised to publish the first volume in record time—three months. In one letter he described how the compositor who was setting *Gulag* told him, with tears in his eyes, "When I die, put this book in my coffin with me." But I kept on nagging at him: What about putting out Volume Two straight after the first, say a month later?—No, out of the question . . . YMCA Press can publish it in May.—No, no! March at the absolute latest!—Impossible, they can't commit themselves to maintaining that rate of work twice in a row.—Well, what if we were to break up the volumes into Parts One, Two, Three, and so on and print them as separate fascicles (the volumes are not important for their own sake), just so long as it speeds up the process? And you must take steps to guard the printing house against a direct attack! The KGB will stop at nothing! And I told Betta: Once Volume One of the Russian-language edition comes out, we are pinning our hopes on the German translation appearing as quickly as possible; if it is delayed, perhaps we should pull out individual chapters and print them in periodicals? "Speed is of the essence, make sure *everyone* knows! Only then will this burning pain pass." That autumn—like salt on an open wound—came the news that the Carlisles had let us down: after five years the American translation was still not ready; it had only just been submitted now, at the end of October, and even that was not the final version. "It needs some more work." On the other hand, Hans Björkegren's Swedish translation was hot on its heels—that would help! But what about security precautions? With three printing houses involved now, there could be a leak. If I could get it published without delay, it would be the irrevocable step I needed, a break so complete that the KGB would not even bother trying to get anything out of me by force. Then another (bizarre) scenario had to be dealt with. What if the KGB should get in first and publish their confiscated copy of *Gulag* before me? (After all, they did just that with Alliluyeva's memoirs.*) If they do, we will prove that they are working from a stolen copy and that their text is an incomplete earlier version. I sent Betta a list of evidence. Or perhaps the Soviet authorities would take the opposite tack and try to have *Gulag* banned in the West? At Heeb's request I sent out, through illicit channels, a new Confirmation of Power of Attorney with *Gulag* specifically in mind; in it I reaffirmed that he was empowered to authorize all and any publications of the book and, at the same time, that he was exempt from personal financial liability for them (he feared that events might take such a turn). Now my will and testament was no longer needed, for this was the start of a period of nonstop publication of all my works, as far as was technically possible. But there was something else, too (can't think of everything at once); we no longer needed to conceal the Lenin chapter from *August 1914*. Was there any chance of having it inserted into one of our publications in time? And another thing—now that radio jamming had been lifted, the moment *Gulag* was published we could have it read out by all the overseas broadcasting services simultaneously. (See how I get ahead of myself! Neither Voice of America nor the BBC would lift a finger, lest they sour diplomatic relations with the Soviet Union. . . .) And as for the film of *Tanks*, let's get a note about it in the press the moment the contract is signed. (No such luck! The film is a long way down the road yet. . . .) Let's detonate it all, as fast as we can! I suggest publishing "Live Not by Lies" in February. (My guess is right on the money!)

We sent *October 1916* to Zurich on film—just as I had left it when I broke off work; I wondered if it would ever be finished now. We also had the collection of essays, *From Under the Rubble*, smuggled out in installments.

But even more urgently still, in mid December I sent Nikita my "Letter to the Soviet Leaders," intending it to be published twenty-five days after the appearance of the first volume of *Gulag*! (I must have been out of my mind! I did not realize that I was sawing off the very branch I was sitting on. Once people in the West read the Letter, then they would have no use for *Gulag* either). And let's organize the translations quickly!

The YMCA Press's printers—I did not know who they were—went straight to work on my "Letter to the Soviet Leaders." But on December 28 *Gulag* exploded into the world, and it dawned on me that publication of the Letter must be held up at all costs! Partly this was due to Ugrimov's warning that it would alienate public opinion in the West. But this was not the main reason for my decision; it was more my realization that the Letter would not sound the same now as it had in September, when I delivered it to the Central Committee. Perhaps in the current context people would suspect me of making conciliatory noises. No, with the repercussions of *Gulag* thundering all around, this was not the moment for the Letter. Absolutely not! ("My head feels like lead, I can't get enough sleep!")

At the beginning of January 1974 we wrote to Nikita and Betta telling them they must hold up the Letter indefinitely, prevent any circulation, even to translators, and halt any translations already in progress!

But our letter arrived too late to stop anything. At YMCA Press Nikita had already finished his print run, and the French translation was ready and on its way to the printers. What did stop it was a cryptic phone call we made, using prearranged signals. It worked! There was no leak! (A bull's-eye? Or a blunder? Everything turned upon chance factors, and my physical and mental faculties were so dulled by now that I could not put things in perspective. If we had failed to hold up the Letter, I would most likely have ended up in jail, rather than being deported—no one in the West would have stood up for me then.)

Yet again it was Betta who was having to shoulder the extra burden of all this frantic to-and-fro—and in the very weeks when she had submitted her translation of Volume One of *Gulag* and was trying to get going on the second! What patience and mental agility it must have taken! At the end of January she wrote her last letter, which only caught up with me after I had left the Soviet Union: "Apart from the extraordinary sense of elation, I feel a terrible weariness and a constant nagging worry that something has been overlooked. I wake up every night with the same nightmare: I've forgotten to do something vital! Sometimes I even leap out of bed. . . . I am so glad that the 'Letter to the Leaders' has been postponed: it would have confused people over here terribly and would even have spoiled their understanding of *Gulag*. You have to know Russia to understand the 'Letter.'"

She writes with justifiable pride of how we "managed to keep *Gulag* secret right to the end." But by now she, too, is exhausted; she will share some of the translating of the second and third volumes with a colleague, since there is no longer any need for secrecy. Her translation is praised by Böll and in *Die Zeit* and *Der Spiegel*.

"But still I am sick at heart with worry over you. . . ."

My letter crosses with hers in the mail: "Do I feel that we shall never see each other again? Certainly not! I am convinced that we shall meet again for a lively, leisurely, fascinating chat. How? That is a mystery. There are many miracles and surprises still in store for us. . . . Let the New Year bring us victories! . . . I hate to say goodbye, but just in case . . . lest by any chance . . ."

And on this last letter Alya writes in a vigorous hand, "Today, February 12, at 5 o'clock Sanya was taken away by eight men. At 10 P.M. they telephoned to say that he was under arrest. Press on and keep up the momentum! Let *all* his works be published, one after the other. That is what matters."

———

Liza arrived to see me on my very first day at Böll's house, as did Heeb—a tall, imposing figure with a sense of his own dignity, puffing away at his pipe. Nikita Struve phoned from Paris as well, offering to come to Germany right away, but I could not digest this rush of events, and I invited him to come when I was in Zurich. When we did meet it was in Heeb's house, and there was an immediate warmth between us: he was both the only Russian in my immediate entourage and a man with whom I had an instant understanding and rapport, whatever the topic and despite the fact that he had been an émigré all his life while I had been a Soviet citizen for the whole of mine.

Here, then, was my entire Supporting Triangle gathered together in one room, and we were talking freely instead of through coded letters. Whoever could have foreseen it a little while before? The house was completely surrounded, they were watching it like hawks—but now *they* were journalists, not Chekists.

What this triangle did for me went beyond anything it actually managed to achieve. It was a source of confidence, an unseen wall at my back, and leaning on it, I was able to stand up against the Dragon without a flicker of hesitation or a moment's regret, fully prepared for whatever fate might befall me.

Nikita Alekseyevich stayed on for another two or three days, accompanying me everywhere—not walking but sprinting through the streets of Zurich with a whole pack of journalists and television correspondents in hot pursuit. He was with me when I entered the vaults of the Canton Bank of Zurich, in whose safe all our microfilms were stored; right there and then I handed over my appeal "Live Not by Lies" to Nikita for publication, after learning, to my delight, that Alya had not flinched from publishing it in Moscow. Meanwhile, the journalists staking out the bank leaped to the conclusion (and duly reported) that I had gone there to count my fortune. Nikita was there, too, when I went to see the film of *One Day in the Life of Ivan Denisovich*, and to visit the house where Lenin had lived, and to the Sternenberg hills to see whether it was somewhere I might be able to work, and to vespers in the Benedictine abbey. Nikita turned out to be someone I could talk to in a relaxed and effortless way; by now I was already telling him about *The Oak and the Calf*, and *The Troubled Waters of the Quiet Don* and other works that I hoped to publish in the near future. Nikita Alekseyevich was profoundly interested in all things Russian and followed them closely. This was the start of my long years of close collaboration with him, both as publisher and as friend.

13

The Foreigners

In the main body of *The Oak and the Calf* I stated that everything that went out to the West was sent by me in person. I wrote this to cover the tracks of Eva, Dima Borisov, and Zhenya Barabanov.

In reality, up to 1968 my sole contact with the West was through Eva: it was she who determined what was possible and how to do it, and I never had to give such matters a moment's thought. After that, the channel set up by Barabanov and Durova was in operation, and again we had a dependable means of sending out manuscripts and exchanging letters with our allies Nikita Struve and Betta. When our appetite grew and we started wanting to receive books from the

West, again it was Eva who tracked down Axel and Jacqueline Krauze. He was an American businessman who was able to receive mail in bulk and free from postal controls. Many people, including us, benefited from the help that he and his wife so generously gave, and indeed, for a long time we regarded this as entirely adequate. Many Muscovites had already felt the need to establish direct contact with foreign correspondents, but as yet I was not inclined to do so; I had refrained from approaching them for many years and I did not anticipate that I might one day need to have recourse to them.

Zhores Medvedev had more than once offered his services in our conspiratorial schemes (but I had always felt it prudent to decline). In autumn 1970 he tried to get me to meet the Norwegian Per Hegge, who was trying to contact me at the time, but again I saw no point in it. But then I was awarded the Nobel Prize, and Hegge, who had somehow managed to track down Rostropovich's telephone number, caught me by surprise with his call, and I reluctantly answered his questions. When, as the latest step in the Nobel saga, I had to send letters to Scandinavia by illegal means, it made sense to continue dealing with Hegge. Zhores Medvedev fixed up one of our meetings and strolled with us for a few blocks along the dimly lit streets. The next time it was just the two of us, Hegge and I, who met among the crowds by the Lenin Library and set off, again along gloomy streets until in some unfamiliar courtyard near Volkhonka Street I passed him the papers I had prepared for the Nobel committee. This was not done with any great speed or dexterity, and when we eventually emerged onto another street, we saw the brightly lit sign of a police station: I had handed the papers over in their backyard.

Soon afterward Per Hegge was expelled from the Soviet Union. Zhores made new arrangements, and this time his contacts were Robert Kaiser of the *Washington Post* and Hedrick Smith of the *New York Times*. Again he offered his services, but again I had no occasion to accept.

Another year passed, and Alya and I managed to get out for an evening at the Conservatoire—a rare occasion. During intermission, I was approached by a persistent and not particularly well-mannered person who asked for an interview: this was Olle Stenholm, another Scanadinavian, but this time from Swedish Radio. I refused. (He was to cause us further difficulties in the future by turning up at Alya's flat, telling her he was going to Zurich to interview Heeb, and asking if we had any messages for him to take. Certainly not! But that left us racing to get word through to Betta so that Heeb should not believe Stenholm had come with our blessing.)

That evening I had many requests for my autograph, and there was no chance to look around properly. In particular, we remained unaware of the intent, pensive gaze of another young Swede, who on this occasion did not come up to us.

He came later and found Alya at home. She was at once favorably impressed by his candor and integrity, even by his apparent lack of journalistic sophistication, all of which could be plainly read in his young yet stern face and blue eyes. Somewhere he had picked up an old peasant custom, and before Alya even had time to notice, he had slipped out of his shoes and was walking into the room in his socks (in fact, this was not a practice we observed in our apartment); the gesture and the impulse behind it would have been unthinkable in a hardened reporter! (A long time afterward, we learned that he was the son of a pastor from southern Sweden.)

He did not even come with the intention of asking for an interview but simply wondered if he could be of any help.

Alya noted down his name and details, and with that the link was forged: Stig Fredrikson, Hegge's successor as correspondent for the Scandinavian press agencies.

Around this time—it was the spring of 1972 and they were bearing down on me in earnest—I had the idea of giving a lengthy interview, my first interview in effect, but we had to offer it to newspapers with a huge readership. Our choice fell (quite correctly) on the two leading American papers, and we contacted their correspondents (indirectly, through Zhores Medvedev) and invited them round on a particular day. Hedrick Smith and Robert Kaiser arrived with a microphone and a list of prepared questions (of surpassing triviality). But I, too, had already prepared the whole substance of the interview (if I could not get this across, the entire exercise would be quite pointless) and I had it all written down. Ignorant as I was about Western journalists and their newspapers, I imagined that they would be content to accept it in this form—after all, it was sensational material, wasn't it? Not a bit of it; they found such a proposal offensive and humiliating. (Later, when I came to understand the Western press, I realized that they could not have reacted otherwise.) The very most they would agree to, out of respect for me and in their eagerness to land a big story, was to take the content I had envisaged—not word for word but the bulk of it at least—and rework it into their own story line, with the sequence, style, and emphasis left to their own literary taste, and I, in exchange, had to let them record my answers to their run-of-the-mill questions (about Yevtushenko and suchlike).

It seemed a pity to let the chance of speaking to two such influential newspapers pass by, so I agreed, having already resolved to give my full text to Stig for him to pass on to his Scandinavian agencies the next day. I had yet to appreciate that "the next day" is yesterday's news and not worth a hill of beans; even with additions to the text, no one would touch it. At the time, I could not see how the author's own authentic text could fail to be of interest. As for Stig, he firmly believed that the agencies would take it.

So that was how it was done. Two major American newspapers made mincemeat of the underlying design of my piece and garnished everything important with their own fatuous observations and arguments. Meanwhile, in Scandinavia, not so much as a line of my text appeared; it was a waste of time, even though Stig had sent it out word for word over the teletype.

Then, a week later, our plans to hold the Nobel ceremony here in Moscow fell through, and I had to make a brief statement, intended specifically for the Scandinavian countries. Naturally, we decided to send it through Stig; we liked him, both for his undoubted integrity and for the spiritual kinship between us.

This time everything went swiftly and splendidly. So it really had been that the agencies had turned him down on the first occasion.

While all this was going on, Stig and I devised an outdoor rendezvous. It was to be in the underground passage at the Belorussian station, through which I always traveled on my way to and from Rostropovich's dacha.

When we met at the end of April, I had in my pocket a film containing the text of the Nobel speech. We had failed to find any other way of sending it out, and once again, its destination was Sweden. I was standing in an inconspicuous spot; he and his wife Ingrid came strolling along arm in arm; I followed, keeping a gap between us, and Alya came behind me, after first watching out for a while from a different spot to make sure that no one was tailing us. Everything turned out fine, so we caught up with them and the four of us set off at a leisurely pace down the Leningrad Prospect. (I had wandered up and down this street many times and it had never had any particular associations for me, yet now I can only think of it as the last street I was driven down as I was being deported from Russia.) As we talked, I asked Stig if he would take the film, and he agreed. I handed it over in a dark courtyard. Folk wisdom has it that seeing a pregnant woman means your plans will come to fruition. Well, we had two of them: both our wives were pregnant, and Stig was taking Ingrid back to Sweden to have her baby. (He told me how he had put the film inside a small transistor radio and taken it out of the country like that, before handing it over to the Swedish Academy. We thought this was ingenious and reminiscent of my earlier years of experimenting with various hiding places.)

Upon his return he told me of the successful outcome. We met again a couple of times before the summer. A contact so honest and so easily established was too valuable to lose. Gradually we (just the two of us now) worked out a method of meeting up: which stairs we would use, what distance I should keep, which way we would turn, and where I would catch him up. In midsummer to our amazement Stig suddenly failed to keep a meeting. Then another Scandinavian journalist left us a touching letter from Stig written in rudimentary Russian: driving back from Finland by car and hurrying to be in time for our meeting that evening, he had been involved in a road accident. "But God was with me at that moment, and I am optimistic that I shall make a complete recovery."

It was this unhappy accident with its happy ending that united us once and for all. All through the autumn and winter of 1972 and into 1973 our meetings continued, always under cover of darkness, always in the gloomy side streets and courtyards around the Belorussian station. (We met at a fixed time of day, and on parting we always agreed the date of the next meeting, as well as an alternative date to be kept in reserve.) And gradually I became aware that these meetings were indispensable to me. I could not even live without them. How could I have existed for nine years without any direct personal contact with anyone from the West? It gave me an unprecedented degree of maneuverability and a rapid means of getting materials abroad; each time we met, there was always something that needed sending or something to be passed on to me. (From now on all my surreptitious letters to Struve, Betta, and my lawyer Heeb went this way, making it *the* channel for my principal communications.) There were little rolls of film, new works, and new variants of existing ones. All this Stig would pass on in the diplomatic bag—but not through his own diplomats (Russians would call them by the zek term *suki*: running dogs who sell out to the Soviet authorities). Instead they went through a different embassy. At various times over many years the staff at this particular embassy were, to the best of my memory, unfailingly honorable people; they helped others as well as us, and no one was ever caught or betrayed. (To this day I know none of them in person or by name, but I want to express my respect and thanks to them.) We called this channel the GNR—the Great Northern Route.

On one of our walks we suddenly came up with an idea: Hans Björkegren was a Swedish writer and outstanding translator, whose superb versions of my *First Circle* and *Cancer Ward* had done much at the end of the 1960s to prepare the ground for my Nobel Prize. What if he were to start straight away on the Swedish translation of *Gulag*? But where would he get the text from? Why not from Heeb? And so our lines of communication joined up in the West, too. Björkegren provided his address for letters to me from the West, and they came the rest of the way by the good old GNR.

In their day the Bolsheviks did not have recourse to foreign journalists for their underground communications, partly because it would never have occurred to them and partly because they would have been unlikely to find correspondents willing to cooperate. It was left to the Bolsheviks themselves to create the sort of society where kindhearted foreigners feel unable to refuse the call to serve as secret couriers, illegal though that may be. And the same is true of diplomats. Whereas Soviet diplomats abroad are, almost to a man, just so many government spies, while Western embassies in Moscow are loyal and ineffectual, individual members of staff and diplomats at the embassies have feelings and a sense of justice that impel them to help us in our miserable plight. Here are some further remarkable instances.

Simultaneously with the Great Northern Route, a second route presented itself of its own accord—or rather, by the grace of God—and went into operation. Long before this, in December 1967, Olga Carlisle had been anxious to come to Moscow for talks with me, but she was refused a visa. Thereupon she asked someone to make a tourist trip to Moscow and meet up with me: this was Stepan Nikolaevich Tatishchev, a young Parisian Slavist who was also a second-generation émigré descended from those who had left Russia in the first wave. Tatishchev had no trouble getting into Russia; once there he immediately phoned Eva (was there *anyone* in the Paris Russian community whom she did not know?), and she brought him around to the Princess's apartment to meet me. On the way, she taught him how to behave on the street and in shops when one is probably being shadowed. At the same time she was testing his nerve. (She concluded that he was apprehensive but was mastering his fear.) The subject of our talks seemed important at the time (he had learned Carlisle's questions by heart and committed my answers to memory, too). In fact, nothing of any significance came of it, but our acquaintance with Tatishchev had been established. That evening he made a good impression on several close friends of ours who had gathered at the Princess's—he was a witty and engaging conversationalist with none of the conspirator's tense and wary manner; he told amusing stories about the left-wing antics of the Paris students and the intelligentsia as a whole. It emerged that he and Nikita Struve taught at the same university. We told him he could lower his guard with Nikita and let him know what was going on.

He made a second trip to Moscow as a tourist, and we met at Eva's, again with nothing of great importance to discuss but feeling more and more at ease with him. We came to feel that we could trust him completely. (On one occasion, as he strolled around Moscow, Stepan was amazed to come to a road junction marked with two nameplates: Tatishchev Street and Shukhov Street.* He took this as a sign.)

Then in the spring of 1971, it was Eva once again who brought us the amazing news: Stepan Tatishchev was to take up the post of French cultural attaché in Moscow and would be here for a full three years! It was an incredible stroke of good fortune at a time when success was in precious short supply. (Stepan Nikolaevich told us later that he had had a telephone call from their Ministry of Foreign Affairs seeking his advice, as a specialist in Slavic studies, on whom they should appoint to Russia for the next three years. Since he was set on going back, he did not beat around the bush but promptly put his own name forward! The recommendation was duly accepted.) To have a trustworthy, reliable channel permanently open to us and for three whole years—that was something we had never expected! (But Asya Durova was not keen to confide in him, and they both continued to work independently of each other, with no one at the embassy aware of what was going on.)

Our hopes were not entirely fulfilled. It seems that Tatishchev (we gave him the code name "Émile," then turned it into the more Russian-sounding "Milka") started off by committing a number of indiscretions, which meant that he had to be especially on his guard for a long time afterward. But then, the style is the man, as they say, and Tatishchev's own particular way of doing things was not quite what we had anticipated. He kept on assuring us that behind this apparently easygoing manner he remained tense and vigilant. (Eva, who herself answered that description to a T, felt, as an outside observer, that Milka was reckless and careless, and she was forever correcting and admonishing him.) Yet it has to be said that he was never once caught, and he served his whole time in Moscow without anything going disastrously wrong. At times our links with him were not especially close, and the timing, speed, and volume of the consignments we were able to send through him were often far from ideal. But that said, there were times when his help was a real boon, especially when it came to passing on letters, instructions, and news. The beauty of it was that they were always delivered straight into Struve's hands, without the need for any intermediaries! On one occasion Milka's help was invaluable in sending out a long list of our "ciphers," indicating who was to receive financial assistance from abroad and who was to be the nominal sender. Having two independent lines of communication is extremely convenient; whenever there is a stoppage in one line, the other makes up for it.

Tatishchev finished his stint as cultural attaché when I was already in the West. But his successor in that post helped us greatly:

Yves Hamant[1] was a native Frenchman, a devout believer who was devoted to Russian culture, so much so that he was prepared to face risks and endure sacrifices for its sake.

When Tatishchev returned to Paris, he was even more useful to us than before. He kept closely in touch with Eva through former colleagues in the French embassy, and throughout 1975, when we were in the West, she sent us further bulky consignments of papers we had left behind in Moscow. Thus, everything that Ugrimov had been storing for me was systematically cleared away, and what was left they burned over there, using the system of identifying marks we had devised. (Alya's old lists of where things were kept and the key to decode it passed to and fro across the Soviet frontier.)[2]

In the spring of 1973, when I was already in the process of moving out of Rostropovich's dacha and was seeing the Belorussian station

---

[1] Unlike Tatishchev, Yves was extremely circumspect and self-possessed, and when he had been in Moscow until 1977 the French Ministry of Foreign Affairs readily renewed his term of office. We were simply overjoyed! We referred to him as "Fei," our fairy king, and never uttered his name indoors, even in the West. In 1975 Yves took a chance and came to see us in Zurich. He turned out to be gentle, reserved, and taciturn. (1978 note)

[2] Tatishchev always readily accepted letters from us for transmission abroad, and this was no small undertaking, since over the years our correspondence between Europe and Russia came to involve dozens of different people. But when he came back to Paris, he left his heart behind in Russia and found he could no longer settle back into his former life. Between 1975 and 1976 he made two more trips to Russia as a tourist without anything going wrong, but he had obviously not taken sufficient care. On his next trip, in summer 1977, the KGB put him under surveillance, following him closely and openly, and warning him, "We'll break your legs for you." He did not panic, and while they were at a market he managed to shake them off—with difficulty but, according to him, completely successfully. He then went to the Princess's apartment to deliver something to her, but as soon as he returned to his hotel he was picked up and deported.

Eight years later he was diagnosed with cancer and died almost immediately, still a young man. Among the last of the services he performed for his homeland, from which he was now excluded, was to found a radio station—"the Voice of the Orthodox Church"—which broadcast to Russia. (1986 note)

for the last time, I proposed to Stig that we transfer our meetings to the Kiev station, which I would now be using on my way to Rozhdestvo, my last place of refuge—or semirefuge, as it was by now. My trips to Rozhdestvo involved a long journey, weighed down with luggage, and I was no longer free to pick what train I pleased. Accordingly, that spring I suggested that we meet in the morning. He boldly agreed, and we did so on two or three occasions. Meeting as we did in the full glare of the morning light at that teeming railroad station, then sitting in a green summerhouse on a working-class suburban street not far from the Studencheskaya subway station, we were wide open to prying cameras, and any fool could have shadowed us. At the same time, it had been a long time since *we* had seen each other by daylight, either! (This was the first time he took my photograph, not for the press but for himself.) There was a striking nobility, intelligence, and honesty about his face, and it was perpetually gaunt and pallid—Scandinavian features, perhaps?

That spring he had the idea of going to meet my lawyer. I gave my approval. (He subsequently spoke with great respect of Heeb's reliability and acumen, which led me to compound the mistakes I had already made.) As a stand-in while he was away for the summer, he proposed Frank Crepeau of the Associated Press—"just in case anything should happen." Happen it did, and at the end of August we had need of Crepeau. By this time, however, Stig was already back from his vacation, and he came to meet me one evening by the Studencheskaya subway station, at a bench under a tree where a streetlamp cast a mottled twilight.

The date was either the nineteenth or twentieth of August. When I arrived for our meeting I already had set out in my head the plan for a whole series of individual actions as part of my intended counterattack. It seemed clear to me that this supreme step was the last I would be permitted to take, and I therefore suggested to Stig that he should now abandon his clandestine role—which put him in danger without in any way enhancing his reputation—

and that, instead, he should come out in the open and conduct an interview with me. (I had yet to grasp that a remote corner of the world like Scandinavia was the worst place to send my interviews.)

I imagined that he would leap at the opportunity—it would strengthen his position and make a name for him. But there in the evening gloom beneath the tree, he thought for scarcely a moment and—refused.

I was amazed. But was it not, in all likelihood, a prudent decision? Stig could stay in his Moscow post for another one and a half years, two and a half even.

Prudent it may have been from a hidebound Western viewpoint, but the way he put his Moscow posting, and even his whole career as a journalist, at risk every time he met me was anything but prudent—in fact, it was desperately brave. He ran that risk every time he set off for a rendezvous bearing illicit papers in his pocket (once he was even stopped by a patrol of the People's Volunteer Militia, but they did not dare to frisk him), and every time he returned with a different batch of papers, no less subversive than the first. Following the promptings of his heart, he acted utterly unselfishly and risked much more than when he moderated his impulses with the familiar Western rationalizations.

Our wonderful Western friends! The position they found themselves in and the decisions they made were so fraught with contradictions.

Stig entered so fully into the stresses and strains of our conspiratorial life that when asked about the danger of his role becoming known, he answered, "*Personally, I don't really care. I just think I'll be more useful to you if word doesn't get out.*"

And so he declined to interview me. And he did so because such a step fell not within the perilous terrain into which his feelings drew him (and his charming wife, Ingrid) but rather in the sphere of mundane reality, where he was required to think logically and act sensibly like everyone else.

Instead, he sent Frank Crepeau along to interview me (a thoroughly nice, decent, honest person), together with, at my own insistence, a correspondent from *Le Monde*, who was extremely self-assured and who inspired little fellow feeling. (I was still hopelessly naive about the wariness and hypocrisy of these various newspapers. We in the East think of them all as much more devoted to freedom that they are in reality. Since we were indoors, we kept our conversation to a minimum, and I wrote a note for the journalists, explaining that I would like to publish a series of articles in *Le Monde* on aspects of Soviet life. I thought they would accept with alacrity, but received instead an indignant refusal from *Le Monde*—why would they want me writing articles for them, when they already had their own Moscow correspondent?)

The battle was about to enter a new phase of intensity, and Stig and I agreed that in September 1973 we would meet every ten days. The dates had been fixed in advance, but so intense was the conflict that I needed more meetings. Having learned of the seizure of *Gulag*, I now had to send word to the West, along with my instructions for printing it. We had a system worked out for emergencies like this: we would telephone Stig early in the morning before his Soviet secretaries arrived. He could recognize Alya's and my voices at once, and the meaning of such a call was clear—I had to meet him that evening (at the time and place we had already agreed). But what were we to say when we called, given that the phones were tapped? Stig had a good idea; we would make it a "wrong number": "Hello, is that the dry cleaner's?" "Hello, grocery order department? . . . It isn't? Oh, I'm sorry!" Just long enough for him to recognize the voice. But if the telephone were out of order or busy for a long period, or if Stig weren't at home . . . what then?

On September 4 everything went well; the "wrong number" was duly dialed amid the crowds surging around the suburban trains at the Leningrad station, and Stig and I met as planned. That evening I had gone to extraordinary lengths to frustrate anyone trying to tail me: I had left the dacha by an unusual route through the back streets, and on the subway I had changed trains more than once at stations that I knew would quickly become clear of passengers—Krasnoselskaya, for instance, where the platform stays completely empty and you can be absolutely sure that you have shaken off any pursuit.

However, when Stig came up to me at our secluded spot near the Studencheskaya subway station, I had a fleeting impression of a figure looking to see that we had met, then taking cover behind a building. I told Stig about it. He laughed out loud. "You're right. That's Udgaard." Udgaard, a Norwegian journalist, was a friend of his and the only person whom he had told about our meetings.

Udgaard was very keen to meet me, too, but it would have been quite unethical to barge in on his friend, so he did not even come and introduce himself.

There was plenty to pass on to Stig that evening of September 4: the news about *Gulag*, the text of the "Letter to the Soviet Leaders," and lots of instructions for my friends in the West, as well as a film with something else of mine on it. I remember feeling as though an enormous burden had been lifted from my shoulders, and that evening Alya and I were in a festive mood—everything was collapsing around us, but we were holding our own. (While this was going on, she was well into her ninth month of pregnancy and—four days later, in the thick of one of those flurries of events so beloved of fate—she did indeed give birth to our Stephan.)

Terrible as that final autumn was, Stig and I went on seeing each other quite uneventfully. For me these meetings were an indispensable safety valve to ease the unremitting pressure I was under. Once when there was a sudden need to send an additional letter, we arranged to keep Stig out of sight by having Ingrid stroll along Naryshkinsky Boulevard and meet Alya coming toward her with our young Ermolai. I was there, too. The two women bent over the child so that from a distance no one could make out what they were doing with their hands, and Alya passed over the letter, while Ingrid handed her a Swedish Christmas candle as a present.

They left to spend Christmas in Sweden, and then the whole tempestuous *Gulag* affair burst upon us, and there was still so long to wait before Stig's return! Every two or three days we would need to get in touch with someone—there were questions to ask, lists of corrections to send. It is true that many journalists came to see us during this time of adversity, some for profit—a photograph or a tidbit of news—others, like John Shaw and Frank Crepeau, to offer help.

For a variety of reasons, a Moscow posting confers a great deal of prestige and privilege upon a Western correspondent, both as a career move and in terms of the material conditions it offers (up to and including a free nanny service, for the Soviet government spares no expense, reckoning that journalists who are well provided for will tone down their reporting in order to hold onto their posts). But I have noticed an amazing change in people educated in the West who have come into contact with our movement: they leave their mercenary habits behind and are ready to risk their necks.

It is not an inherent characteristic of people in the West that they should be calculating to the point of pettiness or that the more amiable they appear on the surface, the more hard-hearted they are in reality. It is all a question of which "force field" they are drawn into. In Russia, despite Soviet oppression, there has long been a field tugging us in the direction of generosity and self-sacrifice, and it is this force that is communicated to certain Westerners and takes hold of them—perhaps not for all time but at least while they are among us. Even though they shared the same Western education and enjoyed the same living conditions, the various members of the foreign press corps showed themselves in widely different colors during those difficult days.

The last secret meeting I was to have with Stig fell on January 14, 1974, the very day that *Pravda* launched a major press campaign against me. There was already a hint in the article that one of the possibilities being considered was not to arrest me but to deport me to the West. If that were to happen, I had it in mind to stay in Norway, and Stig had been such a marvelous friend that I wanted to keep him with me. So I proposed that if they were to exile me and if he were to suffer because of his connection with me, then he should not be afraid of being deported from the Soviet Union or of forfeiting his career as a journalist—he would come to Norway to be my secretary and handle all my communications with the outside world.

In fact, he had already been thinking along similar lines, and the idea appealed to him.

In the entryway to one of the courtyards where we could not be seen, we exchanged a farewell embrace.

Our next meeting had been scheduled for February 14—forty-eight hours after my arrest.

Stig did, however, call on Alya during the events of January, accompanied by Nils Morten Udgaard. Apart from our acute need for help and friendship, such a visit seemed quite natural at the time. This was already the prelude to a period when in the furor following my arrest, our apartment would be swarming with foreign press, giving Alya the chance to save all of my current work—some completed, some unfinished, some temporarily set aside—texts that existed in a single copy, with no time for us to make more. (I do not believe that the KGB had any idea just how much preparatory work on Lenin, the Bolsheviks, and the revolution as a whole I had already completed for my *Red Wheel* and the degree to which all this would have been impossible to replace if it were lost. If they had, I think they would have grabbed the lot the moment I was arrested.) As soon as I was led away, Alya had to clear all of this out of the apartment immediately. For a start, anywhere at all would do, but then she had to get it to a place suitable for possible shipment abroad. As for carrying it all out of the apartment, surely it would be less dangerous for foreigners to take it? Journalists galore were already passing through in a steady stream. This provided some cover, but when journalists trav-

eled around Moscow they were not in the habit of carrying anything
with them; more often than not they arrived empty-handed, and so
of course they could not suddenly emerge from our apartment with
a bag. The only way was for them to fill their pockets with packages,
but not to the extent that they started "putting on weight." Alya said
nothing about this in front of the assembled journalists and handed
nothing over. The presence of so many strangers made it hard for her
to arrange things with the initiated. But she would shut herself away
in a small room with the trusted few, and there they would communicate by writing notes (explaining anything aloud was out of the
question, and to make matters worse, you had to keep up some kind
of vacuous chatter while you were writing). It was there, too, that
the packages were handed over.

   The first person Alya turned to on the day I was deported was
Nils Udgaard, for though a very recent acquaintance, he was a man
of such noble bearing—large-framed, with calm, regular features—
that his every gesture breathed assurance; moreover, as a historian
and academic, he stood out from the general run of less well educated journalists. To him she revealed the nature of the task:
"There's a large, bulky set of archives, and it's imperative that we get
them out of the country. Can you arrange it?" (Bear in mind that
this was a man "with a past"; he had already been the object of
abuse in *Komsomolskaya pravda*, which meant they were keeping
tabs on him.) He thought it over and the next day asked Alya to give
him written authorization for use in any discussions that might
arise. It read:

> I request that Mr. Nils Udgaard be regarded as my authorized
> representative in his dealings with _____. I ask for your assis-
> tance in securing the shipment abroad of Solzhenitsyn's ar-
> chives.

   And from that point on he acted on a grand scale, approaching
the task with the vision of a historian and not as a journalist.

Regrettably, even today the story of this remarkable operation, which rescued my most important manuscripts and ensured that for years I would be able to press on with my *Red Wheel*, must still remain untold.

. . . .

. . . .

What Udgaard had not fully worked out was how he was going to fit everything into the two suitcases he was allowed to take out. It was already obvious that my archives were too big for them. (It also seemed that we were living on borrowed time, for at any moment my family might be thrown out of the country.)

By a fortunate coincidence, returning home from a concert, he found his friend William Odom waiting for him. Odom, a forty-year-old assistant to the American military attaché, had previously taught history at West Point and, like Udgaard, held a doctorate in the subject. Now he brought Nils a pamphlet published by the Novosti Press Agency attacking *Gulag* and me.

It was not safe to speak indoors, and Nil, preoccupied with all the loose ends still remaining, wrote down, "Solzhenitsyn's archive is proving a big problem."

William Odom already had a far-from-superficial acquaintance with the history of the twentieth century and of Russia in particular. He had missed serving in the Korean War only because he had entered West Point that year. From there he had gone on to study Soviet history at Columbia University, completing his research on Sverdlov and the Osoaviakhim.* He had then served with the American mission attached to the Soviet armed forces, followed by two years in Vietnam and now by two years in Moscow, where his posting was coming to an end.

He immediately agreed to help in principle, provided that no one should know of his involvement, "not even Solzhenitsyn himself." He had in any case to pack his personal belongings and send them back to the United States (in the diplomatic pouch), and he would put the archives in among them. This allowed him to act without seeking official permission (and without courting official rejection). Nevertheless, he did tell his friend and superior, the military attaché, Rear Admiral Mayo, what he had in mind.

But everything looked decidedly less auspicious from within our besieged apartment. Confusion reigned not just among my papers but in Alya's mind as she struggled to anticipate what was to come. It was clear within a day or two that a house search could be ruled out, but would those carrying things away from the house be picked up? If so, who was most likely to be stopped? And when would they start doing it?

When they had come for me, not only were pieces of my subversive correspondence with the West lying scattered about on my desk, but on Alya's desk lay the key to the code for our entire system of safekeeping, listing names, locations, and the items stored! Now it fell to Alya to sort out the entire mass of materials we had hidden away, which involved getting through to places we had had no contact with for years, then building up a new system and sorting *every single item* into one of the following categories: definitely send on after me; send if possible; leave hidden in the Soviet Union for eventual recovery; leave hidden permanently; or, finally, destroy.

For this reason it was hardly ever possible to take the simple course and transfer the materials for shipment abroad directly from their place of storage. Instead, Alya had to risk bringing everything back to an apartment that was under constant threat, go through it there, sometimes page by page, sort it into new envelopes, and get it out again. (Alya was the only one capable of doing this job, except for Lyusha, who came round in the evenings and did a great deal of the work as well.)

But before this, when they were still expecting the place to be searched, they followed their first impulse. Get everything out of the house! Store it with someone else! Anyone we can find! On the evening of the day I was arrested, Stig carried out drafts of the essays for *From Under the Rubble* and various letters to the West hidden about his person—he was used to wearing a coat with roomy pockets when meeting me. Then Alya used others of our circle, Soviet citizens, to ferry the rest to various friends' apartments. Our friends would burst out of our home in a boisterous throng (the Pasternaks, neighbors of ours, carried one batch in a bag with onions and cauliflowers sticking out of the top), then they would accompany one another to their destinations. The greatest help and shrewdest counsel during these critical days came from Dima Borisov, Andrei Tyurin, and Aleksandr Ginzburg, the last a newcomer to the business of hiding archives but a familiar figure in the annals of the Russian underground. He took away with him manuscripts earmarked for storage in the Soviet Union and provided an assembly point for them.

Alya went on to send out not only my manuscripts and drafts but rare books and important newspapers from 1917. (There was a Soviet customs regulation banning the export of any books published before 1945, in case they might have taken the "wrong" line. But my books about the revolution consisted exclusively of "wrong" ones. Worse still, they had all been snatched from the flames to which they had officially been consigned.) Another group (including Vilgelmina Germanovna Slavutskaya and Aleksandr Sergeyevich Buturlin) managed to take away books—the bulkiest, albeit least risky, loads to carry. Slavutskaya personally devised a route for sending books out and organized the whole thing herself—a marvelous achievement and more than we had ever expected!

It was felt to be too dangerous for journalists to carry anything directly from our home and safer for them to pick the papers up from other apartments. Stig and Nils were given the addresses so that they could pass them on to the relevant correspondents, while the owners of the apartments in question were warned approximately when to expect them and told how to check that their visitors were genuine by looking for a code penciled on their press cards.

And so, like a puddle of water stamped on by a heavy boot, my archives were scattered to the four winds, ending up in various remote parts of Moscow and even in outlying districts—on the Rublyov Highway and at Medvedkovo. (Within a few days it became clear that this had been a false move, and Alya and the others had to start hauling everything in again, back to our apartment.)

Udgaard himself was the one who went out to collect what had been left at Medvedkovo. The plan was that he would change taxis en route, and instead of driving up to the door of the house he was heading for, he would get out at the house before it and let his taxi go. (This was all intended to cover his tracks.) Once there, he filled all the pockets of his voluminous reporter's jacket, picked up the two heavy shopping bags, and went outside. But the house is well off the beaten path, so how is he to find a taxi back into town? It is three in the afternoon, still broad daylight. A taxi drives by with some soldiers in it, one of them a colonel (but they might be KGB, there's no time to make sure). Udgaard, in his respectable clothes, tries to hitch a lift with them; they pick him up, then strike up a conversation, and of course it is clear that he is a foreigner. (Perhaps it would have been easier to go by bus?)

Such a risk to take, and not at all what Moscow correspondents are used to! And in addition, they still have to keep on top of all their other work every day (making sure their Soviet-appointed secretaries do not know what is going on), and there are still reports to file with their agencies or newspapers.

The foreign correspondents reacted in very different ways during this period. For each it was a test of character, a question of conscience. There was no glory to be had, no congratulations, praise, or promotion at work; instead, they were courting professional ruin, risking all those years spent struggling to establish themselves in their careers. After all, their newspapers had not sent them here to get mixed up in a conspiracy. (After certain interviews I gave to Frank Crepeau, the Associated Press astutely sensed the danger and sent him a stern and pointed warning not to step over the line in his dealings with Solzhenitsyn. Yet he was forever taking documents or films for us, and he would hide them away with an eloquent expression on his face, suggesting how, deep within him, the cogs were turning, and, at the same time, how he was gambling with his own fate, albeit willingly. Again, to get my "Statement in the Event of Arrest" away from Alya's apartment in the dead of night, *Le Figaro's* correspondent, Lacontre, put it inside his sock under the sole of his foot. The European papers and agencies tended to be the more understanding, and their correspondents fared better. For example, Udgaard was convinced that if he should come to grief, his boss would be sympathetic and excuse his actions. (That said, Udgaard carted off incomparably more than the others did, stuffing the side pockets, breast pockets, back pockets of his reporter's jacket with papers and pausing to scrutinize his tall, broad figure closely in the full-length mirror before leaving, in case there were any telltale bulges.) Americans, on the other hand, tend to be career-oriented to a particularly single-minded degree, and if one of them should blunder, he would not earn sympathy or moral support from his boss and colleagues but would be held up to ridicule as a loser. And it was understandable that some refused to help. But of the Americans, three splendid men, Steve Broening, Roger Leddington, and Jim Peipert, took one load after another. As did three trusty Englishmen, Julian Nundy, Bob Evans, and Richard Wallis. But the suitcases that would eventually house all these papers were as large as the journalists' pockets were small, and some of our helpers had to come back for another load of dynamite *every single day*! (I suppose that the KGB, pleased at how my deportation had gone, took a relaxed view of these swarms of correspondents and did not nab any of them because it wanted to avoid a scandal over secondary issues—never imagining, of course, the volume and significance of what was being spirited away.)

Weak and belated as these lines of mine may be, let them stand, nevertheless, as a grateful tribute to these correspondents. Without that handful of Westerners, it would have been years before my work regained its momentum.

Most of what they took away they delivered to Stig, who built up a whole store of my papers in his apartment (which is why he rarely came around in person at that time). But if the foreign correspondents were taking it to Stig, that must mean they all knew about him by then! And the more who knew the secret, the greater was the risk that it would leak out. Yet nobody gave the game away! Neither then nor since.

On February 22 it became known that I had left Sweden, heading for Norway. Of course, Stig could not possibly resist the chance of meeting up for the first time since my expulsion; in Norway we could discuss what had been going on and swap plans and questions.

It was at this point that Alya made a dangerous mistake and nearly brought the whole elaborate operation crashing down around us. She sent me a letter via Stig. (After all, it had worked so well before; for all our barefaced audacity, we had always gotten away with it, and always Stig had been involved. So why change now?) I would in any case get my main information about what had been happening from Stig's verbal account. All that Alya had to say, apart from personal matters, was to explain that she did not intend to leave Russia until she had been able to rescue all my archives and hide them safely (to stop me from pressuring her over the phone to come sooner) and that it was essential that she make a public statement before her departure. But what could have been easier than to pass all this on by word of mouth? Yes, it was a mistake, but when the knife is at your throat and your ribs are cracking, it's hard to avoid taking a false step.

In his last few hours before leaving for Norway, Stig called at our apartment but was soon on his way to the airport. He had used a "tried and true" method to conceal the letter, tucking it, screwed up in a little ball, inside a transistor radio—the same one he had used to smuggle out the Nobel lecture two years before, or one like it. But the customs official went straight for the radio, opened it—and took out the letter. (Mere coincidence? Too obvious a hiding place? Or had Stig once breathed an incautious word in a bugged room?) Humiliated and apprehensive, Stig stood blushing like a little boy caught in the act. And such a petty thing to trip up on! After so many difficult and dangerous missions . . . (And back at home, in his Moscow apartment, lay the entire store of papers waiting to be sent abroad! What if they were to go there now?) However, the KGB agent made a scathing remark, confiscated the letter, but did not prevent Stig from continuing on his journey. In deep despair he boarded the plane and left for Scandinavia.

He did find time, however, to whisper a message to an airline employee, a fellow Swede, who then went round and told Ingrid what had happened. She was at her wits' end. How could she save the threatened archives? She had a guest with her at the time, a diplomat who must remain nameless. She decided to ask him to take charge of this dangerous cargo for a while. Somewhat reluctantly, he drove part of it off in his car. (And were there eyes watching them as the car was being loaded?) The remainder was taken, in stages, by the indefatigable Nils. Some he brought home with him, some he took to the ————— Embassy.

So many unnecessary comings and goings, risky changes of location, sudden dashes across Moscow! When the bodies of certain animals are chopped up, the amputated parts still stir, quiver, and convulse, clinging to life. In much the same way, my archives went on twitching and refused to die.

Somehow the news of Stig's misfortune raced on ahead of him and was brought to me by John Shaw of the London *Times* out at the cottage of the artist Weidemann. But what I heard was an appalling variant: at the airport filmed copies of my manuscripts had been confiscated from Stig! There was nothing implausible about this, since he did have microfilms of mine, so the news came as a bitter blow, and Stig himself was in such great danger! Yet within the hour he turned up in person. Now we learned that the only thing taken had been a letter, yet we still had no idea how serious its contents were. More importantly, my heart shrank at the thought of what this might mean for Stig, and a feeling of guilt came over me such as I had never known throughout our years of surefooted covert operations together. It was not even certain that he would be allowed back into Moscow after this.

But no, the KGB must have dozed off! There was no raid, and Stig was allowed to return without hindrance. Perhaps they had yet to get the full measure of our network and thought Sven's attempt to smuggle the letter was a one-time episode, a casual favor by one of the many journalists who flocked around us? Or perhaps they were simply anxious to contain the scandal provoked by my expulsion?

But there have been many comparable instances in this book, and taken together, they suggest that in its dealings with me the KGB was constantly befuddled, lacking the sense and nerve to take the simplest and most straightforward of measures!

So Stig returned and promptly retrieved the portion of my archives that he had been storing. Again he was sitting on a volcano. But at this point Nils swung into action. . . .

. . . .
. . . .

. . . And no matter how many allies were drawn into our secret operations—and remember, they were from the West, inexperienced in our ways, and were professional sensation-seekers to boot—not one of them ever breathed a word!

———

Alya and I spoke on the telephone and agreed that she and the family would not fly to Zurich by Aeroflot but on a Swiss airline that used the small airport, Sheremetyevo-2. A Swiss official there had promised that their luggage would be accepted at once without the Soviet authorities being allowed to check it. But the KGB had a trick up its sleeve! A few hours before the Swiss airliner was due to arrive, they gave instructions that on this occasion (and this occasion alone) our particular aircraft was to land at Sheremetyevo-1. And all our cases vanished from sight down the big conveyor belt to where the KGB agents were waiting to inspect them. They held them for a long time. (How much they photographed I do not know, but our magnetic tapes were all erased.)

I knew that Alya had sent everything that mattered out by secret channels, so she would not be carrying anything of much importance. Perhaps it was precisely because of this, acting on a subconscious impulse or out of sheer devilry—whatever the reason, when my family arrived with their ten suitcases, their bags and baskets, I dashed for the luggage cart in full view of the waiting press, grabbed two heavy cases full of the innocuous papers Alya was bringing out, and carried them myself. To an outsider it would have seemed as if all my papers had come out legally. (And if the KGB decided that I was not expecting anything important apart from what they had already copied at Sheremetyevo, then that was fine by me. They could pore over it to their heart's content!)

It was not until April 1974 that a young German couple, who were driving to Italy on vacation with their young daughter, called at our Zurich home. The husband unloaded the car (taking care even here to avoid a press photographer), and out came my beloved archives, packed in two suitcases and a carryall. So circumspect was our visitor that he would not even give his name in the presence of Dr. Heeb's son, and he handed me his ID without a word.

We could not have been more delighted to see them if they had been members of our own family. Alya's hands trembled with joy as she checked off the number on each package. It was all here— everything that really mattered, the most priceless things of all! It had arrived! We had saved it all!

Later still, a large number of books that I needed for my work were brought by Mario Corti, a member of the staff of the Italian embassy in Moscow who had taken up the cause of Russia's persecuted Christians. Our thanks to him! Now these books, too, were back on my shelves.

The materials that Odom was keeping took longer to arrive. His luggage had been sent to the States by sea, but he himself spent a few more months in Europe. It was September 1974 before those particular treasures reached us in Zurich.

Before that, at the end of July, Nils and Angelika came to visit us, and he brought with him another, less urgent part of my archives, almost enough to fill another suitcase. More cause for celebration! By now we had our doubts about how safe it was to talk inside our Zurich home; it was child's play even here for the KGB to clamp a listening device onto an outside wall. So I took Udgaard up into the hills, to an isolated house in Sternenberg, and here for the first time he described the whole secret to-and-fro of my archives and gave me the names of those involved. Just being able to talk out loud about such secret matters and to treat them as a thing of the past gave us a wonderful sense of freedom and exhilaration! Here, at least, we could be sure that no one would hear us.

Udgaard interviewed me about my literary work for the newspaper *Aftenposten,* and I gave him a final proof copy of *Troubled Waters of the Quiet Don* to take into the Soviet Union. None of this was at all to the liking of the Soviet authorities. They had been building up evidence against him and Stig for a long time now, but it was still vague. The year 1975 was to mark the end of their time in Moscow, and in the spring *Literaturnaya gazeta* attacked them in an article entitled "Mr. Udgaard's Dossier of Shame." However, their fatuous efforts to incriminate him in the smuggling of works of art only revealed their ignorance of the real substance of that "dossier." Both Udgaard and Stig put up a stout defense and made uncompromising public statements. In Norway the newspapers and the journalists' union took Udgaard's side, protesting to the Soviet embassy and demanding that their own foreign ministry protect him from persecution. There was support for Stig, too, in Sweden. Neither of them lost his position.[3]

During our first months in Zurich we had a number of visits from journalists who had helped us in Moscow. This was my first chance to get to know some of these new friends, and we were delighted to have them as our guests. When they went back, they took letters we had written to our friends in Moscow, and before long they were taking the first installments of the financial assistance we directed to Russia through our Social Fund. Steve Broening came to see us in November on the occasion of the press conference to launch *From Under the Rubble*. It was a year later, in America, that I met William Odom under a shroud of secrecy and was able to express the enormous gratitude I felt toward him.

Only now that I have lived here for a while and had a chance to observe the attitudes and mentality of people in the West can I fully appreciate the heroism they displayed—and I used the word *heroism* advisedly. We Russians were already shuffling along, drenched to the skin from the relentless (sometimes radioactive) torrents, and if we took chances, then all we risked was being doused with a few more bucketfuls from the same downpour. But for those from the West it meant leaping out of their cozy shelter, still dressed in their nice dry little suits, and plunging into the thick of this saturating storm. When things went badly for them, this leap must have struck their friends and acquaintances and the society they came from as simply idiotic and ill considered. The moral chasm that they stepped across was much greater that it was for us, and whenever I remember them or see their faces, my admiration knows no bounds.

---

[3] Nils saw out his posting in the Soviet Union, while Stig even extended his stay and was promoted on his return. (1978 note)

14

Troubled Waters of the Quiet Don

There was an unbearable density to the world in which our movement had to operate, an oppressive sense of danger and need for secrecy, exacerbated by the need of most of its participants to earn their living in the service of the state. So close and constricted was this world that not so much as a sunflower seed—let alone the proverbial apple—could fall far enough to reach the ground. How then could any subject peripheral to our cause induce us to divert our energy and interest in its direction? Yet one such question did present itself—and so, too, did the time and energy needed to cope with it.

This was the question of who actually wrote the novel *The Quiet Don*. For decades anyone expressing doubts about its authorship aloud could have been sure of prosecution under Article 58 of the Criminal Code. After the death of Maksim Gorky, Mikhail Sholokhov was ranked first in the literary hierarchy of the Soviet Union. He was not so much a member of the Party's Central Committee as its living embodiment, and he regularly took the floor, as the Voice of the Party and the People, at Party congresses and sessions of the Supreme Soviet.

Elements of our new task gradually converged from different quarters and coalesced, unpremeditated, unbidden, and uncoordinated. They found their way by chance into the highly charged field of our narrow world, but once there they sparked and flared into life.

As for the mystery itself, in the south of Russia, where I lived, there could hardly have been many people who were not aware of it and intrigued by it. As a child I heard many a conversation on the subject, and everyone was convinced that Sholokhov had not written the book. No systematic work had been done on the question, but sooner or later everyone caught wind of the rumors in one form or another.

It was one of the later rumors that particularly affected me. In the summer of 1965 I was given an account of a story told by Petrov-Biryuk during a dinner at the Central Writers' Club. Around 1932, when he had been president of the Azov and Black Sea Writers' Association, he had been approached by a man who claimed to have conclusive proof that Sholokhov had not written *The Quiet Don*. Petrov-Biryuk was taken aback—what evidence could be so incontrovertible? The stranger had laid before him the missing drafts of the novel. Sholokhov had never had them, never shown them to anyone, and here they were, right in front of him—and in someone else's handwriting! Whatever Petrov-Biryuk's own view of Sholokhov might have been (and, of course, he was afraid—even then Sholokhov inspired fear), he telephoned the agitation and propaganda department of the local Party committee. There he was told, All right, just send this fellow over to us with his papers.

And the man and his papers—disappeared forever.

It was not until thirty years later, not long before Biryuk's death, that he revealed this incident in a drunken conversation with a friend, and not without glancing over his shoulder first.

To the widespread suspicions of plagiarism was now added the destruction of this courageous man, a classic Gulag episode, and this I found so hard to bear. And what of the real author? I seethed with indignation at the thought of how circumstances had conspired against the unfortunate writer, damning him to half a century of oblivion. What I wanted for them both was not just revenge but retribution and justice before the court of history. But who had the strength for such a task?

Unbeknownst to me, that very summer of 1965, another audacious stone had been cast into the stagnant depths of this swamp: far away in my hometown of Rostov-on-Don there had appeared an article by Molozhavenko on the writer F. D. Kryukov.*

For me the Don was not simply a childhood memory but an indispensable strand in my future novel.* Through one particular "son of the Don" (Y. A. Stefanov), its waters surged into my mill-race to power the wheels of my narrative. Stefanov kept bringing me more and more information, filling pages the size of bedsheets with his bold, sprawling handwriting. He was the first to tell me about Molozhavenko's article and a little about who Kryukov was. (I had never so much as heard of him till then.)

By contrast, it was in that trivial and mundane sphere of life where people occasionally make you a present of their books that a package arrived containing an inscribed copy of a book by Irina Nikolaevna Medvedeva-Tomashevskaya. It was a study of Griboedov's play *The Misfortune of Being Clever*, of which I was a great admirer, and I found it interesting.

From yet another direction, through Q's vigorous but chaotic stories and letters, the figure of Irina Nikolaevna also began to emerge, now as a friend from her student past, now as someone who was still her friend in present-day Leningrad (she would come to Leningrad to spend the four winter months, but the rest of the year she lived in the Crimea). And whenever her name cropped up, it was always as a brilliant, tough-minded woman, a gifted literary scholar in the mold of her famous husband, the late Professor Tomashevsky, with whom she had collaborated in editing the Academy edition of Pushkin's works.

It must have been the winter of 1966-67 when I first met her, by which time Irina Nikolaevna was already approaching sixty-five. I was gathering material for *Gulag*, and she had been a witness of the deportation of the Crimean Tatars from their homeland. I met her in that odd building on Cheboksary Lane where writers are housed (not far from the Church of Spas-na-Krovi), and we sat talking for three hours in her study, where her many books were shelved not just along the walls but in bays projecting into the room itself, as in a library. The spines of these volumes alone bespoke a profound and long-established culture. The notes I took as she was speaking cover events in the Crimea in 1944, followed, unexpectedly, by the destruction of the kulaks in 1930, then stories of village life in the Novgorod area in the 1920s. (It emerged that as a young woman from a highly cultured background, Irina Nikolaevna had married a simple Novgorod peasant, Medvedev, and had enjoyed such a wonderful life with him that even when married to her famous second husband, she would not drop the surname of the first.) Next came startling but by no means damning information about Arakcheyev's settlements* (she had lived in those parts, too). Irina Nikolaevna's stern character came through: there was a note of nostalgia for the civic virtues of uprightness and candor, which her whole generation had been denied. After that I was introduced to her daughter, an architect, and what with one thing and another almost the only subject we neglected throughout the entire visit was—literature. As for Sholokhov and the Don, they were not so much as mentioned.

It was quite true: Irina Nikolaevna's intellect poured forth in her speech and showed through the aged, rather sharp features of her dark-complexioned face; hers was a stern, masculine cast of mind. She received me most cordially and invited me to work in her study when she was away and to come and work at her home in Gurzuf (she dearly loved the Crimea and had written a book about it, entitled *Taurida*). But for all her cordiality, we did not easily warm to each other. She was a resolute and imperious woman, and this tended to crowd out her other qualities.

A year went by and she sent me a glorious photograph of her dacha on a hillside in Gurzuf, surrounded by cypress trees. For a long time this picture beckoned to me: here was a free corner of a kindly land, such as I could never experience in my constant race against the clock; I would be welcome there, and I could start work on my big narrative, the project I had been clawing my way toward for so many years, telling myself, Just a bit longer, then I'll start. But if I was to start, surely it would be a good thing to have a complete change of environment?

So in March 1969 I set off to visit Irina Nikolaevna and start my *Red Wheel*. It was a mistake. In order to *start*—especially on something that will be so extraordinarily hard to get off the ground—what one needs is not change but the same old familiar setting so that the only problems that arise are those of the task itself. Yet there I was, banking on finding a new frame of mind in a brand-new setting. I could not get acclimatized, achieved precisely nothing, and before three days were up I was on my way home. You can't put two willful old bears like Irina Nikolaevna and me, each one used to having the run of his own den, under the same roof and expect them to feel at ease. She tried to be a good hostess, while I forced myself to respond to her hospitality, but for both of us the effort swiftly palled. None of it came to anything—my work, the swimming (too cold and too far to walk), my blissful dream of getting away from it all. I begrudged every minute spent sightseeing in the Crimea, wanted nothing but to get down to my work, and could not wait to leave.

The one real event of that trip took place in passing. We met on the veranda in between two rooms and stood there talking for a few minutes, but the subject was—*The Quiet Don*. Before I could mention it, she told me about Molozhavenko's article and the furious response from Moscow. It goes without saying that neither of us believed for one moment that Sholokhov had written the novel. I went on to repeat something I had already said to others on more than one occasion—at gatherings of literary friends, for instance, where I hoped I might stimulate interest and plant the idea in someone's head: I said that it might well be beyond anyone's powers to prove our suspicions to the satisfaction of a court of law, let alone to establish the identity of the true author; too much time had elapsed and the trail was cold. But it was not beyond the powers of a serious and competent literary scholar to demonstrate that Sholokhov *did not* write *The Quiet Don*, nor would it be an especially laborious task. All that was needed was a comparison of the language, style, and the whole range of artistic devices used in *The Quiet Don* with those found in Sholokhov's *Virgin Soil Upturned*. (It never occurred to me to suspect that perhaps *Virgin Soil* itself had been written by someone else!) I was not appealing to her or pushing the point (although the hope did flash through my mind); I just said what I thought, as I had done on other occasions (never to any avail—literary experts have to earn a living, and work like this does not pay; rather, it costs you your neck!). We were not speaking at a telling moment at the beginning or end of my three-day visit; this was merely a passing exchange, and we took the matter no further.

Soon afterward, Irina Nikolaevna made up her mind. (I do not flatter myself that I was the cause; it had been clear from her first words that she was quite worked up over this literary enigma, and now the idea had simply come into its own.) Instead of slaving away at minor assignments for the sake of the money (more for her grown-up children than for herself), she had decided she would rise above all this, and before long she let us know through Q that she was going to start working on *The Quiet Don*. She asked for a copy of the first edition of the novel, which was difficult to come by, as well as certain items on the history of the Cossacks, for the Don was a completely new theme for her and there were many books and other materials she would have to read on the history of the Don region and of the civil war and on the dialects of that area. None of these could she possibly ask for in libraries without giving the game away. Once again we were up to our necks in conspiracy from the very first step we took! For some of the books we even had to look abroad, and they were delivered through our secret channels.

So the work began. And who would provide all the books and information that the "Lady" needed? (No conspiracy is complete without its code names, and we certainly could not use her real name in our letters and phone calls.) Who else but Lyusha Chukovskaya yet again! Lyusha took on each new burden without a murmur, and now there was this onerous chore to add to the rest.

Although the Cossack theme was remote from her interests, Lyusha now undertook the entire external organization of this aspect of the research, an indispensable role both from Irina Nikolaevna's point of view and from mine, for both of us led a largely housebound existence. This latest task of furnishing the Lady with all the materials and information she needed involved Lyusha in a good deal of work in Leningrad and the Crimea—never close to home. True, it was made somewhat easier by the fact that Irina Nikolaevna belonged to the same Moscow and Leningrad literary milieu in which Lyusha had grown up. More than that, Irina Nikolaevna remembered Lyusha's late father well and recalled seeing Lyusha herself as a little girl—all of which immediately put their relationship on a warm and friendly footing.

Lyusha tackled the work with diligence, resourcefulness, and considerable success. Without her, the book *Troubled Waters of the Quiet Don* would never have appeared, not even in the form in which it was eventually published.*

And then there was a secret and miraculous turn of events. The first step had no sooner been taken, the first person had no sooner resolved to enter the lists against Sholokhov than various other elements began to close in for what would be an explosive combination. Help came our way through the good offices of Natalya Milyevna Anichkova, a woman with an unfailingly lucky touch. Natasha Kruchinina, the daughter of a childhood friend of hers, worked as a therapist in Leningrad. "Natanya" (we used this form as there were beginning to be rather too many Natashas in our circle) enjoyed the confidence of a patient, Maria Akimovna Aseyeva, who revealed to her that she had been hounded for years by Sholokhov's gang; they were trying to wrest her cherished "little notebook" from her, containing the first chapters of *The Quiet Don*, written in Saint Petersburg at the beginning of 1917. But where had it come from? Who had written it? Why, Fyodor Dmitrievich Kryukov, the well-known (not to us!) Don Cossack writer. Maria Akimovna's father was the mining engineer Aseyev, and Kryukov had lived in his apartment in Saint Petersburg and left behind his manuscripts and personal archives when he set off "temporarily" to the Don in the spring of 1917, just for a few short weeks. But events took a different turn, and he never returned. It was her father who had discovered the similarity between the notebook and *The Quiet Don*, which came out in the 1920s. "But if I say anything, they'll lynch me." Now Maria Akimovna trusted Natanya so much that she had promised to leave the notebook to her—not now, but in her will.

That was at the end of 1969. Our little circle was shaken by the news. What should we do? Keep out of it? Out of the question! Wait for years? Preposterous! This wrong had already gone unavenged for more than forty years as it was, and they might manage to intimidate Maria Akimovna enough to prize the notebook out of her grip. And was there in fact anything to the story? It would be good to see with one's own eyes. And what might the rest of the archive hold? And if we ask her, then in whose name? Mine? But would my name be a help or a hindrance?

The most sensible course of action would simply have been for me to go and see her. But I was in the very thick of writing *August*. The question of whether I was capable of writing a historical novel or not hung in the balance, and I could not possibly tear myself away. In any case, I might be followed to her house. (This was all happening in the months following my expulsion from the Writers' Union, at a time when there were already hints that I ought to leave the country.)

It should have occurred to us at the time to send someone from the Don. (We even had such a person, but he was a big, obtrusive fellow, talkative and too free and easy—we could not possibly send him.) Lyusha volunteered to make the trip. This was a mistake. But as yet we had no idea what Maria Akimovna herself was like. Lyusha hoped that the Chukovsky family cachet might inspire more trust and less fear than most. Perhaps it would. (As for *my* name, it emerged that Maria Akimovna had scarcely so much as heard of it at that time; it was not until later that she read some of my things.)

Lyusha came back empty-handed and despondent: the woman, she said, was willful and difficult; it was virtually impossible to reach any kind of understanding with her, although it seemed she might be prepared to let the open part of Kryukov's archive be systematized, as almost nothing had been done to it for fifty years and this was preying on her mind. We decided to send out a second expedition in the person of Dima Borisov. Probably we should have sent him in the first place. He was not from the Don, but he immediately won Maria Akimovna's confidence. They even sang Russian songs together, and he succeeded in winning her agreement to let us have the archives. However, they could not simply be taken on the spur of the moment; there were enough papers to fill three hefty knapsacks. This meant a third trip, and this time Dima was accompanied by Andrei Tyurin. They brought back the entire archive that Kryukov had left behind, but only on loan for sorting and classification. However, the *"little notebook"* was for later, they were told. We were not about to insist. What we were getting was a considerable treasure. This was Kryukov's principal archive and, very likely, his only one. After he left it, he lived through three years of upheaval before meeting his death during the Whites' retreat.

With all her experience of looking after her grandfather's archives, Lyusha imagined that she could put Kryukov's papers in order, too. But she could only manage the most superficial classification. This was an archive quite different from what she had known: the literary milieu was unfamiliar, and so was much of the subject matter; the names of people and places, the factual background—everything was obscure, and as if that were not enough, Kryukov's handwriting was not the most legible.

But at this point our "Don Cossack" set to work! It was as if he had been waiting for this archive all his life, as if he had lived for nothing else. He simply fell upon it. As always, he worked without a moment's leisure or a day of rest, totally absorbed by what he was reading, and in one year he did the work of three people, acquiring a detailed knowledge of the papers (copying substantial excerpts for his own use as well), and he presented us with a complete summary of the structure and composition of the archive. (All of this involved many a meeting and transfer of documents from one place to another. Initially, the archive was kept at Galya Tyurina's home, then part of it was moved to Lyusha's apartment, from which it was taken, a little at a time, to the Don Cossack's home and back again, while part went into more remote storage at Lamara's place in the former "Beria" building.* In this case, as always, everything was geared to secrecy and camouflage, and at no stage could we run anything resembling an open office.)

As the documents gradually yielded up their secrets, everything that might be of use to the Lady had to be put at her disposal (but she spent more of her time in the Crimea than in Leningrad, and these materials were not exactly suitable for sending by mail). And I, too, needed to see some of them, both for their treatment of the actual events in the Don region and as the testimony of a quite exceptional eyewitness. (But by now I was incapable of taking it in. I was so completely saturated that I had lost my capacity to absorb anything new. Fascinating as it was to explore what Kryukov had to say, there was simply no room for it. Lyusha had a brainstorm, and I adopted it at once: why not take Kryukov, regardless of whether he was the author of *The Quiet Don* or not, and make him a character in the novel? He was such a vivid, fascinating figure, and we had so much authentic material about him. How often does a literary prototype come complete with such a mass of written evidence? I adopted him as a character, and it was a good decision; it enabled me to bring so much more into the novel! And what an attractive solution—I no longer had to rely on my own inexperience but could approach the whole subject of the Don from the perspective of a local man who had had more than his share of the suffering and anguish of those years.)

As Irina Nikolaevna received fresh materials about the Don, her provisional thesis took shape. On one winter visit, probably early in 1971, she brought with her three small typed pages in the form of a "Draft Outline for a Book," in which she listed all of her main hypotheses: these included the theory that Sholokhov did not simply plagiarize another writer's work but *spoiled* it by cutting up, transposing, and obscuring the original and that the true author was Kryukov.

It is true that Sholokhov's novel has neither a unified structure nor balanced proportions—that much is immediately evident. The idea that more than one person might have been in control is not at all difficult to believe.

Irina Nikolaevna had gone so far as to mark out chapter by chapter the points at which the text can be peeled back to reveal the true author's text. She had even set herself the task of finishing her study with a reconstruction of the original text of the novel!

Her approach showed such impressive flair and authority! Even in its initial stages her research already had a wider sweep than we had ever expected. But she did not have the reserves of health or the extra years of life she needed, nor sufficient free time, for once again she was having to work nonstop to earn her living. For our part, we had no Soviet money to draw on, and since Irina Nikolaevna refused to allow us to have hard currency transferred to her from abroad in someone else's name, there was nothing we could do from 1972 to 1973 to free her from material cares. Otherwise, her book might well have progressed by leaps and bounds.

At first, the conclusion that someone as mild as Kryukov was the author of *The Quiet Don* was disappointing. Some craggy, tragic figure was more what I expected. But our researcher, Irina Nikolaevna, was confident, and gradually, as I got to know everything that Kryukov had published and prepared for publication, I began to agree with her. There are *individual* passages dotted here and there in many different stories where Kryukov comes little short of genius. Only, their effect is diluted by being combined with fairly vacuous or even mawkish writing. (On the other hand, a certain mawkishness survives in the nature descriptions of *The Quiet Don* itself.) But when I gathered together some of the best passages from Kryukov's stories and assembled them in the chapter "From the Notebooks of Fyodor Kovynyov,"* the effect was so dazzling it almost hurt to read them.

I became more and more ready to concede that in the swirling bitter years of Cossack history and the final years of his own life, a writer might experience a marked concentration of his powers, might drain life's bitter cup, and rise above his former self.

Or perhaps the author was not Kryukov, but someone as yet unknown to us?

Once the archive had been organized, we deposited the less precious part of it in the Lenin Library at Maria Akimovna's request and passed on to her the fee of five hundred rubles that they paid. It was a blunder on our part to give it to the library; we were not paid enough for it, which put us in an embarrassing position with Maria Akimovna, and we had left our tracks exposed. They would know that someone close to us was working on Kryukov. But the sheer bulk and weight of the archive was a constant headache—how should we store it and, above all, where?

In June 1971 I was in Leningrad and went to see Maria Akimovna. Our meeting went well. She turned out to be another tough-minded woman, truly unbending in her attitude toward the Bolsheviks; she forgave them nothing, and neither illness nor family misfortunes (her husband had left her) could sap her will. She was genuinely committed to revealing the truth about the Don and about Kryukov himself. We drank wine from the Don region and ate a meal typical of those parts. I had the impression that after this she believed me to be reliable. At the same time, I had come to believe in her "notebook"—it really existed! All that was needed was to fetch it from Tsarskoe Selo out in the suburbs, "from the old lady who is keeping it for me." (Maria Akimovna had failed to stop word about the notebook from leaking out, and since then, she told me, people from Sholokhov's entourage kept coming around with bribes and threats.) She promised to retrieve it before I left Leningrad.

But she did not do so. ("The old lady won't let me have it.") I expressed my regret, but my former doubts resurfaced—did this notebook really exist? Yet if it didn't, then why pull the wool over our eyes? It did not seem in character.

But in conversation with another woman, Faina Terentyeva, whom she knew from the outpatients' department, Maria Akimovna was less grudging with her confidence! She even told her how she had really wanted to give me the notebook but had been afraid to: after all, anything might happen to me; they were trailing me, they would take the book from me. A fatal error! Of course, it was hard for her to weigh the odds and decide where it would be safer. But a fatal error, because we would have sent a photocopy for publication together with samples of Kryukov's handwriting, and if the drafts really had resembled the beginning of *The Quiet Don*, then Sholokhov would not have had a leg to stand on, and Kryukov would have been vindicated once and for all. But now Maria Akimovna and her notebook were tightly boxed in, and dearly as she would have liked to pass it to someone, it was too late. Our omnipotent guardians of national security had replaced the neighbors with whom she shared her communal apartment (just as had happened with Q), installing their own people instead. Now Maria Akimovna was, to all intents and purposes, imprisoned, and a watchful eye followed her every move.

I learned of this postscript to the story in July 1975 from Faina Terentyeva in Toronto, where she had emigrated. She wrote that Maria Akimovna had tried to give her the notebook but that she had been afraid to take it, and she asked what she could do now to help get it out. . . .

Not a thing. The only hope is that the beleaguered Maria Akimovna will cling to her sanity and manage to hold out for what could be many a year.[1]

Well, there it was—we had failed to get hold of the notebook, and now we were waiting for the research itself to be completed. However, it was progressing very slowly: Irina Nikolaevna was inundated with tedious contractual obligations, which exhausted her but did at least pay the bills. Lyusha and I met her more than once on her way through Moscow, and she gave me drafts of individual chapters to read. Lyusha (or Q in Leningrad) would type them out, for although her handwriting was far from easy to decipher and the text was full of interpolations, the task could not be entrusted to anyone else.

[1] Now Maria Akimovna, too, is dead. I still do not know whether she took her secret with her to the grave or whether it even existed. (1986 note)

The last time I saw Irina Nikolaevna was in March 1972. The meeting took place once again in her study in Leningrad, the room where we had first met and in which she had offered to let me work. (But by now events were crowding in on me, and it was worrying to bump into one of her neighbors, a writer, as I was going in. She might have recognized me. Word might get out that I had some connection with Irina Nikolaevna. Not good at all!) Illness had etched its mark more deeply on Irina Nikolaevna's features, but her bearing had lost nothing of its indomitable, almost masculine toughness. Without any prompting, she launched into a monologue: what would she say if *they* were to come and find out what she was up to? (I had crossed the Rubicon so long ago that I had forgotten such dilemmas existed, but everyone has to take that first step at one time or another, and it is no easy matter.) She was already steeling herself to reply with full self-assurance and without yielding an inch. She was not signing any petitions and had stopped meeting people; isolated, she trod her lonely path and faced the trials that lay ahead.

Shortly before the denouement of the whole story Natalya Milyevna Anichkova (who else!) added still more fuel to the fire. She insisted that I come over and meet an old Cossack who, though a Bolshevik, had also been a zek. Apparently he wanted to give me some valuable materials about Filipp Mironov, commander of the Second Cavalry Army, under whom he had served as regimental commissar. I arrived, and it all turned out to have been a misunderstanding. Sergei Pavlovich Starikov had collected a great deal of damning documentary material (working in closed archives and with official blessing) not only about his beloved Mironov, who died thanks to Trotsky, but also concerning the Bolsheviks' systematic destruction of the Cossacks during the civil war. What he wanted to do was immortalize Mironov in a separate monograph, but he was not capable of writing it himself. He was now seriously proposing that I should work for him as a ghostwriter, processing the material he had gathered and writing the actual book, where-upon he would publish it under his own name and repay me out of the royalties. My counterproposal was that he should let me have the materials he had collected, and I would see that Mironov's biography was fed gradually into the general panorama of the epoch. He refused. We were obviously at cross-purposes, and that would have been the end of the matter—but as we were taking our leave we chatted about this and that, and it transpired that Mironov had come from the same Cossack settlement as Kryukov and had been his best friend in their youth. Moreover, Starikov himself was from the same settlement, Ust-Medveditskaya. Not only was Starikov positive that Sholokhov had purloined *The Quiet Don* from Kryukov (he had seen the fifteen-year-old Sholokhov in Vyoshchenskaya and remembered him as an altogether dull and backward boy) but he knew something else besides—namely, who actually "put the finishing touches" to *The Quiet Don* and who wrote *Virgin Soil Upturned*. In both cases the answer was not Sholokhov but his father-in-law, Pyotr Gromoslavsky. In the past, Gromoslavsky had been the ataman of a Cossack settlement (and before that, apparently, a church deacon—until he gave up the cloth), but he also had literary interests. He had sided with the Whites and had to hide from his past for the rest of his life. Gromoslavsky had been close to Kryukov and served with him in the retreat to the Kuban, burying him there after his death and taking possession of the manuscript. He had then, so the story went, passed it on to young Mishka Sholokhov by way of a dowry when Sholokhov married his daughter Maria. (By Starikov's account, she was twenty-five and an old maid, while her new husband was only nineteen.) Then, after Gromoslavsky's death, Sholokhov could no longer write at all.[2]

---

[2] Gromoslavsky was still alive in the 1950s, which is when the second volume of *Virgin Soil Upturned* came out, but for the twenty years following Gromoslavsky's death Sholokhov did not publish another line. I pointed this out in an article on *Virgin Soil Upturned* ("The Don Debate," *Vestnik RKhD*, no. 141, 1984) where I also took the opportunity to respond to the ludicrous attempt by the Norwegian

In the months to come, my negotiations with Starikov cropped up again. It was in the autumn of 1973, a time full of menace for us, when Natalya Anichkova told me that Starikov was close to death and wanted me to come as quickly as possible so that he could arrange to let me have all his materials. I got there, but no—now that he had recovered from his heart attack, he was not exactly pre-occupied with preparations for death, and he embarked once again on the same tedious haggling over documents. I stuck to my line: let me use the materials about Mironov in my big epic. He had been warned about me since our last meeting and been put on his guard. Now he countered with: they say you're distorting Soviet history. (This was the work of Roy Medvedev and his circle of Communist friends; Starikov had, after all, been a member of the Party in the past! Almost immediately after this he would give everything he had collected to Roy, thus inspiring Roy's own book* about the events on the Don—a subject to which he had probably never given more than a few moments' thought in his whole life.) Starikov did nevertheless agree to lend me a number of items for a short while. Strike while the iron is hot! I ought to jump at the offer, but who is going pick the stuff up? We don't have a spare hand among us! And there is Alya with three children to see to. So yet again it fell to Lyusha, who had not really recovered completely from the car crash that had left her with a concussion. She went to Starikov's home and sorted out the papers we wanted, maintaining the same solemn expression throughout so that he should not get a clear sense of what we were interested in. He would only lend them to her for a short period, which he later telephoned to reduce still further. She had to read everything into a Dictaphone before typing it, which added an extra stage to the work. Lyusha was working flat out, typing for me (there is no access to photocopiers in our coun-

---

slavist Geir Kjetsaa and his colleagues to demonstrate Sholokhov's authorship on the basis of computer analysis.* (1986 note)

try, remember!); Starikov's materials were truly mind-boggling, but now he had had second thoughts and was snapping at her heels, demanding that she give everything back—hand it over right away! (After I had been deported, he came to see Alya and kept insisting that she return the excerpts we had copied as well. If they were discovered at customs, they would want to know who had obtained them from secret archives and that would lead them to—Starikov.) But when all is said and done, Sergei Pavlovich Starikov did his bit to recover the true history of our times, and he thoroughly deserves a pat on the back!

That autumn everything came to a head: the loss of *Gulag* and the campaign I launched in response, the death of Q and the fear that she might have exposed the whole network involved with *The Quiet Don*. (She had called to see Irina Nikolaevna in Gurzuf, the last of us to do so—but what a way to call! She had brought with her that same "Gudyakov, the poet," who had latched onto her in the Crimea, an error of judgment that might have had fatal consequences.)

At the beginning of September Irina Nikolaevna was alone in Gurzuf once again. She had just celebrated her seventieth birthday with her son and daughter, and now they had returned home. Tuning in to a Western radio station, she heard about the seizure of *Gulag* and the death of Voronyanskaya and promptly suffered a heart attack. (We were quite unaware of what had happened to her.) But her character was as hard as iron, and she concluded that the best course was not to hide her manuscripts away and stop work, but quite the contrary, to muster all her remaining strength and attempt to complete it! Now, thanks to her incomparable willpower, she was hard at work—now, of all times, flat on her back in bed, unable even to reach for a book without an enormous effort. And by dint of these secret labors she was gradually making up the ground she had lost. She had invited Lyusha to stay with her for the month of September in order to get some serious assistance. But after the car crash Lyusha herself could scarcely walk so that accident also did its share to frustrate the completion of *Troubled Waters of the Quiet Don*.

Lyusha was aware of the danger that under interrogation Q might have disclosed something about Irina Nikolaevna's work and that, as a result, Irina Nikolaevna might be caught red-handed with her manuscripts. With this in mind, Lyusha now turned to Ekaterina Vasilyevna Zabolotskaya, the sixty-year-old widow of the poet Zabolotsky, who knew Irina Nikolaevna very well. Lyusha asked Zabolotskaya to go and help her friend and to see that the manuscripts were removed safely. Ekaterina Vasilyevna acted decisively and, leaving her four grandchildren, flew off to the Crimea at once. There she discovered Irina Nikolaevna, barely over her heart attack but working on regardless, and she stayed to take care of her. In all she spent a month with her before the need to look after her grandchildren drew her back to Moscow. She brought with her part of Irina Nikolaevna's manuscript.

From Leningrad Irina Nikolaevna's daughter engaged a nurse in Gurzuf to come in every day and look after her mother—in addition, of course, to the visits of her regular doctor. On the telephone, Irina Nikolaevna was anxious to know whether anything had happened to her apartment in Leningrad (had there been a search?).

Then came the news that Irina Nikolaevna was dead. Ekaterina Vasilyevna volunteered to fly to Gurzuf once again and try to save the rest of the manuscripts, which she had asked the doctor to take care of in the event of Irina Nikolaevna's death. But the storm clouds were gathering, and for safety's sake she could not go alone. Who could accompany her? Natalya Stolyarova—who was constantly on the go—undertook to be her traveling companion. (Ahead of them lay an unavoidable night's stay in Simferopol, and at this stage, signing in at a hotel was quite out of the question, even if they had been lucky enough to find a vacant room—another example of the endless complications that the Communist system puts in the way of conspirators. I remembered the house in Simferopol where Nikolai Ivanovich Zubov and I had once burned *The First Circle*, and I wrote a quick note to the owners on the off chance . . . Despite their amazement, they did let the two women spend the night there but made a careful note of their names and subsequently told Nikolai Ivanovich about them. However, the Zubovs never found out just who these visitors were and why they had come. The conspiracy at which the three of us had first dabbled some twenty years before had now caught them with a flick of its far-reaching tail.) And the two women's trip was all in vain. The doctor gave them nothing and spoke in vague terms about an arson attack on a shed near Irina Nikolaevna's dacha, adding that in general "there were things he could not talk about." The circumstances of Irina Nikolaevna's death remained something of a mystery to us, nor can we be at all sure that we have all the completed fragments of her book.

And so all we could add to the book was the part of the manuscript we had received earlier. It did not amount to a great deal. Of the bold and well-defined plan that Irina Nikolaevna had originally mapped out, not much had been brought to fruition in the intervening two years. If Lyusha had been well enough to go there in September, then perhaps they might have managed between them to distill another chapter or two from what were still very rough drafts. But no, a curse hung over the treasure of *The Quiet Don*.[3]

Although all these questions relating to the Don were essentially a side issue, they had become a duty that could not be shaken off, and even in the last months remaining to us, in the shadow of the noose, we pressed on and on, trying to force the matter further. For instance, from Riga we were brought a good photocopy of the en-

---

[3] In 1988 and 1989 there appeared in issues 60 and 63 of the Israeli journal *22* a most persuasive textual analysis by Zeev Bar-Sella entitled "*The Quiet Don* Versus Sholokhov." This was the kind of thing we had long been waiting for. (1990 note)

tire first edition of *The Quiet Don*, which had then been subjected to years of drastic chopping and changing by a specially appointed ten-person editorial team. (Stalin himself even supposedly supervised their work; the 1948 edition refers in a note to the "supervising editor G. S. Churov," who, it has been claimed, is actually Stalin.) Then there was the time I spent at Peredelkino in the final days before my exile, finishing off my preface to *Troubled Waters of the Quiet Don*. Or the sheet of published materials I put together from Irina Nikolaevna's various fragmentary notes. (The pseudonym D★, which I gave her, derived both from Don and from "Dama," the Russian for "madame," "lady." She had been in the process of picking a pen name from my list of surnames of the Don region but did not get around to making her choice.)[4]

An inner voice kept telling me that for safety's sake, Kryukov's archive needed to go into separate storage; these materials, along with anything relating to *Troubled Waters of the Quiet Don*, would have to be completely isolated from everything of mine. So ten days before I was deported, in what was probably the last visit I paid while in Russia, I went to Elena Vsevolodovna Vertogradskaya's apartment, on the other side of Krestyanskaya Zastava. She had invited several

---

[4] In the interests of Irina Nikolaevna's children we were forced to conceal the author's true name for another fifteen years, which gave rise to jibes to the effect that I had invented this D★ figure.

Then in 1989 I learned, from a letter by Dr. V. I. Baranov to *Knizhnoe obozrenie*, that when *Troubled Waters of the Quiet Don* came out in the West, a powerful rebuttal was organized in the Soviet Union. First Konstantin Simonov was charged with giving an interview to the West German magazine *Stern*, an assignment that he duly carried out. Then they waited for the West to show interest in it, intending to respond with a broadside of articles in *Literaturnaya gazeta, Voprosy literatury*, and *Izvestia*. The articles were already written, but . . . in the West Simonov's interview passed without comment. They still published the articles that had been prepared, but ostensibly in commemoration of Sholokhov's seventieth birthday and without any reference to the book by D★. Nowadays, the Soviet press blames this book for so disconcerting Sholokhov that it stopped him from finishing his thirty-year-old novel *They Fought for the Motherland*; he was supposedly so upset that he could not add a single line to a book he had started during the war! (1990 note)

young people over, and our task was to decide who would look after the *Quiet Don* archive. Georgi Pavlovich and Tonya Gikalo agreed to take it on, and a few days later at most, the delivery was made by Sasha Gorlov, who by now had been hounded out of every job he had held. It was moved not a moment too soon! When I was arrested, I drew comfort from the knowledge that this archive, at least, had been saved.

A memorial service was held for Irina Nikolaevna in Moscow at the Church of Ilya (Elijah) Obydenny. It was out of the question for me to attend, but Lyusha's friendship with Zoya Tomashevskaya was no secret, so she was able to go. Prior to this, however, Lyusha had passed on to us one of Irina Nikolaevna's dearest wishes, which she had confided to her during Lyusha's last visit: at some time in the future she wanted a requiem to be held for her in the Church of the Elevation of the Cross in Geneva, where she had been baptized. But whom could we entrust with this duty? What chance was there that any of us would ever be in Geneva? But in fact someone *would* be there: I myself, and all too soon. . . .

Alya and I arrived in Geneva one evening in October 1974, but it was a weekday, and since it did not coincide with a church festival, there was no reason for services to be held that day or the next. Still, we walked through the rain to the church on the off chance, hoping at least to touch its doors. When we got there, however, we could hear singing coming from inside. On entering, we discovered that the actual end of the period marking the Elevation of the Cross fell on the following day and that, as this church was dedicated to this holiday, a service was to be held here!

Next morning, after mass, Archbishop Anthoni of Geneva celebrated a requiem at our request. I wrote down the names of the dead: Irina and Fyodor. . . .

It was an attractive stone church, "fair in the sight of the Lord." The autumn sun shone in at the windows. Smoke from the incense rose and drifted in the air. The little choir sang with assurance and fervor; their "At Peace with the Saints" was so heartrending that I could not hold back the tears. Again and again the two names rang out united, offered up in prayer by the archbishop, echoed by the choir. Their fates intertwined—the ill-starred author from the Don and his intercessor, the lady from Saint Petersburg—and they rose together above the murders and deceptions, above the stark oppression of our age.

Grant them, O Lord, to know Thy truth and justice. And roll away the stone that weighs so heavy on their hearts.

1974–1975
Zurich

APPENDIX A

Letter from
Natalya Stolyarova

Paris, October 29, 1977

Dear Aleksandr Isaevich,

. . . Your kind words about my return leave me thoroughly embarrassed—it's like one of those awkward moments when people are singing your praises and you just keep quiet. In fact, it all worked out thanks to you, would you believe it! With your help I was able to spend a year living in the West, scarcely dependent on anyone (I couldn't have endured it otherwise). Thanks to you I was blessed with a unique opportunity to choose calmly and freely after deep and searching reflection; my mind was burdened neither by principles (I've nothing against them, I've just never had any need of them), nor by a "sense of duty" (strictly forbidden—doctor's orders!), nor even by an awareness of the good I might do (I never take a utilitarian view, not even of myself). A year ago that golden autumn in

Paris made me feel that I was back in my own hometown, never to leave it again. Well, it didn't work out that way. I had absolute freedom, it seemed —and with it the "stream more bright than azure skies" and "golden ray of sun,"* and no one could appreciate it more than I! Yet my heart was like an open wound, torn this way and that by love and hate for that great, terrible, tormented, trampled, that immortal, beloved Russia of my dreams.

. . . Today I was wandering through the passages of the subway carrying parcels for posting to Moscow when suddenly I heard a deep voice singing in Russian: it belonged to one of those indigent street musicians who sit on the floor singing and accompanying themselves on the guitar. I looked and saw a young Russian face. He was singing the folk song "O, Dear Plains." And he sang well, with intense longing, and many passersby stopped to listen. To my shame I wept as I listened, turning my head to the wall—wept bitterly as if I had kept my tears bottled up all that year. What was I crying for: for the curse that hangs over our country, forcing people to flee—young and old, good people, all kinds of people—all fleeing. And each of them is right in his own way, for we are all granted but a single life to live. Yet "I feel sorry for Russia."*

You would think that fear and oppression would have reduced the very concept of freedom and human dignity to ashes in our country, but in fact that same inexorable pressure to which the spirit is exposed has unexpectedly increased the *need* for freedom and dignity tenfold. It was not so much the prison camps as the Soviet version of "liberty" that taught me to value *freedom* above everything in this world—the freedom to live, to move about, to think for oneself—the freedom for which we strive so fervently. And it is ultimately for the sake of this passion, this intense life that we "tightrope walkers despite ourselves" endeavor to invest with freedom and dignity, that I am returning home. *Yes, I prefer living there*, listening to the steps on the stairway at night, frantically stripping the apartment of anything subversive because someone kept ringing my doorbell the night before (I discovered later that it was an ambulance crew who had come to the wrong door); I prefer a life spent constantly outwitting the "all-seeing eye" (and ear) and drawing as best I can on the literature in which our land is so rich (and which floats out to me here in Europe with such insultingly effortless ease), a life spent satisfying as best as I can my inexhaustible craving to hear the word of truth. Perhaps *that* is why I so jealously guarded [during travels in the West—A. S.] the chastity of my passport, lest any irregularity should prove an obstacle to my return.

Since this is likely to be my last letter to you, I would ask you, if you wish me well, not to depict me as better than I really am. Remember how greedy I am for life in all its diversity, what a contradictory person I am and how *content* I am to be so, how sybaritic I am, never running away from temptation but always straight into its arms. True, I am grateful to fate for my life, for the remarkable people I have met, none of whom I shall ever forget. You, in particular, were one of my great temptations, as I immediately recognized the very first time we spoke together, and as you will remember, I would not let you go until you had "heard me out."

Of course I shall pass on all your greetings when I get to Moscow, but there are very few people I shall be able to tell about our meeting. We shall *very* much look forward to seeing the small-format edition of your books. Our channels of communication are not looking too good (not many people enjoy walking the high wire in someone else's country for any length of time), but I believe in the miracle of personal contact, and I find that life (mine, at least) is an endless succession of miracles—to such a degree that I have come to take them for granted.

I send you my love and will never forget you.

N. Stolyarova

From Rostov-on-Don to Moscow

or

The KGB Versus Solzhenitsyn

Recollections of a Chekist

by Boris Ivanov[1]

The shrill and unexpected jangling of the telephone was cause for concern. The phone in question, one of three arrayed on a stand next to a huge desk, had a very special function. It had no dial, since it was a direct line, and in off-the-record talk with colleagues it was referred to as the "black" or "boss" line. As a rule it was employed only by the head administrator or "general," and the response was expected to be immediate and appropriately brisk: "Good morning, sir, what can I do for you?" The other two

---

[1] This memoir appeared in abridged form in the Moscow monthly *Sovershenno sekretno*, 1992, No. 4.

Boris Aleksandrovich Ivanov, a professional KGB agent, spent more than three decades in the employ of the state security agency based in the northern Caucasus region, in Georgia, and in Lithuania. From 1967 to 1976 he headed one of the subdivisions of the ideological directorate in the Rostov KGB administration.

phones were of the ordinary kind, one connected to the city switchboard, the other directly linked to the various departments of our agency. (Somewhat later we were given a fourth line for communicating with agency offices located elsewhere.) The assortment of telephones in any given office testified to the position of its occupant within the rigid hierarchy of the security agency. Conversations conducted on these phones had a peculiar style marked by Aesopian allusions, figurative terminology, and conspiratorial tone. In contrast, the brief and infrequent exchanges on the "black" line always had the appearance of absolute harmlessness. . . .

The message conveyed by the familiar, slightly impersonal voice in the receiver was simple: "Please step into my office."

The invitation surprised me greatly. The standard—albeit unwritten—rules specified that any meeting with the chief administrative officer must occur with the permission, and in the presence of, one's immediate superior. So this was clearly irregular.

I entered the spacious, partially darkened reception room and gave a questioning look to the secretary, who did double duty as the general's assistant and adjutant. Though I cannot say we were friends, we had the kind of easy relationship that permitted communicating by means of gestures and facial expressions. I nodded in the direction of the door to the general's office as if to say, "What's going on in there?"

The response was similarly wordless: "I have no idea."

I passed through the massive double door and announced my presence. The general was in a good—I would even say exceptionally fine—mood. An unfamiliar middle-aged man clad in a double-breasted gray suit was sitting next to him. The general motioned for me to take a seat across the desk from the stranger and introduced us to each other, indicating the name, rank, and official duties of each. He then warned us of the top-secret nature of the business at hand, referring to instructions received from the "center"—that is, from KGB headquarters in Moscow. My question as to whether and how this should be made known to my immediate superior received a nod of acknowledgment that signified that I had nothing to worry about. The general then proceeded with the briefing.

"The writer Solzhenitsyn is traveling to our region for unknown reasons. The comrade from Moscow has been sent here in connection with this alarming development. You, Boris Aleksandrovich, are well versed in Solzhenitsyn's years of residence in Rostov and are informed about his former links to people here. I frankly can't think of anyone who could be of greater help to the comrade from Moscow. The other departments of our agency have already been instructed to render you all necessary assistance. Hotel reservations have been made, and a car has been assigned for the guest's needs. I am sure that you will have a pleasant supper together, and I very much regret that I won't be able to join you.

The fact that the general turned down a chance to dine with us made me very uneasy. Could the guest's rank have made this inappropriate in some way? Or was headquarters somehow at odds with the local authorities? In the course of my long service in the KGB, I had fulfilled a great variety of tasks and errands, but this time I intuitively felt that something extraordinary was going on. But it would have been stupid to ask a direct question; the rule in such situations is to keep one's mouth shut so as not to find oneself in an untenable position that might lead to unpleasant consequences. The only thing clear was that the guest from Moscow had been assigned to fulfill a mission focused on the leader of the "dissidents" (a fashionable and much-used term at that time), the writer Aleksandr Solzhenitsyn.

But why should Moscow headquarters become directly involved here, on our territory? Normal procedure would have been to turn the operation over to the Rostov branch. Perhaps they simply did not trust us in view of what they knew of Solzhenitsyn? The point here is that he truly did possess outstanding conspiratorial talents. Perhaps he was a born conspirator, or perhaps a life filled with suffering and deprivation had honed this quality in him, but he often managed to confound even seasoned veterans of the agency's ideological counterintelligence unit. This, in turn, caused the KGB's Fifth (ideological) Directorate to assemble a special operations unit specifically to deal with Solzhenitsyn. I was fully aware of the existence of this group and had a fairly good idea of its composition. Stated in the most general terms, it consisted of "theoreticians" (literary professionals invited from outside), "planners" (career KGB officers who analyzed the information gathered and decided on specific actions to be taken), and "implementers" who had the task of carrying out the decisions of the "planners" with due regard to concrete circumstances.

When Solzhenitsyn began exhibiting more and more hostility toward the socialist system, orders were issued to remove from circulation all his published works as well as to confiscate any samizdat copies. While the literary and social phenomenon of samizdat had existed before Solzhenitsyn, the international renown it achieved is attributable directly to this writer. The tide of dissidence generated by him could not be contained by the border controls of the "most progressive state," and it surged abroad. The state's response was to strengthen the special operations unit within the ideological division of the security agency. I did not know the identities of all the individuals who made up this group, and I believe its overall composition fluctuated considerably in accordance with the demands put on it. But there was an unchanging nucleus that consisted of "planners" and "implementers," some of whom held very high positions and who, following the regulations in force at the time, made contact directly with me. In fact, I established amiable relations with the head of the Moscow unit as well as with his chief assistant. The primary task of this group was to block the dissemination of the literary works of Aleksandr Solzhenitsyn in official and unofficial publications.

The appearance of *One Day in the Life of Ivan Denisovich* had specific ramifications in the Don area, with the local KGB branch asked to undertake an exhaustive study of the writer's life in Rostov. We knew that he had lived in Rostov with his mother, had attended school here, and had studied physics and mathematics at the local university. A detailed scrutiny of the links he had with friends and acquaintances, as well as of any romantic connections, allowed us to determine the character of the persons involved and, above all, the means of approaching them. The circle of identifiable classmates from school and university turned out to be relatively small because of the passage of three decades. These people resided in Rostov, Novocherkassk, Taganrog, and naturally enough represented a wide range of personalities; some now held very substantial positions. The information gathered from them presented the following picture. The writer's mother had been a simple typist in a government agency; as a result the family experienced constant hardship and deprivation. The young man was gifted, conscientious, and literally lived according to a schedule. Girls liked him for his intelligence and straightforward personality but thought his reserve and remoteness excessive and a little absurd.

A distinct pattern emerged in our interviews with Solzhenitsyn's former classmates and acquaintances: the higher the position of the individual, the less information would be forthcoming about his or her relationship with the writer. Some made assiduous efforts to denounce him, but there were also a few obviously courageous individuals who spoke of the great writer with respect and admiration.

Since I headed one of the subdivisions of the Fifth Ideological Directorate of the Rostov KGB bureau, all the information gathered about

Solzhenitsyn's life in Rostov-on-Don was funneled to my desk. The standing instructions were that I should immediately forward all such data to the Fifth Directorate at KGB headquarters in Moscow, addressing it to the special operations unit referred to earlier.

But my duties were by no means limited to this function. Headquarters saw to it that appropriately coached foreign writers were sent to Rostov in order to familiarize themselves with the period of time the writer had spent here. The only purpose of all this was to present material that, when published abroad, would compromise Solzhenitsyn's name. This policy was in effect for many years and in fact was not limited to collaboration with foreigners. Thus, Solzhenitsyn's first wife, Natalya Reshetovskaya, received help from the Fifth Directorate in publishing and distributing a book in which she attempted to discredit her former husband.

But to return to foreign visitors. The first of them to come to Rostov was a Czech national by the name of Tomaš Řezáč, the son of a writer prominent in Czechoslovakia. In 1968, during the so-called Prague Spring, Tomaš had emigrated to Switzerland but was returned to Czechoslovakia by the Czech security services. The reason for this, presumably, was that great hopes had been held for Tomaš in view of his father's literary reputation. About thirty-five years old, a highly sociable man with an attractive accent in Russian and a partiality for good times, Tomaš was a study in likability. He loved to have a drink, a fact much used by the agencies interested in his services.

Řezáč arrived in Rostov accompanied by the head of the Moscow special operations unit as well as by a major of the Czech security agency named Vaclav. During the several days that they spent in the Don region, we acquainted the guests with Rostov and made a trip to the Novocherkassk Institute of Grape Growing and Wine Making (where a branch office of the local KGB was located). In the course of all this we provided the visitors with materials selected by the directors of the special operations unit, each time presented in a tendentious manner. The general scenario here was representative of the standard procedure we were under strict orders to follow. The result was a book by Řezáč entitled *The Spiral of Solzhenitsyn's Betrayal,** a complimentary copy of which was eventually forwarded to me from the center.

Another visit involved a woman writer from Canada. Being less than popular in her own country, she seems to have decided to make use of the lurid Solzhenitsyn theme as a ticket to international renown. A tall, gaunt, coarse-featured lady well past middle age, she did nothing to attract our sympathy.

On this occasion the visitor was nominally hosted by the Rostov branch of the Novosti Press Agency. The Moscow KGB representative who accompanied her had all the documents to support this disguise, even a business card in Russian and German with a telephone number unrelated to KGB headquarters (a fact that suggested the presence of a KGB unit within the Moscow Novosti offices). The Canadian writer was also accompanied by a translator from Moscow, a rather comely woman with brash manners and of indeterminate age. One assumes that she was an actual employee of Novosti, with parallel services rendered to the security agencies. During one of our dinners, washed down as they all were with moderate amounts of alcohol, the man from Moscow headquarters motioned toward the translator and asked me, "D'you know who she is? She's the daughter of Anka the machine-gun girl."

I had no idea what he was talking about.

The woman guffawed. "You mean you don't see the resemblance?" she asked. And then she added in a confidential tone, "My father really was Chapayev."*

As in all such cases, I had received specific instructions about how the Canadian visitor should be entertained. We paid a visit to the tasting room of the "Sun in a Wineglass" shop and to the frozen goods facility number 1, where we were fêted as the dearest of friends. The show continued with a hydrofoil ride along the Don River. The end result was sad enough, though, for as I learned later, the lady from Canada did not justify the hopes and expenses put into her visit and indeed seems to have publicly exposed the KGB's role in the whole enterprise. (In such cases it is always handy to blame the American intelligence agencies.)

The foregoing digression from the principal topic of my memoir is intended to emphasize that the appearance of any visitor sent by Moscow headquarters was invariably preceded by advance notice and specific instructions. But here was a visitor as unannounced as a bolt from the blue. One possible reason for the lack of warning could have been the rapid movement of Solzhenitsyn in his travels, and the visit of the stranger from Moscow might possibly be explained by a leadership change in the surveillance unit. But these were all guesses, and in the meantime, as we sat in the general's office, it was obvious that background information on Solzhenitsyn held little interest for the man from headquarters.

We took leave of the general and came out onto the street. It was a clear, warm late-summer day; we chose to forego the car ride and strolled to the Moskovskaya Hotel, where a luxurious suite had been reserved for the visitor. He stopped at the check-in desk to ask about a person whose name I could not make out. We went up to his room, where my new "chief" deposited the contents of his briefcase in a nightstand, and then we descended to the cafeteria. It should be noted that the dining room in this hotel was viewed as a sort of mecca by our agency's operations. This was the place for exchanging news and the latest gossip; having a couple of shots of vodka or a glass of wine while you were at it was considered perfectly aboveboard. The administration of our agency was well aware of these get-togethers and from time to time made use of them for its own purposes.

We entered the cozy alcove with its two windows and sat at my favorite table to the right of the entrance, a location from which one could observe the entire area. While the visitor studied his menu and asked my opinion about some of the items, I noticed a young man enter, exchange glances with my guest, give me a searching gaze, and saunter over to the counter. I could not help but conclude that the two men were acquainted. As he ordered his dinner, the new arrival glanced our way from time to time.

I had a vague but constant feeling of anxiety and was growing more and more tense. Smaller than average in stature, huskily built, and with a closely cropped head of dark hair, the stranger was probably a member of the seven-man surveillance team—or so it seemed if one were to judge by his appearance and behavior. Regulations forbade surveillance personnel from dealing with other operatives except through their leader, who functioned as a liaison officer.

This tentative conclusion set me somewhat at ease, and I began to pay more attention to my guest. The cleaning lady (who doubled as a waitress for regular customers) came to take our order. We ordered cognac, salads, and a meat dish. Our conversation perked up. After some general comments, my companion cautiously but in a natural enough manner began to ask questions about my background. How long had I worked in state security? Where? What responsibilities did I have? He was particularly interested in my service in Lithuania and whether any "special actions" had been taken there.

The ample servings and the Armenian cognac had their usual effect. My guest leaned back in his chair, loosened his tie, and began to talk more openly. He was a newcomer to state security, had never worked as a rank-and-file KGB operative, and had been assigned to a supervisory position without having to climb the usual rungs of the service ladder. His former job had been in the administrative section of the Komsomol.

It instantly became clear "who and what" was before me. In the 1960s and 1970s, when Shelepin and then Semichastny headed the KGB,* key posts at KGB headquarters as well as in local branch offices were being taken over by former Komsomol functionaries, all of whom landed fat salaries with their high posts. Needless to say, this "rejuvenation" of the cadres produced a hostile—albeit muted—reaction among the regular professionals who had thus been passed over and denied their expected promotions. The Komsomol influx brought a variety of individuals into the KGB, bright men as well as slow, decent individuals and cynical careerists, honest folk and hypocrites, hard workers and sycophants. The one characteristic common to all, however, was a total lack of the professionalism that comes only with long experience and complete devotion to the job.

That same evening after supper my Moscow guest inquired about the distance from Rostov to Kamensk and asked me to accompany him there. He summoned a car, contacted the data center of the Seventh Directorate by phone, introduced himself, and received a report on the location of the "target"—that is, of Solzhenitsyn. Within twenty or thirty minutes, a glistening black Volga was speeding us toward Kamensk along a smooth highway. En route I was told that Solzhenitsyn and his friend had stopped for the night in a pine forest north of Kamensk. The purpose of our trip was to replace the seven-man Muscovite surveillance team that had been tailing our "target" with a similar team based in Rostov, since Solzhenitsyn was planning to visit Rostov, Novocherkassk, and possibly other towns in the area. My role would consist of scrutinizing the "target's" contacts as they were identified by the surveillance team and forwarding this information to Moscow. I quote the subsequent dialogue:

I: Why did you have to come all the way from Moscow for such a routine mission? After all, our "target's" connections in the region have long been established, and this information was forwarded to Moscow some time ago.

He: New contacts could occur, and anyhow I am here for a different reason.

I: How long will you be staying?

He: I'll be flying back as soon as I have accomplished my mission.

This exchange made me prick up my ears once again. Why was this mission being kept secret from me? Could this mean that I might be placed in a vulnerable position? I recalled that I had once been asked to feign a jealous fit in front of an American scholar, a purported CIA agent, and then to attack him physically, but that I had categorically refused. This time, however, I felt the stirrings of professional pride. Knowing the level of the people I was dealing with, I decided to wait it out, keeping a sharp eye on the actions and apparent plans of my "chief."

The lights of Kamensk came into view in the distance. Passing the town, we pulled off the road several kilometers to the north. It was 11:00 P.M., and I could clearly distinguish the jagged outline of the tops of a dense pine forest against a starry sky.

"Stay here," my chief ordered, setting off toward the forest.

I watched him carefully. A man came out of the woods to meet him; they discussed something briefly and parted. My companion returned to my side and announced quietly, "The Moscow surveillance unit has been replaced. Now let's take a look at what our 'target' is up to."

We crossed the highway and entered the forest. It immediately became clear that my companion had no idea of the proper way to move through a nighttime forest. I smiled to myself. Soon we could hear men's voices, talking in calm, even tones. Drawing any nearer would have been stupid and unsafe, since it would have placed us at risk of being detected. I used gestures to communicate this to my companion, and we returned to the car.

"We're now going to Novocherkassk, where we'll be spending the night," my chief rapped out as he dove into the vehicle.

I followed him.

It was long past midnight when we arrived in Novocherkassk. Despite the late hour, the head of the local KGB office was on duty; presumably he had received advance notice. Two rooms had been reserved in the hotel, suggesting that my chief wanted to separate himself from me. I wondered whether this reflected a whim or a necessity, but at the hotel he announced that we would be occupying a single room.

The identity of the person for whom the other room had been set aside was a new puzzle, but I did not think it useful to ask, since I certainly could not expect to receive a straight answer.

In the morning we were informed that Solzhenitsyn and his friend had arrived in Novocherkassk. The surveillance unit had them firmly in their grip. We were sitting in the car and every five or ten minutes received an update by radio on the whereabouts of our "target". Finally the word came that they had stopped in Yermak Square, had parked their vehicle, and were proceeding to the cathedral where a church service was then in progress.

We drove slowly toward the cathedral, getting out of the car some two hundred yards before the entrance to the square. The chief asked me whether I had ever laid eyes on our "target."

"No."

"Do you want to take a look?"

"Naturally."

A solemn and imposing church service was under way as we entered the cathedral. The number of worshippers was relatively small. With faces full of concentration and inner peace, they listened to the choir, some standing motionless, others making the sign of the cross from time to time. Carrying our hats in our hands, we cautiously moved forward.*

Suddenly my "chief" nudged me with his elbow and, with a barely perceptible motion of his head, directed my attention toward one of the interior pillars. I saw a kneeling middle-aged man with a large open fore-head and a horseshoe-shaped reddish beard. Oblivious to his surroundings, he was crossing himself and making prostrations, while a lanky man of about fifty-five stood next to him. I could not tear my eyes away from our kneeling "target" and must confess that I was deeply shocked by what I saw. In fact, I would never have believed it if this had been related to me by others. I have always regarded religious believers calmly and with under-standing, since I consider that everyone has the inviolable right to profess their own beliefs. Since I knew a great deal about Solzhenitsyn by virtue of my job—having read all his published works as well as those circulating in samizdat, to say nothing of all the reports about him—I was of course aware that we were dealing with a prodigious and unusual personality. But the scene I had just witnessed seemed so incomprehensible that it did not spark my sympathy. On the contrary, it was disconcerting and raised doubts about my previous evaluations of the man.

We did not linger in the cathedral. As we were descending the steps on our way out, my chief asked me what I thought. I did not reply.

Several hours later, the surveillance unit reported that our "target" had stopped at some addresses that we did not have in our records. I would need to establish the identities of the individuals he had contacted, what kind of people they were, together with the exact character of the relationship of each to the writer.

By mid-afternoon we received a message to the effect that our "target" and his friend were on the town's main street and were about to enter a store. My chief suddenly leaped into action urging the driver to get our vehicle as quickly as possible to the downtown area. But on the way he ordered the driver to stop several times, going off somewhere briefly and seeming quite nervous. One of these stops produced a great surprise: I saw my chief meeting with the stranger from the dining room at the hotel in Rostov. That implied that this man could not have been a representative of the surveillance unit from Moscow, as I had assumed earlier, since those men had surely left the area long ago. It also answered my question about the second reservation in the Novocherkassk hotel.

The gestures of the two men indicated that they were disagreeing over something. I was unable to draw even a minimally useful conclusion from all this—I had simply nothing to go on. I stepped out of the car and made my way toward the arguing men, hoping to catch at least some part of their conversation. It was too late. Without seeing me, the stranger uttered one last phrase to my chief, turned sharply, and set off in the direction of a store. But at this very moment I saw our "target" and his friend emerging from the door. The stranger passed them by, then turned and began to follow.

The time for being a passive observer was over. I went up to my chief and asked, "Can I be of assistance?"

"Possibly . . . Let's go."

It was a procession of sorts, the "target" leading, followed by the stranger then by my chief and myself, as we moved along the city's main street. In a little while, our "target" and his friend entered a specialty food store, a large facility by local standards. We followed, all five of us now finding ourselves in the same confined space. The stranger was standing very close behind our "target," who was in line in front of the pastry counter. My chief stood next to the stranger, partially blocking him from view as the latter made some sort of movement with his hands behind the back of our "target." I was unable to see exactly what he was doing, but I clearly remember the movements of his gloved hands and an object of some kind that he held in one of them. In any case, something I could not understand was taking place next to me, right in the middle of Novocherkassk. The whole operation lasted only a couple of minutes.

The stranger now left the store, and my chief's face broke into a smile. He looked around, nodded at me, and strode toward the exit. I followed. Once on the street, he said quietly but firmly, "That's it. It's all over. He won't last very long now."

Sitting in the car he could not conceal his delight. "The first attempt failed, you see, but on the second pass everything went OK."

Then he looked at the driver and myself and stopped short.

We drove to the hotel, then to the main office of the local KGB, where my chief left instructions about checking out the personal contacts that our "target" had made in town. We said our good-byes and set off for Rostov.

My mind was in turmoil. My chief's words about the "second pass" having gone well shed new light on the scene I had just witnessed. The episode in the store was no longer strange and incomprehensible; it was in fact the culmination of a criminal act planned against the great writer and dissident by the highest levels of the state's punitive agency. What could I do? Keeping my mouth shut was the only way I could preserve my own life and that of my family.

Upon arriving in Rostov, my chief and I took leave of each other at the door to the general's office. His parting words were pronounced with exaggerated cheerfulness: "Everything went just fine. Do forward the Novocherkassk materials to headquarters."

I have no information on the subsequent fate of the stranger. My cautious questions about my "chief" elicited the information that he was later sent abroad. Needless to say, tourism was not the purpose.

One naturally wants to know what happened to Aleksandr Solzhenitsyn after the Novocherkassk episode. I don't have the answer. Perhaps he became seriously ill; possibly he was close to death. The answer will have to be provided by him or by persons in his immediate entourage.*

AFTERWORD

The above is a factual narrative, albeit one written from memory. All the events described actually took place, and they have weighed on my conscience for nearly two decades. I keep asking: what else could I have done?

I have no direct, irrefutable proof, to say nothing of physical evidence. I could only have cried out. But would I have been given the chance to do so? I doubt it; indeed, I am convinced that my "discovery" would have been buried forever at its inception.

The first chapter of G. A. Arbatov's book, *Testimony of a Contemporary*, contains the following passage: "I think that as long as those who witnessed this important and complex period of our history are still with us, they must be allowed to speak out, especially those among them who participated in the events of the day, no matter how modest their role might have been."

I have deliberately avoided naming the principal actors in the events described, since I believe it crucial to give them the opportunity to make their own statements, correcting inaccuracies, filling out the picture, and naming the instigators of this criminal act, men who unquestionably belong to the very highest levels of government.

It is time we looked one another squarely in the eyes.

Translators' Notes

On February 12, 1974, Aleksandr Solzhenitsyn was arrested in his Moscow apartment, subjected to the routine indignities of a Soviet inmate in Lefortovo prison, officially charged with treason, and on the next day expelled from his homeland. He settled first in Zurich, Switzerland, and it was there, in 1974-75, that he wrote the fourteen sketches that make up *Invisible Allies*.

The book was conceived as a supplement to the author's *The Oak and the Calf*, itself completed in Zurich in 1974. But while the parent volume was published almost immediately after it was finished (Russian edition, Paris, 1975; English translation, 1980), *Invisible Allies* could not appear at the time for the simple reason that it discloses the names of the numerous individuals who had lent their support to Solzhenitsyn in the course of his long career as an "underground" writer and bitter opponent of the Soviet regime.

With the virtual collapse of the Soviet system in the second half of 1991, Solzhenitsyn deemed it safe to publish the greater part of this text, and *Invisible Allies*—the Russian title is *Nevidimki*—was serialized in two issues of the Moscow literary monthly *Novy Mir* (nos. 11 and 12, 1991). The translation offered here follows the *Novy Mir* text, but also takes into account certain further emendations introduced by the author.

In the annotations that follow, the most frequent reference is to the main body of *The Oak and the Calf*. The text cited is Aleksandr I. Solzhenitsyn, *The Oak and the Calf: Sketches of Literary Life in the Soviet Union*, translated by Harry Willetts (New York: Harper & Row, 1980). Another work repeatedly mentioned in the notes is Aleksandr I. Solzhenitsyn, *The Gulag Archipelago*, 3 vols., trans. by Thomas P. Whitney (vols. 1 and 2) and Harry Willetts (vol. 3) (New York: Harper & Row, 1974-78).

All the explanatory notes have been compiled by the translators. These annotations must be clearly distinguished from the footnotes introduced by Solzhenitsyn, which in almost all cases present material that came to the author's attention after the main body of his text was completed.

PAGE

4, *go to the people*: The chief goal proclaimed by the Russian radical populists in the nineteenth century. It reflected both the desire to serve the peasant majority and the belief in the fundamental soundness of the peasant way of life.

6, *M. P. Yakubovich*: A Menshevik turned Bolshevik. See *The Gulag Archipelago*, vol. 1, pp. 401-7.

7, *zek*: Soviet slang for inmate of a prison or labor camp.

9, *my camp sentence*: Natalya Reshetovskaya filed for divorce from the imprisoned Solzhenitsyn in 1949, at first to protect herself from the discrimination to which wives of "enemies of the people" were subjected. Somewhat later, while Solzhenitsyn was still in prison camp, she married another man whom she then divorced to remarry Solzhenitsyn after the writer was released from Central Asian exile. The final break between Solzhenitsyn and Reshetovskaya came only in 1973, after several years of estrangement.

9, *pop up everywhere*: The reference is to Article 58 of the U.S.S.R. Criminal Code, which was notorious as the specific instrument of political repression. Its numerous subheadings listed various types of "counter-revolutionary activity."

9, *Beria's last*: Lavrenti Beria, the head of Stalin's security apparatus, was arrested and shot during the struggle for power that followed Stalin's death in 1953.

9, *for years*: On the method invented by Solzhenitsyn to help his memory, see *The Gulag Archipelago*, Vol. 3, pp. 99-101.

10, *another person*: See the *The Oak and the Calf*, p. 4.

11, *death there*: Solzhenitsyn's cancer was diagnosed in the late fall of 1953, and he was given only a few weeks to live by the examining doctors.

12, *Republic of Labor*: A politically sanitized version of this play is known as *The Love-Girl and the Innocent* in the English translation. The unexpurgated text is not available in English.

14, *1965 debacle*: This is a reference to the confiscation of Solzhenitsyn's papers held by V. L. Teush. See Chapter Three.

15, *Torfoprodukt*: During the 1956-57 school years Solzhenitsyn taught physics and mathematics in this village, located about a hundred miles east of Moscow.

15, *Ryazan*: Solzhenitsyn moved to Ryazan in 1957. The town is located about a hundred miles southeast of Moscow.

17, *considered complete*: The First Circle exists in two significantly different versions. The eighty-seven-chapter edition appeared in the West in 1968, while the politically much more caustic ninety-six-chapter version is not available in English.

17, *Tvardovsky*: Aleksandr Tvardovsky, the editor in chief of *Novy Mir*, maneuvered *One Day in the Life of Ivan Denisovich* into print in 1962. The story is told in *The Oak and the Calf*, pp. 21-46.

18, *Ekibastuz*: On the rebellion in Ekibastuz, see *The Gulag Archipelago*, vol. 3, pp. 249 ff.

18, *Susi*: See Chapter Four.

19, *first broke*: Nikita Khrushchev was ousted from power in a coup headed by Leonid Brezhnev.

20, *Teush*: See Chapter Three.

20, *own purposes*: The play was deemed seditious, and the point of printing it for restricted internal distribution was to provide Party propagandists with textual evidence of Solzhenitsyn's anti-Soviet views.

20, *Rozhdestvo*: In 1965 Solzhenitsyn purchased a plot of land with a small summer house in the village of Rozhdestvo, some forty miles southwest of Moscow.

23, *second wife*: Solzhenitsyn married Natalya Svetlova (Alya) in 1973.

25n, *Tomaš Řezáč*: A Czech associate of the Soviet security agency, published a scurrilous attack on Solzhenitsyn; in Russian translation: Tomash Rzhezach, *Spiral'izmeny Solzhenitsyna* [*The Spiral of Solzhenitsyn's Treachery*] (Moscow: Progress, 1978).

30, *historical epic*: The planned series of volumes or "knots" of which *August 1914* was the first. (Solzhenitsyn refers to the whole series variously as *R-17* and *The Red Wheel*.)

30, *February Revolution*: The revolutionary events of February 1917 resulted in the abdication of Tsar Nicholas II and the onset of a chaotic period that led to the Bolshevik seizure of power eight months later.

31, *From Under the Rubble*: Edited by Solzhenitsyn, this volume (which also includes three of his own essays) addresses issues bearing on the condition of the country after decades of Communist misrule. The Russian-language edition was published in Paris in 1974; the English-language version appeared a year later.

34, *literary underground*: See the further description of this state in *The Oak and the Calf*, pp. 10-12.

34, *Lev Kopelev*: Specialist in German literature, and prison-mate of Solzhenitsyn, depicted as Lev Rubin in *The First Circle*.

35, *at the time*: Shch-854 is the main protagonist's prison identification number.

35, *Shukhov Street*: Shukhov is the surname of Ivan Denisovich, Solzhenitsyn's main protagonist in *One Day*.

35, *Tsezar Markovich*: One of Ivan Denisovich's fellow prisoners in *One Day*. He is an intellectual who seems to be Jewish, and he is unusual because he is relatively well supplied with parcels from the outside.

36, *Twenty-second Party Congress*: Held in October 1961, this represented the high-water mark of Khrushchev's de-Stalinization campaign.

39, *for the drawer*: That is, without having publication in mind due to political circumstances.

40, *Dyomichev*: Solzhenitsyn's 1965 meeting with P. N. Dyomichev (Demichev), a high Party official in charge of ideology, is described in *The Oak and the Calf*, pp. 92-97.

40, *the ceiling*: The popular assumption was that any hidden microphones would most likely have been implanted in the ceiling.

42, *Zilberberg*: Solzhenitsyn describes how he brought the *First Circle* typescript to the Teushes in *The Oak and the Calf*, pp. 100-102.

44, *A Necessary . . .*: The Russian title is *Neobkhodimyi razgovor s*

Solzhenitsynym. The book has not been translated into English.

45, *name Teush publicly*: See *The Oak and the Calf*, p. 466.

45, *Lakshin*: A literary critic at *Novy Mir* who is often mentioned in *The Oak and the Calf*, Lakshin sets forth his position in his *Solzhenitsyn, Tvardovsky, and "Novy Mir"* (Cambridge, Mass.: MIT Press, 1980).

45, *Gestapo*: In 1957 Solzhenitsyn was officially cleared of the charges that had led to his arrest in 1945 and to the eight years he subsequently spent in prison and labor camp. (He had criticized Stalin in letters to a friend.) Starting in the mid 1960s, however, the KGB made systematic attempts to discredit the writer by planting false rumors about his war record. See, for example, *The Oak and the Calf*, p. 461.

46, *meddle*: During the Russian Civil War, a relatively small force of Whites under General Nikolai Yudenich launched an unsuccessful drive toward Bolshevik-held Petrograd from what had become independent Estonia.

47, *these men*: On Susi, see, for example, *The Gulag Archipelago*, vol. 1, pp. 205 and 213. On Tenno, see especially vol. 3, pp. 126-92.

47, *Dolgun*: An American-born former employee of the U.S. Embassy in Moscow, who spent eight years in the prison camps. See Alexander Dolgun and Patrick Watson, *Alexander Dolgun's Story: An American in the Gulag* (New York: Knopf, 1975). Dolgun's testimony is included in *The Gulag Archipelago*, e.g. vol. 1, pp. 126-27.

55, *author's sheets*: Units of text containing 40,000 typographical characters.

55, *Dahl Dictionary*: Vladimir Dahl (Dal') was a nineteenth-century lexicographer whose four-volume dictionary of the Russian language remains an unsurpassed source of popular idiom and proverbial expressions. Solzhenitsyn has studied this text closely and has often expressed his great admiration for it. See, for example, *The Oak and the Calf*, p. 114.

57, *the Seine*: The quote comes from Nikolai Gumilev's 1921 poem "The Streetcar That Lost Its Way."

59, *APN*: Agentstvo Pechati Novosti, the official Soviet news agency.

60, *Congress*: The Fourth Congress of Soviet Writers convened in Moscow in May 1967. Solzhenitsyn mailed some 250 copies of his open letter to members of the presidium and to selected delegates. For the text, see *The Oak and the Calf*, pp. 458-62.

61, *diary*: See Chapter Five.

62, *Writers' Union*: Solzhenitsyn gives an account of this meeting in

The Oak and the Calf, pp. 182–86 and 463–81.

62, *Molotov:* Vyacheslav Molotov, Stalin's trusted right-hand man, lived for many years after his fall from power. He died in 1986.

62, *Pirita:* The ruins of a medieval cathedral in a northeastern suburb of Tallinn.

63, *Paris:* After the death of Voronyanskaya [see Chapter Five], Solzhenitsyn sent a signal to Paris to the effect that *The Gulag Archipelago* should be published immediately. The first volume appeared there at the end of 1973, causing a worldwide sensation.

66, *Krushchev's "miracle":* This refers to the de-Stalinization campaign launched by Khrushchev, with its far-reaching political and cultural repercussions.

66, *Founding Fathers:* Marx and Engels.

67, *If it be love . . . :* Lines drawn from an untitled 1854 poem by A. K. Tolstoi.

70, *Petrograd:* Solzhenitsyn's purpose was to acquaint himself with the locales where the events of the February Revolution had been played out. (This research was later used in the writer's *March 1917.*)

73, *Irina Tomashevskaya's manuscript:* This is a partially completed study questioning Mikhail Sholokhov's authorship of *The Quiet Don* (a long novel published in English in two volumes as *And Quiet Flows the Don* and *The Don Flows Home to the Sea*). See Chapter Fourteen.

75, *Big House:* This was the nickname for KGB headquarters in Leningrad.

75, *Vorozheikina:* The name "Vorozheikina," while it reflects part of Voronyanskaya's surname, is also a play on *vorozheia,* meaning sorceress or fortune-teller.

77, *Avtorkhanov:* Abdurakhman Avtorkhanov, an émigré political scientist of Chechen origin, has published several studies on the structure of the Soviet system.

78, *Vlasovite:* General Andrei Vlasov was captured by the Germans in 1942 and agreed to lend his name to anti-Soviet military units within the German Army, made up mostly of POWs in German hands. Captured Vlasovites were treated with particular harshness by Soviet authorities.

89, *Pavel Korin:* Famous mainly for a series of portraits of Russian Orthodox monks, nuns, and clergy; the series is referred to as *Vanishing Russia.*

91, *Lysenko campaign:* Trofim Lysenko became head of the Soviet

Academy of Agricultural Sciences under Stalin, instituting a reign of terror against all those who questioned his attempts to synthesize genetics with Marxism. One of his many victims was the celebrated geneticist Nikolai Vavilov.

92, *She also translated*: The books referred to are Hermann von François, *Marneschlacht und Tannenberg* (Berlin, 1920); Wassili [Vasilii] Gurko, *Russland, 1914-1917: Erinnerungen an Krieg and Revolution* (Berlin, 1921); Z. A. B. Zeman and W. B. Scharlau, *Freibeuter der Revolution* (Cologne, 1964).

94, *compilation*: Available in English translation in Leopold Labedz (ed.), *Solzhenitsyn: A Documentary Record*, enlarged edition (Bloomington: Indiana University Press, 1973), pp. 44-62.

97, *project*: The White Sea Canal was built by convict labor at huge human cost. See *The Gulag Archipelago*, vol. 2, pp. 80-102.

97, *Vladimir Korolenko*: Korolenko (1853-1921) wrote bitterly about the human suffering caused by the revolution.

97, *Palchinsky*: A prominent engineer and technocrat before the revolution, P. A. Palchinsky (1878-1929) remained in Soviet Russia after 1917, working as a leading technical expert. He was shot in Stalin's purge of the old intelligentsia.

97, *Svechin*: A. A. Svechin (1878-1938), a high-ranking military officer in the tsarist army, joined the Bolshevik cause in 1918 and became a leading theoretician of strategy and tactics in the 1920s. Shot in Stalin's purge of the Red Army.

97, *Tambov*: A provincial city some 250 miles southeast of Moscow, and the center of a major anti-Bolshevik peasant uprising in 1920-21. It was Solzhenitsyn's intention to dedicate a volume in his *Red Wheel* series to this episode.

98, *The Quiet Don*: The Cossack writer Fyodor Kryukov (1870-1920) was known to have been working on a major manuscript at the time of his death during the Russian Civil War. The text has been lost, but there have been persistent rumors that Mikhail Sholokhov may have plagiarized it in the production of *The Quiet Don*. See Chapter Fourteen.

99, *rescue operation*: See Chapter Four.

100, *evict me from Zhukova*: See *The Oak and the Calf*, pp. 337-39.

101, *had been shot*: See *The Gulag Archipelago*, vol. 1, p. 488.

105, *Old Bolsheviks*: Members of the Party who had joined prior to 1917.

106, *late Kadetism*: "Kadetism" here stands for something like doctrinaire liberalism. "Kadet" was the popular appellation for members of the Constitutional Democratic Party of Russia. (The term derives from the Russian initials "K. D.," pronounced "kah-deh.") Formed by left-wing liberals in 1905, the Kadets became a major opposition force in the State Duma before 1917.

110, *Bunin*: Ivan Bunin was the first Russian writer to receive the Nobel Prize for Literature. Since he was an émigré at the time (1933), this caused great displeasure in the U.S.S.R.

110, *listing*: "Letopis' literaturnykh sobytii," in *Russkaia literatura kontsa XIX—nachala XX vv.*, 3 vols. (Moscow: Nauka, 1968-72). M. G. Petrova's contribution is acknowledged in volumes one and three.

111, *Vasily Shukshin*: Shukshin (1929-74) was a very popular prose writer, actor, and film director.

114, *Kornei Ivanovich Chukovsky*: Chukovsky (1882-1969) was a literary critic, translator, and celebrated writer of children's verse.

120, *Carlisles*: Henry and Olga Carlisle were entrusted with overseeing the English-language translation of *The Gulag Archipelago*. On their subsequent dispute with Solzhenitsyn, see *The Oak and the Calf*, p. 320n.

121, *Zhores Medvedev*: When the geneticist Zhores Medvedev was confined in a psychiatric institution for his dissident activities in 1970, Solzhenitsyn expressed his outrage in one of his most militant statements. For the text, see *The Oak and the Calf*, pp. 494-95.

122, *Aeroport*: Many writers with sympathy for liberal and dissident views resided in the area of Moscow near the Aeroport subway station.

123, *Irina*: In her old age Irina Shcherbak lived in extreme poverty, and Solzhenitsyn regularly helped her with money and food parcels.

123, *Guchkov . . . Polivanov*: Aleksandr Guchkov (1862-1936) was a prominent prerevolutionary politician who played a major role in Tsar Nicholas II's decision to abdicate. K. M. Polivanov was a relative of Aleksei Polivanov, a reform-minded Russian Minister of War during part of World War I. For Palchinsky, see our note to p. 97.

126, *mausoleum*: Khrushchev's somewhat haphazard campaign to debunk Stalin began in 1956.

126, *anyone at all*: A play on a line from Pushkin's *Eugene Onegin* (Ch. 3), where the heroine is said to be ready to fall in love with anyone.

127, *Prose Miniatures*: A series of seventeen extremely short stories that Solzhenitsyn has also referred to as poems in prose. All have a strong philosophical orientation.

128, *Alexander Herzen*: A. I. Herzen (1812-70) was a famous essayist and one of the founders of Russian populism. Lidia Chukovskaya has published a monograph on Herzen's memoirs: *"Byloe i dumy" Gertsena* (Moscow, 1966).

130, *Zvorykina*: Ekaterina Fyodorovna Zvorykina, the wife of Efim Etkind.

130, *samizdat essays*: The Russian title is *"Avgust chetyrnadtsatogo" chitaiut na rodine* (Paris: YMCA Press, 1973). The book has not been translated into English.

130, *Pimen*: An English translation of the "Lenten Letter" appears in John B. Dunlop et al. (eds.), *Aleksandr Solzhenitsyn: Critical Essays and Documentary Materials*, second edition (New York: Macmillan, 1975), pp. 550-56.

131, *P. A. Zaionchkovsky*: A professor at Moscow University and a leading specialist on the history of imperial Russia.

132, *mail*: On this campaign, see *The Oak and the Calf*, pp. 340-41, 378.

133, *Western correspondents*: For the text of Solzhenitsyn's interview with correspondents representing the Associated Press news agency and the Paris newspaper *Le Monde*, see *The Oak and the Calf*, pp. 516-29.

134, *encounter battle*: "The name given by military tacticians to a form of warfare distinct from ordinary offensive and defensive engagements: the two sides, each ignorant of the other's intentions, simultaneously decide to attack and unexpectedly collide. . . . Such was the battle that took place in the Soviet public arena in late August and September 1973, a battle so little expected that not only did the opposing sides have no knowledge of each other, but on one side there were two columns (Sakharov's and mine), neither of which knew anything of the other's movements and plans." (*The Oak and the Calf*, p. 335)

137, *bureaucrats*: Lidia Chukovskaya was expelled from the Union of Soviet Writers on January 9, 1974. She responded with a scathing essay, an English translation of which appears in *Survey*, vol. 20, No. 2/3 (1974), pp. 229-31.

140, *Chukokkala*: A "handwritten almanac" consisting of entries made by well-known writers, painters, and other members of the cultural elite—such as Gorky, Mayakovsky, Repin, and a host of others—into a journal kept by K. I. Chukovsky. The whimsical title is a conflation of Chukovsky's surname and Kuokkala, the name of the Finnish village where the Chukovsky family resided at the time the almanac was launched. An abridged facsimile edition of *Chukokkala* was brought out in Moscow in 1979.

143, *Frank*: Semyon Lyudvigovich Frank (1877-1950) was a leading Russian philosopher, one of a group of brilliant intellectuals expelled from Soviet Russia by Lenin's regime in 1922.

144, *back now*: The assassination of Sergei Kirov, a high Party official, is widely believed to have been secretly ordered by Stalin. The dictator then used Kirov's death as a pretext for launching the bloody purges that swept through all levels of Soviet society, culminating in the Great Terror of 1937-38.

145, *Peshkova*: Ekaterina Pavlovna Peshkova (1876-1965) was the wife of Maksim Gorky.

146, *Boris Zaks*: Managing editor of *Novy Mir* in the 1950s and 1960s.

147, *already written*: A number of strikes and mutinies swept through many Soviet "special" prison camps between 1953 and 1955. Solzhenitsyn has dedicated a substantial section of *The Gulag Archipelago* to this theme (v. 3, pp. 228-331). A camp revolt is also the subject of Solzhenitsyn's film scenario *Tanks Know the Truth*, written in 1959. ("Special" camps were organized in 1948 for the purpose of isolating those who had been arrested on political charges from all other prisoners.)

149, *Leonid Nikolaevich Andreyev*: Andreyev (1871-1919) was a playwright and writer of short stories. He rejected the Bolshevik seizure of power and died in exile.

151, *Collective Leadership*: The original name of the group headed by Leonid Brezhnev that engineered the overthrow of Khrushchev.

155, *Grani*: In April 1968 the Russian émigré journal *Grani* sent a telegram to the offices of *Novy Mir*, informing the Moscow journal that a certain Victor Louis had brought a manuscript of *Cancer Ward* to the West with the help of the KGB, and that *Grani* intended to publish it. See *The Oak and the Calf*, pp. 206-210, 483.

156, *Sinyavsky*: In a case that represented the Brezhnev regime's effort to cow the intelligentsia, the writers Andrei Sinyavsky and Yuli Daniel were sentenced to harsh prison terms for publishing their allegedly anti-Soviet fiction abroad.

156, *Archipelago*: In late August 1973 Solzhenitsyn's former wife requested a meeting with the writer at Moscow's Kazan Station and tried, with promises and thinly veiled threats, to persuade him not to publish *The Gulag Archipelago*. See *The Oak and the Calf*, pp. 361-67.

166, *ingenuity*: The Russian Social Fund was constituted in 1974 as a charitable organization under Swiss law; its principal aim was to distribute material aid to Soviet political prisoners and their families. The fund is sustained primarily by the royalties received by Solzhenitsyn from the sales of *The Gulag Archipelago* (in all languages).

170, *patronymic:* "Tsarevich Ivan" is a stock protagonist in Russian folklore, while Tsarevich Dmitri was a real historical figure (the son of Ivan the Terrible) whose death in 1591 raised suspicions made famous by Pushkin's *Boris Godunov.*

171, *Shafarevich:* Igor Rostislavovich Shafarevich (b. 1923), mathematician, Lenin Prize winner, corresponding member of the Academy of Sciences. Author of *The Socialist Phenomenon.*

173, *writer:* Veniamin Kaverin (1902-1989) was a noted prose writer.

174, *samizdat:* An English translation of "Live Not by Lies" appears in Leopold Labedz, ed., *Solzhenitsyn: A Documentary Record*, rev. ed. (Harmondsworth: Penguin, 1974), pp. 375-79.

176, *MIFLI:* The Moscow Institute of Philosophy, Literature, and Art was considered one of the Soviet Union's top institutions for the study of the humanities.

177, *dispersed:* In February 1970 Tvardovsky's chief assistants on the editorial board of *Novy Mir* were replaced by order of the Writers' Union, after which Tvardovsky resigned his post as editor in chief.

178, *behind bars:* This appears to refer to an episode when a manuscript copy of *Cancer Ward* was taken into Czechoslovakia to be published in Bratislava in 1968. Pavel Ličko is a Czech journalist who interviewed Solzhenitsyn in Ryazan in March 1967. He is an acquaintance of Nicholas Bethell, who was subsequently involved in bringing a copy of the novel from Czechoslovakia to the West.

179, *Gvozdev . . . Shlyapnikov:* Kozma Gvozdev, a Menshevik, became the Minister of Labor in Kerensky's Provisional Government, and later spent more than two decades as an inmate of Soviet prison camps.

Aleksandr Shlyapnikov (1884-1937) was a Bolshevik labor organizer who opposed the Party's suppression of an independent labor movement. Died in prison.

180, *apartment:* For the text, see *The Oak and the Calf*, pp. 484-93.

187, *Shch-854:* The original title of *One Day in the Life of Ivan Denisovich.*

189, *customs:* This was a statement condemning the forthcoming Western publication of *Cancer Ward.* See *The Oak and the Calf*, pp. 211-12, 483-84. Vittorio Strada was a prominent Italian Communist, a specialist in Soviet literature. *L'Unità* is an Italian Communist newspaper published in Milan.

189, *Medvedev*: Historian who has done much to reveal the crimes of the Stalinist regime, but who has done so from a consistently "neo-Leninist" perspective.

189, *Proffer*: Literary scholar and head of Ardis, a publishing house based in Ann Arbor, Michigan, that has specialized in books bearing on Russian literature.

190, *The White Sea–Baltic Canal*: A book glorifying this construction project, which was carried out by zek labor under the direct supervision of the security agencies, was published in 1934. Solzhenitsyn comments on it in detail in *The Gulag Archipelago*, vol. 2, pp. 80-100.

194, *an interview*: The reference is to Solzhenitsyn's interview with correspondents of the Associated Press and *Le Monde*. See *The Oak and the Calf*, pp. 516ff.

197, *demonstration in Red Square*: On August 25, 1968, four days after the Soviet invasion of Czechoslovakia, a group of demonstrators (including Natalya Gorbanevskaya, Larisa Bogoraz-Daniel and Pavel Litvinov) were arrested after staging a peaceful protest on Red Square.

198, *Short Course*: *The History of the Communist Party of the Soviet Union (Bolsheviks): Short Course*, as the title is officially translated, was approved for publication by the Party's Central Committee in 1938. It reflected the Stalinist mythologization of Soviet history and was promulgated as a prescribed text and ultimate authority.

200n, *Bulgarian umbrella*: On September 11, 1978, the exiled Bulgarian author Georgi Markov was assassinated in London with the aid of an umbrella adapted to deliver a poisoned pellet.

202, *Paris edition*: This was the Russian-language first edition of *August 1914*, published by the YMCA Press, Paris, in 1971.

205, *chapters*: The Lenin chapters were published in Russian as a separate volume (Paris: YMCA Press, 1975). The English translation, *Lenin in Zurich*, followed in 1976 (New York: Farrar, Straus & Giroux).

205, *"knot"*: Although only four "knots" of *The Red Wheel* were completed, Solzhenitsyn at one stage envisaged writing twenty. The fourteenth "knot" would have been entitled *March 1919*.

209, *Zurich*: For Solzhenitsyn's dealings with Dr. Fritz Heeb, see Chapter Twelve.

210, *1937*: In 1937 Stalin's "Great Terror" reached its full ferocity.

213, *Panin*: Panin (who preferred the spelling "Dimitri") was one of Solzhenitsyn's fellow zeks in the Marfino special scientific prison in the late 1940s and was the prototype for the figure Sologdin in *The First Circle*.

214, *Vestnik*: On *Vestnik* and its editor, Nikita Struve, see Chapter Twelve.

215, *Russian Responses*: Borisov's essay "Molva i spory" appeared under the pseudonym "A. Veretennikov" in *"Avgust chetyrnadtsatogo" chitaiut na rodine* (Paris: YMCA Press, 1973). The volume has not been translated into English.

222, *home*: On Victor Louis and the *Grani* telegram see the annotation to page 155.

223, *émigré literature*: Pyotr Berngardovich Struve (1870-1944), an economist and political thinker, contributed to two influential collections of essays, *Landmarks* (1909) and *De Profundis* (1921). His son, Gleb Petrovich Struve (1898-1985), wrote a number of books on Russian literature, among them *Russkaya literatura v izgnanii* [Russian Literature in Exile] (New York: Chekhov Publishing House, 1956).

223, *Tyutchev*: "In Russia one can but believe" is the last line of a well-known poem, "The Mind Can Never Fathom Russia," by Fyodor Tyutchev (1803-73).

224, *RSKhD*: The Russian-language émigré journal that Nikita Struve edits in Paris formerly bore the title *Vestnik Russkogo Studencheskogo Khristianskogo Dvizheniia* (Herald of the Russian Student Christian Movement), abbreviated to *Vestnik RSKhD*. In 1974 the adjective "student" was dropped from the title and the abbreviation became *Vestnik RKhD*. Whenever Solzhenitsyn writes simply *Vestnik* it is this journal that he has in mind.

227, *delays*: The Soviet Union's adherence to the International Copyright Convention became effective from May 27, 1973.

229, *Gurko . . . Melgunov*: Vasilii (Wassili) Iosifovich Gurko, *Russland, 1914–1917. Erinnerungen an Krieg und Revolution* (Berlin, 1921). General Gurko figures in both *March 1917* and *April 1917*. Sergei Petrovich Melgunov (1879-1956), a historian and political figure exiled from the Soviet Union in 1923, was the author of *The Bolshevik Seizure of Power* and other books.

229, *Zilberberg*: On Zilberberg and the Teushes see Chapter Three.

231, *Dark Avenues*: Ivan Bunin's cycle of short stories *Dark Avenues* (1943) tells of a series of doomed romantic encounters.

231, *Ulyanov*: "Zagadka Solzhenitsyna," *Novoe russkoe slovo* (New York), August 1, 1971.

234, *R-17 Diary*: In this still-unpublished work, Solzhenitsyn describes the stages of writing this multivolume epic.

236, *August 1914*: Luchterhand was the publisher of the official German translation, Alexander Solschenizyn, *August Vierzehn* (Darmstadt and Neuwied, 1974).

236, *bad translation*: The edition referred to is Alexander Solzhenitsyn, *August 1914,* translated by Michael Glenny (London: The Bodley Head, 1972).

237, *"Lake Segden"*: One of Solzhenitsyn's "Prose Miniatures."

238, *Die Zeit*: The excerpts from *Prussian Nights*, translated by R. Drommert, appeared in *Die Zeit*, December 9, 1969. (Solzhenitsyn has asserted elsewhere that *Die Zeit* had received this text from the magazine *Stern*.)

238, *panic*: *Time* magazine (March 21, 1969, p. 28) broke the story that *The Gulag Archipelago* was in the West.

238, *Index*: The verses appeared under the title "God Keep Me from Going Mad," *Index*, vol. 1, no. 2 (Summer 1972), pp. 149-51. Michael Scammell was then editor of *Index*.

238, *essay*: The essay "Solzhenitsyn and the Spiritual Mission of the Writer," which Teush wrote under the pseudonym "D. Blagov," is discussed in Chapter Three. It reached the West and was published in two installments in the Russian-language émigré journal *Grani* (Frankfurt am Main), nos. 64 and 65 (1967). The essay has not been translated into English.

238, *biography*: The book in question is David Burg and George Feifer, *Solzhenitsyn: A Biography* (New York: Stein & Day, 1972).

239, *Bakhrushinsky Street*: The offending instructions were reproduced in Zhores A. Medvedev, *Desiat' let posle "Odnogo dnia Ivana Denisovicha"* [*Ten Years After "Ivan Denisovich"*], but omitted from the subsequent English translation (London: Macmillan, 1973).

239, *my letters*: A product of this collaboration was Natalya A. Reshetovskaya, *Sanya: My Life with Aleksandr Solzhenitsyn* (Indianapolis/ New York: Bobbs-Merrill, 1975).

240, *future letters*: In Evgeni Zamyatin's dystopian novel *We* (1920-21) inhabitants of the future "Single State" are known by a non-Russian form of the word "numbers," here rendered as "ciphers."

246, *memoirs*: When Stalin's daughter, Svetlana Alliluyeva, published her *Twenty Letters to a Friend* in New York in 1967, unauthorized versions appeared in several countries, prompting a copyright battle.

258, *Shukhov Street*: The junction of Shukhov and Tatishchev Streets is not far from the Shabolovskaya subway station. Tatishchev was struck by the felicitous combination of his own surname with that of Ivan Denisovich.

268, *Osoaviakhim*: Y. M. Sverdlov (1885-1919) became titular chief of state of the Soviet Union after the Revolution. Osoaviakhim is an abbreviation for the Society for the Promotion of National Defense and the Aeronautical and Chemical Industries (1927-1948). It was a precursor of DOSAAF, the Voluntary Society of collaboration with the Army, Air Force, and Navy.

281, *Fyodor Kryukov*: (1870-1920) A Cossack, author of numerous stories, sketches and essays. Was known to have been working on a major manuscript at the time of his death during the retreat of the White forces from the Kuban. There have been persistent rumors that Mikhail Sholokhov plagiarized the lost manuscript in producing his *The Quiet Don*. V. Molozhavenko's article "On an Undeservedly Forgotten Name" was originally published in *Molot* (Rostov-on-Don), August 13, 1965. An English translation appeared in the *Times Literary Supplement* (London), October 4, 1974, p. 1057.

281, *my future novel*: *August 1914* opens in the Don region, and other parts of *The Red Wheel* are set in the same area.

282, *settlements*: Count A. A. Arakcheyev, powerful Minister of War (1801-25) under Tsar Alexander I. From 1817 he headed the system of "military colonies" that attempted to combine farming and soldiering under harsh military discipline.

286, *published*: D★, Stremia *"Tikhogo Dona" (Zagadki romana)*, with a foreword by Solzhenitsyn (Paris: YMCA Press, 1974). The book has not been translated into English. The literal translation of its title is *The Current of "The Quiet Don" (Riddles of a Novel)*.

288, *"Beria" building*: The Beria connection is explained in Chapter Ten.

290, *Kovynyov*: Chapter Fifteen of *October 1916*.

295, *book*: Roy Medvedev, *Problems in the Literary Biography of Mikhail Sholokhov* (Cambridge University Press, 1977).

295n, *analysis*: Geir Kjetsaa *et al.*, *The Authorship of the Quiet Don* (Oslo: Solum Forlag; Atlantic Heights, N.J.: Humanities Press, 1984).

304, *ray of sun*: The quotes are from "The Sail," a famous poem by

Lermontov that expresses romantic dissatisfaction with the status quo.

304, *sorry for Russia*: In Solzhenitsyn's *August 1914*, one of the novel's protagonists says these words to explain why he is volunteering for service in the army after the outbreak of World War I.

310, *Betrayal*: The Russian title is *Spiral' izmeny Solzhenitsyna*. The book was printed in tiny numbers, and it has not been translated into English.

311, *Chapayev*: Vasili Chapayev (1887-1919) commanded a Red Army unit during the Russian Civil War. He became a hero in Soviet mythology thanks to a highly popular film devoted to him (*Chapayev*, 1934). The machine-gunner Anka is an important secondary character in the film. The film is based on the novel of the same title written by Dmitri Furmanov in 1923.

313, *KGB*: Aleksandr Shelepin headed the KGB between 1958 and 1961; Vladimir Semichastny took over until 1967. Both had previously held high posts in the Communist Youth League (Komsomol).

315, *moved forward*: Traditional Russian Orthodox churches have no pews, permitting movement of the type described.

317, *entourage*: The reminiscences of KGB agent Boris Ivanov in *Sovershenno sekretno* are accompanied by a substantial investigative report compiled by the journalist Dmitri Likhanov. On the basis of published memoirs of individuals who had seen Solzhenitsyn in the period soon after the events described by Ivanov, as well as an interview with a doctor who had treated the writer, Likhanov shows that the August 1971 episode in Rostov must have been an attempt to assassinate Solzhenitsyn by injecting a toxic substance into his body. Solzhenitsyn became acutely ill, with recovery taking more than two months, but before the Ivanov statement the writer seems not to have suspected that foul play was involved.

Index